P9-CLR-816

T H E

Age of Reform

TO

Beatrice

THE
Age of Reform

FROM *BRYAN* TO *F. D. R.*

by

Richard Hofstadter

VINTAGE BOOKS
A DIVISION OF RANDOM HOUSE
New York

L. C. catalog card number: 54-7206

© RICHARD HOFSTADTER, 1955

Copyright 1955 by RICHARD HOFSTADTER. All rights reserved.
No part of this book may be reproduced in any form without
permission in writing from the publisher, except by a reviewer
who may quote brief passages in a review to be printed in a
magazine or newspaper. Manufactured in the United States
of America.

60 59 58 57 56 55

Contents

THE

Age of Reform

❀

INTRODUCTION

❁

Just as the cycle of American history running from the Civil War to the 1890's can be thought of chiefly as a period of industrial and continental expansion and political conservatism, so the age that has just passed, running from about 1890 to the second World War, can be considered an age of reform. The surge of reform, though largely turned back in the 1890's and temporarily reversed in the 1920's, has set the tone of American politics for the greater part of the twentieth century. The reform movements of the past sixty-five years fall readily into three main episodes, the first two of which are almost continuous with each other: the agrarian uprising that found its most intense expression in the Populism of the 1890's and the Bryan campaign of 1896; the Progressive movement, which extended from about 1900 to 1914; and the New Deal, whose dynamic phase was concentrated in a few years of the 1930's.

This book has been inspired not by a desire to retell the familiar story of the primary movements of reform in the United States since 1890, but by the need for a new analysis from the perspective of our own time. My first interest was in the period from 1890 to the beginning of the first World War, but the more I worked upon the problems of that period, the more it was impressed upon me that its character could be far better understood if it was briefly compared and contrasted with the New Deal.

Hence I have added a final chapter, which should not be taken as a full exploration of that relationship. Today we are more remote in time from the first inaugural address of Franklin D. Roosevelt than Roosevelt himself was on March 4, 1933, from the first inaugural address of Woodrow Wilson. As we begin to view the New Deal in more ample perspective, even the reforms that preceded it take on new meanings. We are now in a position to see things we have not hitherto seen, and to realize the importance of things that once seemed incidental.

Our conception of Populism and Progressivism has in fact been intimately bound up with the New Deal experience. The Populist-Progressive age came to an end only with the first World War, and by the time we began to get serious histories of that age, we had been plunged into a new phase of reform brought about by the Great Depression. The views, therefore, of Populism and Progressivism that one finds in histories written during and shortly after the New Deal era bear inevitably the stamp of this second wave of reform. This is not merely to say that they were usually sympathetic, but that they were pervaded by the assumption that in some way the New Deal was both an analogue and a lineal descendant of the Populist-Progressive tradition, an assumption which is by no means totally false but which tends none the less to direct our attention away from essential differences and hence seriously to distort the character of our history. I have been at some pains to emphasize these differences.

I should perhaps explain the unusually broad sense in which I use the terms "Populism" and "Progressivism." By "Populism" I do not mean only the People's (or Populist) Party of the 1890's; for I consider the Populist Party to be merely a heightened expression, at a particular moment of time, of a kind of popular impulse that is endemic in American political culture. Long before the rebellion of the 1890's one can observe a larger trend of thought, stemming from the time of Andrew Jackson, and crystallizing after the Civil War in the Greenback, Granger, and anti-monopoly movements, that expressed the discontents of a great many farmers and businessmen with the economic changes of the late nineteenth century. The Populist spirit captured the Democratic Party in 1896, and continued to play an important part in the politics of the Progressive era. While its special association with agrarian reforms has now become attenuated, I believe that Populist thinking has survived in our own time, partly as an undercurrent of provincial resentments, popular and "democratic" rebelliousness and suspiciousness, and nativism.

Similarly, by "Progressivism" I mean something more than the Progressive (or Bull Moose) Party formed by the Republican insurgents who supported Theodore Roosevelt for the presidency in 1912. I mean rather that broader impulse toward criticism and change that was everywhere so conspicuous after 1900, when the already forceful stream of agrarian discontent was enlarged and redirected by the growing enthusiasm of middle-class people for social and economic reform. As all observant contemporaries realized, Progressivism in this larger sense was not confined to the Progressive Party but affected in a striking way all the major and minor parties and the whole tone of American political life. It was, to be sure, a rather vague and not altogether cohesive or consistent movement, but this was probably the secret of its considerable successes, as well as of its failures. While Progressivism would have been impossible without the impetus given by certain social grievances, it was not nearly so much the movement of any social class, or coalition of classes, against a particular class or group as it was a rather widespread and remarkably good-natured effort of the greater part of society to achieve some not very clearly specified self-reformation. Its general theme was the effort to restore a type of economic individualism and political democracy that was widely believed to have existed earlier in America and to have been destroyed by the great corporation and the corrupt political machine; and with that restoration to bring back a kind of morality and civic purity that was also believed to have been lost.

The center of attention in these pages is neither the political campaigns, the enactments of legislatures, the decisions of the courts, nor the work of regulatory commissions, but the ideas of the participants—their conception of what was wrong, the changes they sought, and the techniques they thought desirable. My theme, then, is the conception the participants had of their own work and the place it would occupy in the larger stream of our history. While my book is, in this sense, primarily a study of political thinking and of political moods, it is not a study of our high culture, but of the kind of thinking that impinged most directly upon the ordinary politically conscious citizen. Morton G. White in his *Social Thought in America* has analyzed the impact of the Progressive era upon more advanced speculation in philosophy, political theory, sociology, and history. My chief concern is not with such work, not with the best but with the most characteristic thinking, with the middlebrow writers, and with the issues as they were presented in the popular magazines, the muckraking articles, the campaign speeches, and the essays of the representative journalists and influential publicists. Of course the high culture and the ordinary culture overlapped and interacted, as they always do, and there were men capable of playing a part in both. At some points, too, the more speculative thinkers who could be classed as Progressives were themselves critical of important aspects of what I have called Progressive thinking. For instance, when I argue that the goals of most Progressives were profoundly individualistic, I do not forget that some of the most important speculative writing of the age in politics, psychology, and philosophy drew upon the same events and concerns to arrive at opposite conclusions. Nor do I intend to ignore the fact that some Progressive thinkers, like Herbert Croly, and even a few Progressive political leaders, like Theodore Roosevelt, were astute critics of this predominant yearning for individualism. Intellectuals, and often indeed some of our shrewdest politicians, keep a certain distance even from the political and social movements with which they sympathize, and their work becomes a criticism both of these movements and of the institutions they are directed against. One of the ironic problems confronting reformers around the turn of the century was that the very activities they pursued in attempting to defend or restore the individualistic values they admired brought them closer to the techniques of organization they feared. The most penetrating thinkers of the age understood somewhat more of this situation than was understood in common discourse.

The Populist and Progressive movements took place during a rapid and sometimes turbulent transition from the conditions of an agrarian society to those of modern urban life. Standing much closer to the completion of this change, we have in some respects a clearer judgment of its meaning, but we are likely to lose sight of the poignancy with which it was experienced by earlier generations. The American tradition of democracy was formed on the farm and in small villages, and its central ideas were founded in rural sentiments and on rural metaphors (we still speak of "grass-roots democracy"). For reasons I will try to explore, the American was taught throughout the nineteenth and even in the twentieth century that rural life and farming as a vocation were something sacred. Since in the beginning the majority of the people were farmers, democracy, as a rather broad abstraction, became in the same way sacrosanct. A certain complacency and self-righteousness thus entered into rural thinking, and this complacency was rudely shocked by the conquests of industrialism. A good deal of the strain and the sense of anxiety in Populism results from this rapid decline of rural America.

And yet it is too little realized that the farmers, who were quite impotent as a special interest when they were numerous, competing, and unorganized, grew stronger as

they grew relatively fewer, became more concerted, more
tenaciously organized and self-centered. One of the
clichés of Populism was the notion that, whatever the
functions of the other vocations, the function of the farmer
was pre-eminent in importance because he fed, and thus
supported, all the others. Although it has been heard
somewhat less frequently of late, and a counter-ideology
of urban resentment has even begun to appear, our national folklore still bears the heavy imprint of that idea.
In reality something like the opposite has become true—
that the rest of us support the farmer; for industrial and
urban America, sentimentally and morally committed to
the ideal of the family farm, has undertaken out of its
remarkable surpluses to support more farm-owners on
the farm than it really needs under modern agricultural
technology. It is in part because of the persistence of our
agrarian traditions that this concession to the farmers
arouses less universal antagonism than do the efforts of
other groups menaced by technological changes—say, the
musicians and the building-trades workers—to set up
artificial safeguards for themselves. My opening pages are
given to the exploration of this long-range swing from
the pastoral legends of early nineteenth-century democracy
to the complexities of modern American life.

Another circumstance attending the rise of Populism and
Progressivism in America was unique in the modern
world. Here the industrialization and urbanization of the
country were coupled with a breakdown in the relative
homogeneity of the population. American democracy,
down to about 1880, had been not only rural but Yankee
and Protestant in its basic notions, and such enclaves of
immigrants as had thus far developed were too small and
scattered to have a major nationwide impact upon the
scheme of its civic life. The rise of industry, however,
brought with it what contemporaries thought of as an
"immigrant invasion," a massive forty-year migration of
Europeans, chiefly peasants, whose religions, traditions,
languages, and sheer numbers made easy assimilation im-

possible. Populism and Progressivism were in considerable part colored by the reaction to this immigrant stream among the native elements of the population. Out of the clash between the needs of the immigrants and the sentiments of the natives there emerged two thoroughly different systems of political ethics, the nature and interactions of which I have tried briefly to define. One, founded upon the indigenous Yankee-Protestant political traditions, and upon middle-class life, assumed and demanded the constant, disinterested activity of the citizen in public affairs, argued that political life ought to be run, to a greater degree than it was, in accordance with general principles and abstract laws apart from the superior to personal needs, and expressed a common feeling that government should be in good part an effort to moralize the lives of individuals while economic life should be intimately related to the stimulation and development of individual character. The other system, founded upon the European backgrounds of the immigrants, upon their unfamiliarity with independent political action, their familiarity with hierarchy and authority, and upon the urgent needs that so often grew out of their migration, took for granted that the political life of the individual would arise out of family needs, interpreted political and civic relations chiefly in terms of personal obligations, and placed strong personal loyalties above allegiance to abstract codes of law or morals. It was chiefly upon this system of values that the political life of the immigrant, the boss, and the urban machine was based. In many ways the struggles of the Progressive era were influenced by the conflict between the two codes elaborated on one side by the highly moral leaders of Protestant social reform and on the other by the bosses, political professionals, and immigrant masses. Since they stemmed from different views not only of politics but of morals and even of religion, it is hardly surprising that the conflicts of the period, often so modest in actual substance, aroused antagonisms so intense and misunderstandings so complete.

The political value and the ideas of government that had been formed in the rural Yankee world were profoundly influenced by entrepreneurship and the ideal of individual success. The side of the left in American political history —that is, the side of popular causes and of reform—had always been relatively free of the need or obligation to combat feudal traditions and entrenched aristocracies. It had neither revolutionary traditions, in the bourgeois sense (the American Revolution itself was a legalistic and socially conservative affair), nor proletarianism and social democracy of the kind familiar in all the great countries of the West in the late nineteenth century. American traditions of political revolt had been based upon movements against monopolies and special privileges in both the economic and the political spheres, against social distinctions and the restriction of credit, against limits upon the avenues of personal advancement. Because it was always possible to assume a remarkable measure of social equality and a fair minimum of subsistence, the goal of revolt tended to be neither social democracy nor social equality, but greater opportunities. At the turn of the century the world with which the majority even of the reformers was most affectionately familiar was the passing world of individual enterprise, predominantly small or modest-sized business, and a decentralized, not too highly organized life. In the Progressive era the life of business, and to some degree even of government, was beginning to pass from an individualistic form toward one demanding industrial discipline and engendering a managerial and bureaucratic outlook. The protests of reformers against this state of affairs often took the form of demands for the maintenance of the kind of opportunity that was passing rather than for the furtherance of existing tendencies toward organization. Most Americans who came from the Yankee-Protestant environment, whether they were reformers or conservatives, wanted economic success to continue to be related to personal character, wanted the economic system not merely to be a system for the production of sufficient goods and services but to be an effectual system of incentives and rewards. The great corporation, the crass plutocrat, the calculating political boss, all seemed to defy these desires. Success in the great corporation seemed to have a very dubious relation to character and enterprise; and when one observed the behavior of the plutocracy, it seemed to be inversely related to civic responsibility and personal restraint. The competitive process seemed to be drying up. All of society was felt to be threatened—not by economic breakdown but by moral and social degeneration and the eclipse of democratic institutions. This is not to say, however, that the men of the age gave way to despair; for they believed that, just as the sinner can be cleansed and saved, so the nation could be redeemed if the citizens awoke to their responsibilities. This mood of hope, in which the Progressive agitations were conducted, lasted until the first World War.

The next episode in the history of reform, the New Deal, was itself a product of that overorganized world which had so much troubled the Progressives. The trend toward management, toward bureaucracy, toward bigness everywhere had gone so far that even the efforts of reform itself had to be consistent with it. Moreover, as the New Deal era went on, leadership in reform had to be shared increasingly with an organized working class large enough to make important demands and to wield great political power. The political and moral codes of the immigrant masses of the cities, of the political bosses, of labor leaders, of intellectuals and administrators, now clashed with the old notions of economic morality. Some of the social strata and many of the social types that had seen great merit in the more limited reforms of the Progressive era found themselves in a bewildering new situation and, especially after the passing of the most critical depression years, grew increasingly offended by the novelties with which they were surrounded. The New Deal, with its pragmatic spirit and its relentless emphasis upon results, seemed to have carried them farther than ever from the kind of society in which economic life was linked to character and to distinctively entrepreneurial freedoms and opportunities.

In the attempts of the Populists and Progressives to hold on to some of the values of agrarian life, to save personal entrepreneurship and individual opportunity and the character type they engendered, and to maintain a homogeneous Yankee civilization, I have found much that was retrograde and delusive, a little that was vicious, and a good deal that was comic. To say this is not to say that these values were in themselves nonsensical or bad. The ideal of a life lived close to nature and the soil, the esteem for the primary contacts of country and village life, the cherished image of the independent and self-reliant man, even the desire (for all the snobberies and hatreds it inspired) to maintain an ethnically more homogeneous nation—these were not negligible or contemptible ideals, and to those who felt most deeply about them their decline was a tragic experience that must be attended to with respect even by those who can share it only through some effort of the imagination. My comments, then, on the old agrarian and entrepreneurial aspirations are not intended to disparage them as ultimate values but to raise some safeguards against the political misuse of them that was and sometimes still is attempted, and perhaps to shed some indirect light on the methods by which that part of them that is still meaningful can be salvaged.

I find that I have been critical of the Populist-Progressive tradition—more so than I would have been had I been writing such a study fifteen years ago. I say critical, but not hostile, for I am criticizing largely from within. The tradition of Progressive reform is the one upon which I was reared and upon which my political sentiments were formed, as it is, indeed, the tradition of most intellectuals in America. Perhaps because in its politics the

United States has been so reliably conservative a country during the greater part of its history, its main intellectual traditions have been, as a reaction, "liberal," as we say —tnat is, popular, democratic, progressive. For all our conservatism as a people, we have failed to develop a sound and supple tradition of candidly conservative thinking. As Lionel Trilling remarks in *The Liberal Imagination,* our conservatives, with only a few exceptions, have not sought to express themselves in ideas, as opposed to action; they have only manifested "irritable mental gestures which seek to resemble ideas." The American businessman is expected to be a conservative in his politics. The conservative American politician can expect widespread recognition, frequently a long tenure in office, and usually a rewarding sense of public usefulness, even though we usually reserve our highest acclaim for the politician who has in him a touch of the liberal reformer. A conservative politician who has sufficient gifts—Theodore Roosevelt is the best example—can in fact enjoy both respectability and the financial support of the great interests and all the satisfactions of the conservative role in public affairs and yet exert his maximal influence by using the rhetoric of progressivism and winning the plaudits of the reformers. In times past, however, the conservative intellectual, and with him the conservative politician who attempted to give to his actions the support of reasoned belief, has been rather out of touch with the main lines of thought and with the primary public that he wanted to reach. The flow of criticism between conservatives and liberals in the United States has been somewhat blocked, with the consequence that men on both sides have grown excessively complacent about their intellectual positions. In the absence of a formidable and reasoned body of conservative criticism, liberals have been driven, for that exercise of the mind which intellectuals seek, to self-criticism, which has been of less value to them than powerful and searching opposition.

In our own day, perhaps for the first time since the

1890's, this situation is changing, for there are some signs that liberals are beginning to find it both natural and expedient to explore the merits and employ the rhetoric of conservatism. They find themselves far more conscious of those things they would like to preserve than they are of those things they would like to change. The immense enthusiasm that was aroused among American intellectuals by such a circumspect and sober gentleman as Adlai Stevenson in 1952 is the most outstanding evidence of this conservatism. Stevenson himself remarked during the course of his campaign that the liberals have become the true conservatives of our time. This is true not because they have some sweeping ideological commitment to conservatism (indeed, their sentiments and loyalties still lie mainly in another direction) but because they feel that we can better serve ourselves in the calculable future by holding to what we have gained and learned, while trying to find some way out of the dreadful impasse of our polarized world, than by dismantling the social achievements of the past twenty years, abandoning all that is best in American traditions, and indulging in the costly pretense of repudiating what we should not and in fact cannot repudiate.

My criticisms of the Populist-Progressive tradition, in so far as they are at all tinctured by conservatism, are no doubt in part a response to this mood. I do not like to think of these criticisms as being associated with the "New Conservatism" of our time, which seems so modish that I find myself uncomfortable with it. The use of such a term as "*New* Conservatism" only suggests to me how uneasy Americans still are in the presence of candidly conservative ideas. I should have thought that anything that was good in conservatism was very old indeed, and so that finest of American conservatives, John Adams, would tell us if he could. To propagate something called "*New* Conservatism" sounds to me too much like the crasser forms of salesmanship. It is in itself a capitulation to the American demand for constant change, and hence a betrayal of conservatism at the outset. We Americans love to have everything labeled "new" and "big," and yet what is of most value in conservatism is its feeling for the past and for nuances of thought, of administration, of method, of meaning, that might be called "little." What appeals to me in the New Conservatism, in so far as anything does at all, is simply the old liberalism, chastened by adversity, tempered by time, and modulated by growing sense of reality. Hence, to the degree that I have been critical in these pages of the Populist-Progressive tradition, it is criticism that aims to reveal some of the limitations of that tradition and to help free it of its sentimentalities and complacencies—in short, to carry on with a task so largely shirked by its opponents that it must be performed by its supporters.

It would be unfair not to add—indeed, to emphasize as much as it is possible to do here—that most of the failings in the liberal tradition that have attracted my interest are also failings of American political culture in general, and that they are usually shared by American conservatives. The most prominent and pervasive failing is a certain proneness to fits of moral crusading that would be fatal if they were not sooner or later tempered with a measure of apathy and of common sense. Eric Goldman, in his history of American reform, *Rendezvous with Destiny*, criticizes Progressive intellectuals for propagating a moral relativism that, by making all moral judgments the products of particular locales and particular historical situations, eventually undermined confidence in the significance of moral judgments as such. "The real trouble with us reformers," he quotes J. Allen Smith as having said, "is that we made reform a crusade against standards. Well, we smashed them all and now neither we nor anybody else have anything left." This accusation has, in my view, a certain pertinence to some liberals in our time, and particularly to those who were known a few years ago as "totalitarian liberals"—that is, to the type of professed liberals who failed to demand of their own side

the civic principles they expected of others, who exempted
movements deemed to be "historically progressive" from
the moral judgments to which all other movements were
subjected, and who in particular denied or granted special
indulgences to the barbarities and tyrannies of Soviet
politics that they freely recognized and condemned in
the fascist countries. But this kind of thing, lamentable as
it was, has not been the characteristic failing of most
modern American reform movements, and certainly was
not widely characteristic of the Populist-Progressive thinking of the period from 1890 to 1917. My criticism of the
Progressivism of that period is the opposite of Smith's—
not that the Progressives most typically undermined or
smashed standards, but that they set impossible standards,
that they were victimized, in brief, by a form of moral
absolutism. It is possible that the distinction between
moral relativism and moral absolutism has sometimes been
blurred because an excessively consistent practice of either
leads to the same practical result—ruthlessness in political
life.

A great part of both the strength and the weakness of
our national existence lies in the fact that Americans do
not abide very quietly the evils of life. We are forever
restlessly pitting ourselves against them, demanding
changes, improvements, remedies, but not often with
sufficient sense of the limits that the human condition
will in the end insistently impose upon us. This restlessness is most valuable and has its most successful consequence wherever dealing with *things* is involved, in technology and invention, in productivity, in the ability to
meet needs and provide comforts. In this sphere we have
surpassed all other peoples. But in dealing with human
beings and institutions, in matters of morals and politics,
the limits of this undying, absolutist restlessness quickly
became evident. At the so-called grass roots of American
politics there is a wide and pervasive tendency to believe
—I hasten to add that the majority of Americans do not
habitually succumb to this tendency—that there is some

great but essentially very simple struggle going on, at the heart of which there lies some single conspiratorial force, whether it be the force represented by the "gold bugs,' the Catholic Church, big business, corrupt politicians, the liquor interests and the saloons, or the Communist Party, and that this evil is something that must be not merely limited, checked, and controlled but rather extirpated root and branch at the earliest possible moment. It is widely assumed that some technique can be found that will really do this, though there is always likely to be a good deal of argument as to what that technique is. All too often the assumption prevails among our political and intellectual leaders that the judgment of the people about such things must of necessity be right, and that it is therefore their own business not to educate the public or to curb its demands for the impossible but to pretend that these demands are altogether sensible and to try to find ways to placate them.

So we go off on periodical psychic sprees that purport to be moral crusades: liberate the people once and for all from the gold bugs, restore absolute popular democracy or completely honest competition in business, wipe out the saloon and liquor forever from the nation's life, destroy the political machines and put an end to corruption, or achieve absolute, total, and final security against war, espionage, and the affairs of the external world. The people who attach themselves to these several absolutisms are not always the same people, but they do create for each other a common climate of absolutist enthusiasm. Very often the evils they are troubled about do exist in some form, usually something can be done about them, and in a great many historical instances something has been done. It is the merit of our reform tradition that it has usually been the first to point to the real and serious deficiencies in our economic system and that it has taken the initiative in making improvements. It is its limitation that it often wanders over the border between reality and impossibility. This was, I believe, pre-eminently true of

the Progressive generation. It is hardly an accident that
the generation that wanted to bring about direct popular
rule, break up the political machines, and circumvent
representative government was the same generation that
imposed Prohibition on the country and proposed to make
the world safe for democracy.

I believe it will be clear that what I am trying to
establish is not that the Populist and Progressive movements were foolish and destructive but only that they had,
like so many things in life, an ambiguous character. Of
their substantial net value in the main stream of American political experience I have no doubt. There has always
been in the United States a struggle against those forces
which were too exclusively preoccupied with the organization of economic life and the milking of our resources to
give much thought to the human costs or to expend much
sympathy on the victims of their work. It has been the
function of the liberal tradition in American politics, from
the time of Jeffersonian and Jacksonian democracy down
through Populism, Progressivism, and the New Deal, at
first to broaden the numbers of those who could benefit
from the great American bonanza and then to humanize
its workings and help heal its casualties. Without this
sustained tradition of opposition and protest and reform,
the American system would have been, as in times and
places it was, nothing but a jungle, and would probably
have failed to develop into the remarkable system for
production and distribution that it is. If we were to follow
the history of but one issue alone—that of taxation in all
its aspects—we would be quickly reminded of the enormous debt we owe to the liberal tradition for shifting the
costs of society to those who are best able to bear them.
Fifty or sixty years ago our social system had hardly
begun to be touched by the gentle hands of remorse or
reform. Today, as a result of an unintended, intermittent,
and usually hostile collaboration of the opposing forces
of matter-of-fact profit-seeking, engineering, and salesmanship on one hand and dissent and reform on the

other, it has been altered and softened in countless ways. The place of the progressive tradition in this achievement is so secure that it should now be possible to indulge in some critical comments without seeming to impugn its entire value.

While it is always both feasible and desirable to formulate ideal programs of reform, it is asking too much to expect that history will move, so to speak, in a straight line to realize them. Liberal intellectuals, who have rather well-rationalized systems of political beliefs, tend to expect that the masses of people, whose actions at certain moments in history coincide with some of these beliefs, will share their other convictions as a matter of logic and principle. Intellectuals, moreover, suffer from a sense of isolation which they usually seek to surmount by finding ways of getting into rapport with the people, and they readily succumb to a tendency to sentimentalize the folk. Hence they periodically exaggerate the measure of agreement that exists between movements of popular reform and the considered principles of political liberalism. They remake the image of popular rebellion closer to their heart's desire. They choose to ignore not only the elements of illiberalism that frequently seem to be an indissoluble part of popular movements but also the very complexity of the historical process itself. In theory we may feel that we can in most cases distinguish without excessive difficulty between reforms that are useful remedies for the evils and abuses of our society and changes that are in fact only additions to or aggravations of such abuses. Popular movements do not always operate with the same discrimination, and it is often hard to tell when such a movement has passed beyond the demand for important and necessary reforms to the expression of a resentment so inclusive that it embraces not only the evils and abuses of a society but the whole society itself, including some of its more liberal and humane values. One can hardly read such works as Reinhard Luthin's recent study of twentieth-century American

demagogy or Albert D. Kirwan's treatise on Mississippi
politics, *Revolt of the Rednecks*, without finding abundant
evidence of this coexistence of illiberalism and reform,
and of its continuity in our history.

These points are, I believe, applicable to the history of
twentieth-century American reform movements. We tend,
for instance, to think of both Populism and Progressivism
in connection with the many ways in which they can be
considered precursors of the more useful reforms of the
New Deal era. Actually, as I suggest in my final chapter,
the spirit of the Progressive era was quite different from
that of the New Deal. While there are genuine points of
similarity and continuity, which I do not wish to deny
or minimize, my own interest has been drawn to that side
of Populism and Progressivism—particularly of Populism
—which seems very strongly to foreshadow some aspects
of the cranky pseudo-conservatism of our time. Somewhere
along the way a large part of the Populist-Progressive
tradition has turned sour, become illiberal and ill-
tempered. Since most of my concern in this volume has
been with the period before 1917, and since the greater
part of this souring process took place after 1917, and
even after 1930, I have not attempted to deal in any
detail with this transformation. And yet I think it might
well be a leading preoccupation of any history of American
political movements since the first World War. What I
have tried to do, in my treatment of the earlier history of
reform, is to show that this process of deconversion from
reform to reaction did not require the introduction of anything wholly new into the political sensibilities of the
American public but only a development of certain
tendencies that had existed all along, particularly in the
Middle West and the South.

Such tendencies in American life as isolationism and the
extreme nationalism that usually goes with it, hatred of
Europe and Europeans, racial, religious, and nativist
phobias, resentment of big business, trade-unionism, intellectuals, the Eastern seaboard and its culture—all these

have been found not only in opposition to reform but also at times oddly combined with it. One of the most interesting and least studied aspects of American life has been the frequent recurrence of the demand for reforms, many of them aimed at the remedy of genuine ills, combined with strong moral convictions and with the choice of hatred as a kind of creed. The history of this characteristic of our political experience has never been studied on the folk level, but it has been reflected in the caliber of our leadership. One finds it, for instance, in the families of the two Charles A. Lindberghs, and the two Martin Dieses, where in both cases the fathers were populistic or Progressive isolationists and the sons became heroes of the extreme right. One finds it in the careers of such Western and Midwestern Senators as Burton K. Wheeler, Gerald P. Nye, Lynn Frazier, and William Lemke, and in such Southerners as Tom Watson, Pitchfork Ben Tillman, Cole Blease, James K. Vardaman, and Huey Long. Nor is it confined to practical politics. It has its representatives in literature, like Jack London, and in journalism, like William Randolph Hearst.

We have all been taught to regard it as more or less "natural" for young dissenters to become conservatives as they grow older; but the phenomenon I am concerned with is not quite the same, for it involves not so much the progression from one political position to another as the continued coexistence of reformism and reaction; and when it takes the form of a progression in time, it is a progression very often unattended by any real change in personal temper. No doubt the precise line between useful and valid criticism of any society and a destructive alienation from its essential values is not always easy to draw. Some men, and indeed some political movements, seem to live close to that line and to swing back and forth across it more than once in their lives. The impulses behind yesterday's reform may be put in the service of reform today, but they may also be enlisted in the service of reaction.

I am fully aware of the dangers of overemphasizing here the resemblances and the continuities between the currents of political feeling that trouble liberals today and their counterparts in earlier reform movements—the danger of becoming too present-minded to have a sound sense of historical veracity, of pushing an insight beyond the bounds of its valid application. Populism, for all its zany fringes, was not an unambiguous forerunner of modern authoritarian movements; nor was Progressivism, despite the fallible concept of mass democracy it some-times sought to advance, an unambiguous harbinger of our most troublesome contemporary delusions. Among those things which must be kept in mind when we think of the period between 1890 and 1917 is that it had about it an innocence and relaxation that cannot again be known, now that totalitarianism has emerged. Mr. Dooley, one of the shrewdest commentators of that age, saw its character quite clearly when he said, even at the height of the Progressive ferment: "Th' noise ye hear is not th' first gun iv a rivolution. It's on'y th' people iv the United States batin' a carpet."

There are, however, complexities in our history which our conventional images of the past have not caught, and we need to know more than we do about our political traditions before our own generation can finish its portraits of earlier reformers. For this reason I hope that my ob-servations will be taken as a prelude and a spur to further studies of American reform movements and not as an attempt to render a final judgment.

CHAPTER I
THE AGRARIAN MYTH
AND COMMERCIAL REALITIES

1 · The Yeoman and the Myth

The United States was born in the country and has moved
to the city. From the beginning its political values and
ideas were of necessity shaped by country life. The early
American politician, the country editor, who wished to
address himself to the common man, had to draw upon a
rhetoric that would touch the tillers of the soil; and even
the spokesman of city people knew that his audience had
been in very large part reared upon the farm. But what
the articulate people who talked and wrote about farmers
and farming—the preachers, poets, philosophers, writers,
and statesmen—liked about American farming was not,
in every respect, what the typical working farmer liked.
For the articulate people were drawn irresistibly to the
noncommercial, nonpecuniary, self-sufficient aspect of
American farm life. To them it was an ideal. Writers like
Thomas Jefferson and Hector St. Jean de Crèvecœur admired the yeoman farmer not for his capacity to exploit
opportunities and make money but for his honest industry,
his independence, his frank spirit of equality, his ability
to produce and enjoy a simple abundance. The farmer
himself, in most cases, was in fact inspired to make money,
and such self-sufficiency as he actually had was usually
forced upon him by a lack of transportation or markets,
or by the necessity to save cash to expand his operations
For while early American society was an agrarian society

it was fast becoming more commercial, and commercial goals made their way among its agricultural classes almost as rapidly as elsewhere. The more commercial this society became, however, the more reason it found to cling in imagination to the noncommercial agrarian values. The more farming as a self-sufficient way of life was abandoned for farming as a business, the more merit men found in what was being left behind. And the more rapidly the farmers' sons moved into the towns, the more nostalgic the whole culture became about its rural past. The American mind was raised upon a sentimental attachment to rural living and upon a series of notions about rural people and rural life that I have chosen to designate as the agrarian myth.[1] The agrarian myth represents a kind of homage that Americans have paid to the fancied innocence of their origins.

Like any complex of ideas, the agrarian myth cannot be defined in a phrase, but its component themes form a clear pattern. Its hero was the yeoman farmer, its central conception the notion that he is the ideal man and the ideal citizen. Unstinted praise of the special virtues of the farmer and the special values of rural life was coupled with the assertion that agriculture, as a calling uniquely productive and uniquely important to society, had a special right to the concern and protection of government. The yeoman, who owned a small farm and worked it with the aid of his family, was the incarnation of the simple, honest, independent, healthy, happy human being. Because he lived in close communion with the beneficent nature, his life was believed to have a wholesomeness and integrity impossible for the depraved populations of cities. His well-being was not merely physical, it was moral; it was not merely personal, it was the central source of

---

[1] By "myth," as I use the word here, I do not mean an idea that is simply false, but rather one that so effectively embodies men's values that it profoundly influences their way of perceiving reality and hence their behavior. In this sense myths may have varying degrees of fiction or reality. The agrarian myth became increasingly fictional as time went on

civic virtue; it was not merely secular but religious, for God had made the land and called man to cultivate it. Since the yeoman was believed to be both happy and honest, and since he had a secure propertied stake in society in the form of his own land, he was held to be the best and most reliable sort of citizen. To this conviction Jefferson appealed when he wrote: "The small land holders are the most precious part of a state." [2]

In origin the agrarian myth was not a popular but a literary idea, a preoccupation of the upper classes, of those who enjoyed a classical education, read pastoral poetry, experimented with breeding stock, and owned plantations or country estates. It was clearly formulated and almost universally accepted in America during the last half of the eighteenth century. As it took shape both in Europe and America, its promulgators drew heavily upon the authority and the rhetoric of classical writers— Hesiod, Xenophon, Cato, Cicero, Virgil, Horace, and others—whose works were the staples of a good education. A learned agricultural gentry, coming into conflict with the industrial classes, welcomed the moral strength that a rich classical ancestry brought to the praise of husbandry. In France the Physiocrats preached that agriculture is the only true source of wealth. In England the rural entrepreneurs, already interested in breeding and agricultural improvement, found the praise of husbandry congenial. They enjoyed it in James Thomson's *Seasons,* or in Dryden's translation of Horace:

> *How happy in his low degree,*
> *How rich in humble poverty, is he,*
> *Who leads a quiet country life,*
> *Discharged of business, void of strife,*
> *And from the griping scrivener free?*
> *Thus, ere the seeds of vice were sown,*

---

[2] *Writings*, ed. by Paul L. Ford (New York, 1892–9), Vol. VII, p. 36. For a full statement of the agrarian myth as it was formulated by Jefferson see A. Whitney Griswold: *Farming and Democracy* (New York, 1948), chapter ii.

Lived men in better ages born,
Who plough'd with oxen of their own,
Their small paternal field of corn.

"There is, indeed, scarcely any writer," declared Samuel
Johnson in 1751, "who had not celebrated the happiness
of rural privacy." [3]

Wherever the peasantry was being displaced by industry
or commercial farming, and particularly in England, where
rustic life was devastated by the enclosures, such literature
took on special poignancy. Oliver Goldsmith's classic
statement, "The Deserted Village," became well over a
hundred years later the unchallenged favorite of American
Populist writers and orators. Chiefly through English experience, and from English and classical writers, the
agrarian myth came to America, where, like so many other
cultural importations, it eventually took on altogether
new dimensions in its new setting. In America such men
as Jefferson and Crèvecœur, Thomas Paine, Philip Freneau,
Hugh-Henry Brackenridge, and George Logan propagated
the myth, and after them a multitude of writers whose
lives reach well into the nineteenth century. [4] So appealing

---

[3] Quoted by Paul H. Johnstone: "Turnips and Romanticism," *Agricultural History*, Vol. XII (July 1938), p. 239. This article and the same
author's "In Praise of Husbandry," ibid., Vol. XI (April 1937), pp.
80–95, give an excellent brief history of the entire agrarian tradition.

   With Dryden's Horace compare Benjamin Franklin's almanac, quoted
by Chester E. Eisinger: "The Farmer in the Eighteenth Century
Almanac," ibid., Vol. XXVIII (July 1954), p. 112:

> *O happy he! happiest of mortal Men!*
> *Who far remov'd from Slavery, as from Pride,*
> *Fears no Man's Frown, nor cringing waits to catch*
> *The gracious Nothing of a great Man's Nod;*
>
> *Tempted nor with the Pride nor Pomp of Power,*
> *Nor Pageants of Ambition, nor the Mines*
> *Of grasping Av'rice, nor the poison'd Sweets*
> *Of pamper'd Luxury, he plants his Foot*
> *With Firmness on his old paternal Fields,*
> *And stands unshaken.*

[4] The prevalence of the myth in eighteenth-century America is shown
by Chester E. Eisinger: "The Freehold Concept in Eighteenth-Century
American Letters," *William and Mary Quarterly*, third series, Vol. IV
(January 1947), pp. 42–59

were its symbols that even an arch-opponent of the agrarian interest like Alexander Hamilton found it politic to concede in his *Report on Manufactures* that "the cultivation of the earth, as the primary and most certain source of national supply, . . . has intrinsically a strong claim to pre-eminence over every other kind of industry." [5] And Benjamin Franklin, urban cosmopolite though he was, once said that agriculture was "the only *honest way*" for a nation to acquire wealth, "wherein man receives a real increase of the seed thrown into the ground, a kind of continuous miracle, wrought by the hand of God in his favour, as a reward for his innocent life and virtuous industry." [6]

Among the intellectual classes in the eighteenth century the agrarian myth had virtually universal appeal. It was everywhere: in tracts on agricultural improvement and books on economics, in pastoral poetry and political philosophy. At once primitivist and rationalist, it could be made congenial to almost every temperament. Some writers used it to give simple, direct, and emotional expression to their feelings about life and nature; others linked agrarianism with a formal philosophy of natural rights. The application of the natural-rights philosophy to land tenure became especially popular in America. Since the time of Locke it had been a standard argument that the land is the common stock of society to which every man has a right—what Jefferson called "the fundamental right to labour the earth"; that since the occupancy and use of land are the true criteria of valid ownership, labor expended in cultivating the earth confers title to it; that since government was created to protect property, the property of working landholders has a special claim to be fostered and protected by the state.[7]

---

[5] *Works*, Vol. III, pp. 215–16.
[6] *Writings*, ed. by Albert H. Smyth (New York, 1906), Vol. V, pp. 200–2.
[7] Chester E. Eisinger: "The Influence of Natural Rights and Physiocratic Doctrines on American Agrarian Thought during the Revolutionary Period," *Agricultural History*, Vol. XXI (January 1947), pp. 12–23. Cf. Griswold, op. cit., pp. 36–45.

At first, as I have said, the agrarian myth was a notion of the educated classes, but by the early nineteenth century it had become a mass creed,[8] a part of the country's political folklore and its nationalist ideology. The roots of this change may be found as far back as the American Revolution, which, appearing to many Americans as the victory of a band of embattled farmers over an empire, seemed to confirm the moral and civic superiority of the yeoman, made the farmer a symbol of the new nation, and wove the agrarian myth into its patriotic sentiments and republican idealism. Still more important, the myth played a role in the first party battles under the Constitution. The Jeffersonians appealed again and again to the moral primacy of the yeoman farmer in their attacks on the Federalists. The family farm and American democracy became indissolubly connected in Jeffersonian thought,[9] and was inherited from the Jeffersonians by exponents of popular causes in the Jackson era. By 1840 even the more conservative party, the Whigs, took over the rhetorical appeal to the common man, and elected a

---

[8] It is, of course, no more than a plausible guess what working farmers actually believed, as opposed to what politicians and other opinion-makers told them. Eisinger notes ("The Farmer in the Eighteenth Century Almanac," p. 108) that even in the eighteenth century the editors of the farmers' almanacs neglected the practical aspects of farming to publish large amounts of pastoral verse employing the familiar agrarian themes. Apparently these editors felt that it was easier or more important to reassure the farmer about the value of his role in society than to advise him how to run his farm. If the premises of the agrarian myth did not appeal to the farmers, then they were completely misunderstood by all those who spoke to and for them. For an excellent illustration of the acceptance of the agrarian myth in the nineteenth century by an influential editor, see Roland Van Zandt: "Horace Greeley: Agrarian Exponent of American Idealism," Rural Sociology, Vol. XIII (December 1948), pp. 411–19. For the place of the myth in Emerson's thought, see Douglas C. Stenerson: "Emerson and the Agrarian Tradition," Journal of the History of Ideas, Vol. XIV (January 1953), pp. 95–115.

[9] Cf. Griswold's conclusion that Jefferson's view of the small farmers as "the most precious part of a state," is "the classic American statement of the political theory of the family farm. . . . [Jefferson's] ideal of democracy as a community of family farms has lived on to inspire the modern lawmakers and color the thoughts of their constituents when they turn their minds to rural life." Op. cit., pp. 45–6.

President in good part on the strength of the fiction that
he lived in a log cabin.

The Jeffersonians, moreover, made the agrarian myth
the basis of a strategy of continental development.[1]
Many of them expected that the great empty inland regions would guarantee the preponderance of the yeoman
—and therefore the dominance of Jeffersonianism and the
health of the state—for an unlimited future. In his first
inaugural address Jefferson spoke of the United States as
"a chosen country, with room enough for our descendants
to the thousandth and thousandth generation." The opening of the trans-Allegheny region, its protection from slavery, and the purchase of the Louisiana Territory were the
first great steps in a continental strategy designed to establish an internal empire of small farms. Much later the
Homestead Act, though temporarily blocked by the South
(the only section of the country where the freehold concept was seriously contested as an ideal), was meant to
carry to its completion the process of continental settlement by small homeowners. The failure of the Homestead
Act "to enact by statute the fee-simple empire"[2] was, as
we shall see, one of the original sources of Populist grievances, and one of the central points at which the agrarian
myth was overrun by the commercial realities.

Above all, however, the myth was powerful because the
United States in the first half of the nineteenth century
consisted predominantly of literate and politically en-
franchised farmers. Offering what seemed harmless flattery
to this numerically dominant class, the myth suggested a
standard vocabulary to rural editors and politicians.[3]

---

[1] For a remarkable exposition of the fate of the agrarian myth as a
source of political measures and strategies, see Henry Nash Smith: *Virgin
Land* (Cambridge, 1950), Book Three, "The Garden of the World."
[2] Ibid., p. 170.
[3] In fact agricultural spokesmen have long fallen into two types. The
flatterers, usually politicians and journalists, are agrarians whose objective
is political and whose approach is to reassure the farmers about the importance and the nobility of their role in society. The *self-critics*, usually
to be found among agricultural editors and some rural professional people, are not agrarians but agriculturists. Their objectives are not political

Although farmers may not have been much impressed by what was said about the merits of a noncommercial way of life, they could only enjoy learning about their special virtues and their unique services to the nation, could hardly mind hearing that their life was intrinsically more virtuous and closer to God than the lives of many people who seemed to be better off. Moreover, the editors and politicians who so flattered them need not in most cases have been insincere. More often than not they too were likely to have begun life in little villages or on farms, and what they had to say stirred in their own breasts, as it did in the breasts of a great many townspeople, nostalgia for their early years, and perhaps relieved some residual feelings of guilt at having deserted parental homes and childhood attachments.[4] They also had the satisfaction in the early days of knowing that in so far as it was based upon the life of the largely self-sufficient yeoman the agrarian myth was a depiction of reality as well as the assertion of an ideal.

Oddly enough, the agrarian myth came to be believed more widely and tenaciously as it became more fictional. At first it was propagated with a kind of genial candor, and only later did it acquire overtones of insincerity. There survives from the Jackson era a lithograph that shows Joseph Ritner, Governor of Pennsylvania, standing by a primitive plow at the end of a furrow. There is no pretense that the Governor has actually been plowing—he wears broadcloth pants and a silk vest, and his tall black beaver hat has been carefully laid in the grass beside him—but the picture is meant as a reminder of both his rustic origin and his present high station in life. By

---

but economic and technological. They tell the farmers that they are neglectful and ignorant, that they largely earn their own misfortunes, and that they must save themselves by studying science and improving their methods.

[4] This nostalgia is a leading theme in the works of James Whitcomb Riley, the most popular of American folk poets. Some of Hamlin Garland's stories in *Main-Traveled Roads* (Boston, 1891) deal with the sense of guilt connected with migration from country to city.

contrast, Calvin Coolidge posed almost a century later for a series of photographs that represented him as haying in Vermont. In one of them the President sits on the edge of a hay rig in a white shirt, collar detached, wearing highly polished black shoes under a fresh pair of overalls; in the background stands his Pierce Arrow, a secret-service man on the running board, plainly waiting to hurry the President away from his bogus rural labors.[5] That the second picture is so much more pretentious and disingenuous than the first is a measure of the increasing hollowness of the myth as it became more and more remote from the realities of agriculture. Well on into the twentieth century eminent Americans continued to pay this ritualistic obeisance to what one writer has called "agricultural fundamentalism." [6] Coolidge himself, who showed monumental indifference to the real problems of farmers in the 1920's, none the less declared: "It has been attested by all experience that agriculture tends to discouragement and decadence whenever the predominant interests of the country turn to manufacture and trade." [7] Likewise Bernard Baruch, a metropolitan financier whose chief contact with agriculture consisted in the absentee ownership of a country estate, asserted: "Agriculture is the greatest and fundamentally the most important of our American industries. The cities are but the branches of the tree of national life, the roots of which go deeply into the land. We all flourish or decline with the farmer." [8]

Throughout the nineteenth century hundreds upon hundreds of thousands of farm-born youths had set the example that Coolidge and Baruch only followed: they sang the praises of agriculture but eschewed farming as a

[5] On the survival of the agrarian myth in politics, see Roger Butterfield's amusing essay "The Folklore of Politics," *Pennsylvania Magazine of History and Biography*, Vol. LXXIV (April 1950), pp. 165–70; the pictures may be found facing pp. 166 and 167.

[6] Joseph S. Davis has discussed this survival in an essay on "Agricultural Fundamentalism" in *On Agricultural Policy* (Stanford, 1939), pp. 24–43.

[7] Ibid., p. 38.

[8] Ibid., p. 25.

vocation and sought their careers in the towns and cities.
For all the rhetoric of the pastoral tradition, nothing could
keep the boys on the farm, and nothing could conceal
from the farm population itself the continuous restless
movement not merely to farms farther west but to urban
areas, East and West. Particularly after 1840, which
marked the beginning of a long cycle of heavy country-
to-city migration, farm children repudiated their parents'
way of life and took off for the cities, where in agrarian
theory, if not in fact, they were sure to succumb to vice
and poverty. Farm journals were full of editorials, stories,
and poems voicing the plaintive theme: "Boys, Stick to
the Farm!" and of advice to farmers on how to rear their
sons so that farming as a way of life would be attractive
to them.[9] A typical bit of this folklore runs:[1]

> The great busy West has inducements,
>   And so has the busiest mart,
> But wealth is not made in a day, boys,
>   Don't be in a hurry to start!
>
> The bankers and brokers are wealthy,
>   They take in their thousands or so;
> Ah! think of the frauds and deceptions—
>   Don't be in a hurry to go.
>
> The farm is the safest and surest;
>   The orchards are loaded today,
> You're free as the air of the mountains,
>   And monarch of all you survey.
>
> Better stay on the farm a while longer,
>   Though profits come in rather slow;
> Remember you've nothing to risk, boys—
>   Don't be in a hurry to go.

---

[9] Albert J. Demaree: The American Agricultural Press, 1819–1860 (New York, 1941), pp. 86–8, 183 ff.; Richard Bardolph: Agricultural Literature and the Early Illinois Farmer (Urbana, 1948), pp. 162–4.
[1] Quoted by Bardolph, op. cit., p. 164 n.

In the imagery of these appeals the earth was characteristically a mother, trade a harlot, and desertion of ancestral ways a betrayal that invited Providential punishment. When a correspondent of the *Prairie Farmer* in 1849 made the mistake of praising the luxuries, the "polished society," and the economic opportunities of the city, he was rebuked for overlooking the fact that city life *"crushes, enslaves,* and *ruins so many thousands of our young men* who are insensibly made the victims of *dissipation,* of *reckless speculation,* and of *ultimate crime."* [2] Such warnings, of course, were futile. "Thousands of young men," wrote the New York agriculturist Jesse Buel, "do annually forsake the plough, and the honest profession of their fathers, if not to win the fair, at least from an opinion, too often confirmed by mistaken parents, that agriculture is not the road to wealth, to honor, nor to happiness. And such will continue to be the case, until our agriculturists become qualified to assume that rank in society to which the importance of their calling, and their numbers, entitle them, and which intelligence and self-respect can alone give them." [3]

Rank in society! That was close to the heart of the matter, for the farmer was beginning to realize acutely not merely that the best of the world's goods were to be had in the cities and that the urban middle and upper classes had much more of them than he did but also that he was losing in status and respect as compared with them. He became aware that the official respect paid to the farmer masked a certain disdain felt by many city people. In time the eulogies of country life that appeared in farm journals lost their pleasantly complacent tone and took on some of the sharpness of a "defensive gesture

---

[2] Paul H. Johnstone: "Old Ideals versus New Ideas in Farm Life," in *Farmers in a Changing World,* U.S. Department of Agriculture Yearbook (Washington, 1940), p. 119. I am much indebted to this penetrating study of the changing identity of the American farmer.

[3] Quoted by P. W. Bidwell and John I. Falconer: *History of Agriculture in the Northern United States* (New York, 1941), p. 205.

against real or imagined slurs." [4] "There has . . . a certain class of individuals grown up in our land," complained a farm writer in 1835, "who treat the cultivators of the soil as an inferior caste . . . whose utmost abilities are confined to the merit of being able to discuss a boiled potato and a rasher of bacon." The city was symbolized as the home of loan sharks, dandies, fops, and aristocrats with European ideas who despised farmers as hayseeds. One writer spoke in a magnificent stream of mixed metaphor of "the butterflies who flutter over them in British broadcloth, consuming the fruits of the sweat of their brows." [5]

The growth of the urban market intensified this antagonism. In areas like colonial New England, where an intimate connection had existed between the small town and the adjacent countryside, where a community of interests and even of occupations cut across the town line, the rural-urban hostility had not developed so sharply as in the newer areas where the township plan was never instituted and where isolated farmsteads were more common. As settlement moved west, as urban markets grew, as self-sufficient farmers became rarer, as farmers pushed into commercial production for the cities they feared and distrusted, they quite correctly thought of themselves as a vocational and economic group rather than as members of a neighborhood. In the Populist era the city was totally alien territory to many farmers, and the primacy of agriculture as a source of wealth was reasserted with much bitterness. "The great cities rest upon our broad and fertile prairies," declared Bryan in his Cross of Gold speech. "Burn down your cities and leave our farms, and your cities will spring up again as if by magic; but destroy our farms, and the grass will grow in the streets of every city in the country." Out of the beliefs nourished by the agrarian myth there had arisen the notion that the city was a parasitical growth on the country. Bryan spoke for a people raised for generations

---

[4] Johnstone: "Old Ideals versus New Ideas," op. cit., p. 118.
[5] Ibid., p. 118, for both quotations.

on the idea that the farmer was a very special creature, blessed by God, and that in a country consisting largely of farmers the voice of the farmer was the voice of democracy and of virtue itself. The agrarian myth encouraged farmers to believe that they were not themselves an organic part of the whole order of business enterprise and speculation that flourished in the city, partaking of its character and sharing in its risks, but rather the innocent pastoral victims of a conspiracy hatched in the distance. The notion of an innocent and victimized populace colors the whole history of agrarian controversy, and indeed the whole history of the populistic mind.

For the farmer it was bewildering, and irritating too, to think of the great contrast between the verbal deference paid him by almost everyone and the real status, the real economic position, in which he found himself. Improving his economic position was always possible, though this was often done too little and too late; but it was not within anyone's power to stem the decline in the rural values and pieties, the gradual rejection of the moral commitments that had been expressed in the early exaltations of agrarianism. It was the fate of the farmer himself, as we shall see, to contribute to this decline. Like almost all good Americans he had innocently sought progress from the very beginning, and thus hastened the decline of many of his own values. Elsewhere the rural classes had usually looked to the past, had been bearers of tradition and upholders of stability. The American farmer looked to the future alone, and the story of the American land became a study in futures. In the very hours of its birth as a nation Crèvecœur had congratulated America for having, in effect, no feudal past and no industrial present, for having no royal, aristocratic, ecclesiastical, or monarchical power, and no manufacturing class, and had rapturously concluded: "We are the most perfect society now existing in the world." Here was the irony from which the farmer suffered above all others: the

United States was the only country in the world that began with perfection and aspired to progress.

II · The Farmer and the Realities

To what extent was the agrarian myth actually false?
When it took form in America during the eighteenth
century, its stereotypes did indeed correspond to many of
the realities of American agricultural life. There were
commercial elements in colonial agriculture almost from
the earliest days, but there were also large numbers of
the kind of independent yeomen idealized in the myth,
men who had remarkable self-sufficiency and bequeathed
to their children a strong penchant for craftsmanlike improvisation and a tradition of household industry. For a
long time the commercial potentialities of agriculture
were held in check by severe obstacles. Only the farmers
very near to the rivers and the towns had adequate
transportation. The small industrial population provided
a very limited domestic market, and the villagers raised a
large part of their own food. Outside the South operations
above the size of the family farm were cramped by the
absence of a force of wage laborers. At the beginning of
the nineteenth century, when the American population
was still living largely in the forests, poised at the edge
of the Appalachians, and standing on the verge of the
great drive across the prairies that occupied settlers for
half a century, the yeoman was by no means a fiction.

The early panegyrists of the agrarian myth were, of
course, aware of the commercial farmers, but it was this
independent yeoman who caught their fancy. Admiring
the natural abundance produced and consumed by the
family on its own farm, they assumed that the family
farm would always be, as it so frequently was in the early
days, a diversified and largely self-sufficient unit. Even
Jefferson, who was far from a humble yeoman, and whose
wants were anything but simple, succeeded to a remarkable degree in living up to the ideal of self-sufficiency.

Like many planters, he numbered among his slaves a balanced group of craftsmen; and even if the luxuries of Jefferson the planter had to be imported, the necessities at least of Jefferson the farmer, and of all his "people," were yielded by his own land.[6] This was also the goal set by the theorists for the yeoman. Making at home almost everything he needed, buying little, using each year but a pocketful of cash, he would be as independent of the marketplace as he was of the favors of others. The yeoman, too, valued this self-sufficiency and the savings it made possible, but he seems to have valued it more often than not as a means through which he could eventually enter the marketplace rather than as a means of avoiding it. "My farm," said the farmer of Jefferson's time, "gave me and my family a good living on the produce of it; and left me, one year with another, one hundred and fifty silver dollars, for I have never spent more than ten dollars a year, which was for salt, nails, and the like. Nothing to wear, eat, or drink was purchased, as my farm provided all. With this saving, I put money to interest, bought cattle, fatted and sold them, and made great profit."[7] Here, then, was the significance of self-sufficiency for the characteristic family farmer: "great profit." Commercialism had already begun to enter the American Arcadia.

From colonial days there had always been before the eyes of the yeoman farmer in the settled areas alluring models of commercial success in agriculture: the tobacco, rice, and indigo planters of the South, the grain, meat, and cattle exporters of the middle colonies. In America the spirit of emulation was exceptionally strong, the opportunities were considerable. The farmer knew that without cash he could never rise above the hardships and squalor of pioneering and log-cabin life. Self-sufficiency produced savings, and savings went into the purchase of more land, of herds and flocks, of better tools; they erected barns

---

[6] Albert J. Nock: *Jefferson* (Washington, 1926), pp. 66–8; cf. Wilson Gee: *The Social Economics of Agriculture* (New York, 1942), p. 39.

[7] Quoted by Griswold, op. cit., p. 136.

and silos and better dwellings, and made other improvements. When there was spare time, the farmer often
worked off the farm to add to his cash resources, at first
in trapping, hunting, fishing, or lumbering, later in the
maintenance and repair of railroads. Domestic politics
were persistently affected by his desire for the means of
getting a cash crop to market, for turnpikes and canals.
The foreign policy of the early Republic was determined
again and again by the clamor of farmers to keep open
the river outlets for American produce.

Between 1815 and 1860 the character of American
agriculture was transformed. The independent yeoman,
outside of exceptional or isolated areas, almost disappeared
before the relentless advance of commercial agriculture.
The rise of native industry created a home market for
agriculture, while at the same time demands arose abroad,
at first for American cotton and then for American food-
stuffs. A network of turnpikes, canals, and railroads linked
the planter and the advancing Western farmer to these
new markets, while the Eastern farmer, spurred by
Western competition, began to cultivate more thoroughly
the nearby urban outlets for his products. As the farmer
moved out onto the flat, rich prairies, he found possibilities
for the use of machinery that did not exist in the forest. Before long he was cultivating the prairies with horse-drawn
mechanical reapers, steel plows, wheat and corn drills, and
threshers. The cash crop converted the yeoman into a
small entrepreneur, and the development of horse-drawn
machinery made obsolete the simple old agrarian symbol
of the plow. Farmers ceased to be free of what the early
agrarian writers had called the "corruptions" of trade.
They were, to be sure, still "independent," in the sense
that they owned their own land. They were a hardwork-
ing lot in the old tradition. But no longer did they grow
or manufacture what they needed: they concentrated on
the cash crop and began to buy more and more of their
supplies from the country store. To take full advantage
of mechanization, they engrossed as much land as they

could. To mechanize fully, they borrowed cash. Where they could not buy or borrow they might rent: by the 1850's Illinois farmers who could not afford machines and large barns were hiring itinerant jobbers with machines to do their threshing. The shift from self-sufficient to commercial farming varied in time throughout the West and cannot be dated with precision, but it was complete in Ohio by about 1830 and twenty years later in Indiana, Illinois, and Michigan. All through the great Northwest, farmers whose ancestors might have lived in isolation and self-sufficiency were surrounded by jobbers, banks, stores, middlemen, horses, and machinery; and in so far as this process was unfinished in 1860, the demands of the Civil War brought it to completion. As the *Prairie Farmer* said in 1868: "The old rule that a farmer should produce all that he required, and that the surplus represented his gains, is part of the past. Agriculture, like all other business, is better for its subdivisions, each one growing that which is best suited to his soil, skill, climate and market, and with its proceeds purchas[ing] his other needs." [8]

The triumph of commercial agriculture not only rendered obsolete the objective conditions that had given to the agrarian myth so much of its original force, but also showed that the ideal implicit in the myth was contesting the ground with another, even stronger ideal—the notion of opportunity, of career, of the self-made man. The same forces in American life that had made Jacksonian equalitarianism possible and had given to the equalitarian theme in the agrarian romance its most compelling appeal had also unleashed in the nation an entrepreneurial zeal proba-

---

[8] Quoted by Paul H. Johnstone: "On the Identification of the Farmer," *Rural Sociology*, Vol. V (March 1940), p. 39. For this transformation in agriculture, see Bidwell and Falconer, op. cit., pp. 126–32, 164–5, chapters xiii, xix, xxiii, and Everett E. Edwards: "American Agriculture —the First 300 Years," in *Farmers in a Changing World*, esp. pp. 202– 8, 213–22, 228–32. On the foreign market see Edwin G. Nourse: *American Agriculture and the European Market* (New York, 1924), pp. 8–16, and on the disappearance of household industry, Rolla M. Tryon: *Household Manufactures in the United States, 1640–1860* (Chicago, 1917), chapters vii and viii.

bly without precedent in history, a rage for business, for profits, for opportunity, for advancement. If the yeoman family was to maintain itself in the simple terms eulogized in the myth, it had to produce consistently a type of character that was satisfied with a traditional way of life. But the Yankee farmer, continually exposed to the cult of success that was everywhere around him, became inspired by a kind of personal dynamism which called upon the individual to surpass traditions. He was, in terms that David Riesman has made familiar, not a tradition-directed but an inner-directed man.[9] Agrarian sentiment sanctified labor in the soil and the simple life, but the prevailing Calvinist atmosphere of rural life implied that virtue was rewarded, after all, with success and material goods.

From the standpoint of the familiar agrarian panegyrics, the supreme irony was that the immense interior that had been supposed to underwrite the dominion of the yeoman for centuries did as much as anything else to destroy the yeomanlike spirit and replace it with the spirit of the businessman, even of the gambler. Cheap land invited extensive and careless cultivation. Rising land values in areas of new settlement tempted early liquidation and frequent moves, and made of the small entrepreneur a land speculator. Already in the late eighteenth century writers on American agriculture noticed that American farmers were tempted to buy more land than they could properly cultivate. George Washington wrote apologetically to Arthur Young about the state of American farming, admitting that "the aim of farmers in this country, if they can be called farmers, is not to make the most they can from the land, which is, or has been, cheap, but

---

[9] David Riesman: *The Lonely Crowd* (New Haven, 1950). It should be added, however, that the idea of career, as it reached country youth before the Civil War, was strongly tinctured by Yankee intellectualism and did not as yet exalt businessmen. Farm boys were encouraged to emulate inventors, scientists, writers, philosophers, and military figures. Of course all these pointed toward urban life. Johnstone: "Old Ideals versus New Ideas," pp. 137–8.

the most of the labour, which is dear; the consequence of which has been, much ground has been scratched over and none cultivated or improved as it ought to have been. . . ." [1] This tendency was strengthened by the rapid march of settlement across the prairies. In 1818 the English immigrant Morris Birkbeck wrote from Illinois that merchants, professional men, and farmers alike were investing their profits and savings in uncultivated land. "The farmer, instead of completing the improvement of his present possessions, lays out all he can save in entering more land. In a district which is settling, this speculation is said to pay on the average, when managed with judgment, fifteen per cent. Who then will submit to the toils of agriculture, further than bare necessity requires, for fifteen per cent? Or who would loan his money, even at fifteen per cent, where he can obtain that interest by investing it in land? Thus every description of men, almost every man, is poor in convertible property." [2]

Frequent and sensational rises in land values bred a boom psychology in the American farmer and caused him to rely for his margin of profit more on the process of appreciation than on the sale of crops. It took a strong man to resist the temptation to ride skyward on lands that might easily triple or quadruple their value in one decade and then double again in the next.[3] It seemed ultraconservative to improve existing possessions if one could put savings or borrowings into new land. What developed in America was an agricultural society whose real attachment was not to the land but to land values. In the 1830's Tocqueville found this the prevailing characteristic of American agriculture: "Almost all the farmers of the United States combine some trade with agriculture; most of them make agriculture itself a trade. It seldom

[1] Bidwell and Falconer, op. cit., p. 119.
[2] Ibid., p. 154; cf. pp. 82–3, 115, 166.
[3] Benjamin H. Hibbard: *History of Agriculture in Dane County, Wisconsin* (Madison, 1904), pp. 195 ff.

happens that an American farmer settles for good upon the land which he occupies: especially in the districts of the far West he brings land into tillage in order to sell it again, and not to farm it: he builds a farmhouse on the speculation that, as the state of the country will soon be changed by the increase of population, a good price will be gotten for it.. . . . Thus the Americans carry their business-like qualities into agriculture; and their trading passions are displayed in that as in their other pursuits." [4]

The penchant for speculation and the lure of new and different lands bred in the American farmer a tremendous passion for moving—and not merely, as one common view would have it, on the part of those who had fail], but also on the part of those who had succeeded. For farmers who had made out badly, the fresh lands may have served on occasion as a safety valve, but for others who had made out well enough on a speculative basis, or who were beginning a farming "career," it was equally a risk valve— an opportunity to exploit the full possibilities of the great American land bubble. Mobility among farmers had serious effects upon an agricultural tradition never noted for careful cultivation: in a nation whose soil is notoriously heterogeneous, farmers too often had little chance to get to know the quality of their land; they failed to plan and manure and replenish; they neglected diversification for the one-crop system and ready cash.[5] There was among them little attachment to land or locality; instead there developed the false euphoria of local "boosting," encouraged by railroads, land companies, and farmers themselves; in place of village contacts and communal spirit

[4] *Democracy in America* (New York, ed. 1899), Vol. II, p. 644.

[5] Some aspects of agrarian mobility and mechanized agriculture for the market are discussed by James C. Malin in "Mobility and History," *Agricultural History*, Vol. XVII (October 1943), pp. 177–91. The general characteristics of American agriculture in the period after the Civil War are discussed by Fred A. Shannon: *The Farmer's Last Frontier* (New York, 1945), *passim*.

based upon ancestral attachments, there was professional optimism based upon hopes for a quick rise in values.[6]

In a very real and profound sense, then, the United States failed to develop (except in some localities, chiefly in the East)[7] a distinctively *rural* culture. If a rural culture means an emotional and craftsmanlike dedication to the soil, a traditional and pre-capitalist outlook, a tradition-directed rather than career-directed type of character, and a village community devoted to ancestral ways and habitually given to communal action, then the prairies and plains never had one. What differentiated the agricultural life of these regions from the practices widespread in European agriculture—or, for that matter, from the stereotype of the agrarian myth—was not simply that it produced for a market but that it was so speculative, so mobile, so mechanized, so "progressive," so thoroughly imbued with the commercial spirit.

Immigrant farmers, who really were yeomen with a background of genuine agrarian values, were frequently bewildered at the ethos of American agriculture. Marcus Hansen points out: "The ambition of the German-American father, for instance, was to see his sons on reaching manhood established with their families on farms clustered about his own. To take complete possession of a township with sons, sons-in-law and nephews was not an unrealizable ideal. To this end the would-be patriarch dedicated all his plodding industry. One by one, he bought adjacent farms, the erstwhile owners joining the current to the farther West. Heavily timbered acres and swamp lands

---

[6] Thorstein Veblen, who not only wrote about farmers as an economist but lived among them, deals penetratingly with "the independent farmer" and "the country town" in *Absentee Ownership* (New York, 1923), pp. 129–65.

[7] Compare Arthur F. Raper's account of the people of these localities in Carl C. Taylor et al.: *Rural Life in the United States* (New York, 1949), chapter xxvi, with the similar picture of the old yeoman farmer. For an excellent account of the transformation in farming by one who saw it at both ends, see Rodney Welch: "The Farmer's Changed Condition," *Forum*, Vol. X (February 1891), pp. 689–700.

which had been lying unused were prepared for cultivation by patient and unceasing toil. 'When the German
comes in, the Yankee goes out,' was a local proverb that
varied as Swedes, Bohemians or other immigrant groups
formed the invading element. But the American father
made no such efforts on behalf of his offspring. To be a
self-made man was his ideal. He had come in as a 'first
settler' and had created a farm with his ax; let the boys
do the same. One of them perhaps was kept at home as
a helper to his aging parents; the rest set out to achieve
beyond the mountains or beyond the river what the father
had accomplished in the West of his day. Thus mobility
was fostered by family policy." [8] The continuing influx of
immigrants, ready to settle on cleared and slightly improved land, greatly facilitated the Yankee race across
the continent.[9]

American agriculture was also distinguishable from
European agriculture in the kind of rural life and political
culture it sustained. In Europe the managers of agriculture and the owners of land were characteristically either
small peasant proprietors, or substantial landholders of
traditional and conservative outlook with powerful political
and military connections. The American farmer, whose
holdings were not so extensive as those of the grandee
nor so tiny as those of the peasant, whose psychology
was Protestant and bourgeois, and whose politics were
petty-capitalist rather than traditionalist, had no reason
to share the social outlook of the rural classes of Europe.
In Europe land was limited and dear, while labor was
abundant and relatively cheap; in America this ratio
between land and labor was inverted. In Europe small

---

[8] Marcus Lee Hansen: *The Immigrant in American History* (Cambridge, 1940), pp. 61–2.
[9] Ibid., pp. 63–71. I do not wish to imply that the immigrant was in
every respect the superior farmer. He took better care of the land, but
was not so quick as the Yankee to take advantage of mechanization or
scientific farming. This pattern persisted for a long time. See John A.
Hawgood: *The Tragedy of German-America* (New York, 1940), chapter i, esp. pp. 26–33; Edmund de S. Brunner: *Immigrant Farmers and
Their Children* (New York, 1929), chapter ii.

farmers lived in villages, where generations of the same
family were reared upon the same soil, and where careful cultivation and the minute elimination of waste were
necessary to support a growing population on a limited
amount of land. Endless and patient labor, including the
labor of peasant women and children exploited to a degree
to which the Yankee would not go except under the stress
of pioneering conditions, was available to conserve and
tailor the land and keep it fertile. On limited plots cultivated by an ample labor force, the need for machinery
was not urgent, and hence the demand for liquid capital
in large amounts was rare. Diversification, self-sufficiency,
and the acceptance of a low standard of living also contributed to hold down this demand. Much managerial
skill was required for such an agricultural regime, but it
was the skill of the craftsman and the traditional tiller
of the soil. Village life provided a community and a co-
operative milieu, a pooling of knowledge and lore, a basis
of common action to minimize risks.

In America the greater availability of land and the
scarcity of labor made for extensive agriculture, which was
wasteful of the soil, and placed a premium on machines
to bring large tracts under cultivation. His demand for
expensive machinery, his expectation of higher standards
of living, and his tendency to go into debt to acquire extensive acreage created an urgent need for cash and
tempted the farmer into capitalizing more and more on
his greatest single asset: the unearned appreciation in
the value of his land. The managerial skill required for
success under these conditions was as much businesslike
as craftsmanlike. The predominance in American agriculture of the isolated farmstead standing in the midst of
great acreage, the frequent movements, the absence of
village life, deprived the farmer and his family of the advantages of community, lowered the chances of association
and co-operation, and encouraged that rampant, suspicious,
and almost suicidal individualism for which the American
farmer was long noted and which organizations like the

Grange tried to combat.[1] The characteristic product of
American rural society was not a yeoman or a villager, but
a harassed little country businessman who worked very
hard, moved all too often, gambled with his land, and
made his way alone.

III · *The Frontier or the Market?*

The American farmer was unusual in the agricultural
world in the sense that he was running a mechanized and
commercialized agricultural unit of a size far greater than
the small proprietary holdings common elsewhere, and
yet he was running it as a family enterprise on the assumption that the family could supply not only the necessary capital and managerial talent but also most of the
labor. This system, however applicable to the subsistence
farm or the small yeoman's farm, was hardly adequate
to the conditions of commercial agriculture.[2] As a businessman, the farmer was appropriately hardheaded; he
tried to act upon a cold and realistic strategy of self-
interest. As the head of a family, however, the farmer felt
that he was investing not only his capital but his hard
work and that of his wife and children, that when he
risked his farm he risked his home—that he was, in short,
a single man running a personal enterprise in a world
of impersonal forces. It was from this aspect of his situation—seen in the hazy glow of the agrarian myth—that
his political leaders in the 1890's developed their rhetoric
and some of their concepts of political action. The farmer's
commercial position pointed to the usual strategies of the
business world: combination, co-operation, pressure politics, lobbying, piecemeal activity directed toward specific
goals. But the bathos of the agrarian rhetoric pointed in
a different direction: broad political goals, ideological mass
politics, third parties, the conquest of the "money power,"

---

[1] There is an excellent comparison of American and European agriculture in Wilson Gee, op. cit., chapter iii.
[2] Malin: "Mobility and History," pp. 182 ff.

the united action of all labor, rural and urban. When times were persistently bad, the farmer tended to reject his business role and its failures to withdraw into the role of the injured little yeoman. This made the differences between his situation and that of any other victim of exploitation seem unimportant to him. As a Southern journalist wrote of the situation in the cotton country: "The landowner was so poor and distressed that he forgot that he was a capitalist . . . so weary of hand and sick of spirit that he imagined himself in precisely the same plight as the hired man. . . ." [8]

The American farmer thus had a dual character, and one way of understanding our agrarian movements is to observe which aspect of the farmer's double personality is uppermost at a given time. It is my contention that both the Populist rhetoric and the modern liberal's indulgent view of the farmers' revolt have been derived from the "soft" side of the farmer's existence—that is, from agrarian "radicalism" and agrarian ideology—while most farm organizations since the decline of the Populists have been based primarily upon the "hard" side, upon agricultural improvement, business methods, and pressure politics. Populism itself had a hard side, especially in the early days of the Farmers' Alliance and the Populist Party, but this became less and less important as the depression of the nineties deepened and other issues were dropped in favor of the silver panacea.

Most of our views of the historical significance of Populism have been formed by the study of the frontier process and the settlement of the internal empire. This approach turned attention to some significant aspects of American agrarian development, but also diverted attention from others. To a writer like Frederick Jackson Turner the

---

[8] Quoted by C. Vann Woodward: *Origins of the New South* (Baton Rouge, 1951), p. 194. During the late 1880's, when farm discontent was not yet at its peak, such farm organizations as the Farmers' Alliances developed limited programs based upon economic self-interest; in the 1890's, when discontent became most acute, it produced a national third-party movement.

farmer on the plains was significant above all as the
carrier of the traditions of the frontier. To Turner the
frontier, or the West, was the primary source of most of
"what has been distinctive and valuable in America's
contributions to the history of the human spirit. . . ." [4]
Hence the primary interest of the Populist lay in the fact
that he was "a survival of the pioneer, striving to adjust
present conditions to his old ideals." [5] While Turner did
on occasion comment on the capitalistic and speculative
character of the farmer, he saw this as something of no
special importance, when compared with the farmer's role
as the bearer of the yeoman tradition and "the old pioneer
ideals of the native American. . . ." [6] The chief difference
between Populist thinking and the pioneer tradition,
Turner felt, was that the Populists showed an increasing
sense of the need for governmental help in realizing the
old ideals. His explanation of this change in philosophy—
indeed, of the entire agrarian revolt of the 1890's—was
formulated in the light of the frontier theory and the
alleged exhaustion of "free" land. "Failures in one area
can no longer be made good by taking up land on a new
frontier," he wrote in 1896. "The conditions of settled
society are being reached with suddenness and with confusion. . . . The frontier opportunities are gone. Discontent is demanding an extension of governmental activity in its behalf. . . . A people composed of heterogeneous materials, with diverse and conflicting ideals and
social interests, having passed from the task of filling
up the vacant spaces of the continent, is now thrown back

---

[4] Frederick Jackson Turner: *The Frontier in American History* (New
York, 1920; ed., 1947), preface, p. ii; cf. pp. 211, 266.
[5] Ibid., p. 155.
[6] Ibid., p. 148. Note his comments on another writer's characterization
of the commercial nature of settlement, p. 211. Turner himself, it
should perhaps be added, was not a Populist. He disapproved of the
"lax financial integrity" of the Populists, though he thought it was too
much to expect "a primitive society" to show "an intelligent appreciation of the complexity of business interests in a developed society."
Ibid., p. 32.

upon itself and is seeking an equilibrium." [7] The idea that the agrarian uprising was precipitated by the disappearance of the frontier and the exhaustion of the public domain has also been given the scholarly support of John D. Hicks's standard history of *The Populist Revolt*. Earlier discontents, Hicks concluded, had been lightened by the departure of the restless and disgruntled for the West, a process that created new opportunities for them and eased the pressure on those they left behind. But by the nineties, "with the lands all taken and the frontier gone, this safety valve was closed. The frontier was turned back on itself. The restless and discontented voiced their sentiments more and fled from them less." [8]

The conclusion that it was the West, the frontier spirit, that produced American democracy, and that Populism was the logical product of this spirit, is a deceptive inheritance from the Turnerian school. The decisive role played by the South in Populism suggests instantly the limitations of this view. Terms that are superficially appealing when applied to Kansas become meaningless when applied to Georgia. Southern Populism, which could hardly have been close to the frontier spirit, was at least as strong as the Western brand and contained the more radical wing of the agrarian revolt of the nineties.[9] Moreover, the extent to which "the West" as a whole supported the agrarian revolt has commonly been exaggerated, as the distribution of Populist votes in 1892 and of Bryan votes in 1896 clearly shows.[1] Populism had only three compact centers.

---

[7] Ibid., pp. 219–21; cf. pp. 147–8, 218, 276–7, 305–6.

[8] John D. Hicks: *The Populist Revolt* (Minneapolis, 1931), p. 95; cf. also p. vii: "The rôle of the farmer in American history has always been prominent, but it was only as the West wore out and cheap lands were no longer abundant that well-developed agrarian movements began to appear." But the Granger movement of the 1870's, while it may perhaps be dismissed as an undeveloped agrarian movement, manifested acute agrarian unrest long before the disappearance of the frontier line in 1890.

[9] Woodward: *Origins of the New South*, p. 200; cf. pp. 277–8 on the greater staying power of Southern Populism.

[1] See chapter iii, section 1.

Each was overwhelmingly rural. Each was dominated by a
product whose price had catastrophically declined: the
South, based chiefly upon cotton; a narrow tier of four
Northwestern states, Kansas, Nebraska, and the two Da-
kotas, based upon wheat; and the mountain states, based
chiefly upon silver. Silver is a special case, though stra-
tegically an important one, and we can for the moment
postpone consideration of it, except to remark that the
free-silver Populism of the mountain-states variety was
not agrarian Populism at all, but simply silverism. Elsewhere agrarian discontent, where it reached a peak of local
intensity sufficient to yield an independent Populist Party
of notable strength or to win a state for Bryan in 1896,
was roughly coterminous with the cash-staple export crops
and the burden of heavy mortgage indebtedness.

The common tendency to focus upon the internal frontier as the matrix of Populism has obscured the great importance of the agrarian situation in the external world,
which is profoundly relevant to both Southern and Western Populism. The frontier obsession has been identified
in America with a kind of intellectual isolationism.[2] The
larger and more important answer to the causes of the
agrarian crisis of the 1890's must be found not in the
American West, but in the international market. While
American Populism has been seen almost solely in terms
of domestic events and the internal frontier, the entire
European and American world was shaken by an agrarian
crisis that knew no national boundaries and that struck
at several nations without internal frontiers on the verge
of real or imagined exhaustion. "Almost everywhere," declared an English observer in 1893, "certainly in England,
France, Germany, Italy, Scandinavia, and the United

---

[2] As an illustration of the misleading consequences of the "closed space"
obsession, see Turner's comment in 1910 that "the pressure of population upon the food supply is already felt." Op. cit., p. 279. This at a
time when the United States was rapidly losing its place in the world
market because of a surfeit of total world agricultural production.
Nourse, op. cit., pp. 28–42.

States, the agriculturists, formerly so instinctively conservative, are becoming fiercely discontented, declare they gain less by civilization than the rest of the community, and are looking about for remedies of a drastic nature." [8]

During the last three decades of the nineteenth century a revolution took place in international communications. For the first time the full effects of steam locomotion and steam navigation were felt in international trade. In 1869 the Suez Canal was opened and the first transcontinental railroad in the United States was completed. Europe was connected by submarine cable with the United States in 1866, and with South America in 1874. A great network of telegraph and telephone communication was spun throughout the world. Huge tracts of new land being settled in Argentina, Australia, Canada, and the American West were now pulled together in one international market, while improvements in agricultural technology made possible the full exploitation of areas susceptible to extensive and mechanized cultivation. Agrarian depressions, formerly of a local or national character, now became international, and with them came international agrarian discontent, heightened by the almost uninterrupted international price decline that occurred from the early 1870's to the 1890's. [4] It is hardly accidental that the products of the American

[8] Quoted from *Spectator*, Vol. LXX, p. 247, by C. F. Emerick, "An Analysis of Agricultural Discontent in the United States," *Political Science Quarterly*, Vol. XI (September 1896), p. 433; see this series of articles for a valuable contemporary account of the international aspect of agricultural upheaval, ibid., pp. 433–63, 601–39; Vol. XII (1897), pp. 93–127.

[4] For a review of the literature on the Communication Revolution, see Lee Benson: "The Historical Background of Turner's Frontier Essay," *Agricultural History*, Vol. XXV (April 1951), pp. 59–64. The point of view expressed here was originally stated by James C. Malin: "Notes on the Literature of Populism," *Kansas Historical Quarterly*, Vol. I (February 1932), pp. 160–4; the term "Communication Revolution" was first used by Robert G. Albion: "The 'Communication Revolution,'" *American Historical Review*, Vol. XXXVII (July 1932), pp. 718–20. See also Hans Rosenberg: "Political and Social Consequences of the Great Depression of 1873–1896 in Central Europe," *Economic History Review*, Vol. XIII (1943), pp. 58–73.

staple-growing regions showing the highest discontent were
the products most dependent upon exports.[5]

The notion that the unavailability of free land for further expansion of the American farming system was chiefly
responsible for the remarkable surge of agrarian discontent no longer seems credible. It is true that many Americans, including some Populist spokesmen, were concerned
during the 1890's about what they thought to be the im-
minent disappearance of the public domain.[6] There was
also a school of thought among those interested in the
agrarian problem that took pleasure in the prospect that
the approaching exhaustion of new lands would lower
the expansion of the agricultural economy to the point
at which the values of already settled land would begin
to rise sharply, and thus put an end to the problem of
settled farmers.[7] However, the entire conception of ex-
hausted resources has been re-examined and found to be
delusive; actually an abundance of new land was available
long after the so-called disappearance of the frontier in
1890. During the decade 1890–1900, in which the discontent was most acute, 1,100,000 new farms were settled, 500,000 more than the number in the previous
decade. In the twenty years after the farmers' organizations met in 1890 at Ocala, Florida, to formulate their demands, 1,760,000 new farms and 225,600,000 new acres
were added to the nation's agricultural domain.[8] More

---

[5] Wheat-growers were dependent for about 30 to 40 per cent of their
gross annual income upon the export market; cotton-growers for about
70 per cent; raisers of pork and pork products for about 15 to 23 per
cent. Frederick Strauss: "The Composition of Gross Farm Income since
the Civil War," National Bureau of Economic Research Bulletin No. 78
(April 28, 1940), esp. pp. 15–18.
[6] Cf. Senator William A. Peffer as quoted by Elizabeth N. Barr in William E. Connelley, ed.: A Standard History of Kansas and Kansans
(Chicago, 1919), Vol. II, p. 1159; Hamlin Garland: Jason Edwards
(Boston, 1892), p. v; Mary E. Lease: The Problem of Civilization
Solved (Chicago, 1895), pp. 177–8.
[7] An excellent account of speculations about the approaching exhaustion
of the public domain is given by Benson, op. cit., pp. 59–82.
[8] A. W. Zelomek and Irving Mark: "Historical Perspectives for Post-
War Agricultural Forecasts," Rural Sociology, Vol. X (March 1945), p.

land, indeed, was taken up after 1890 under the terms
of the Homestead Act and its successors than had been
taken up before. True, a high proportion of this was suitable only for grazing and dry farming, but the profitability
of land is a result not merely of soil chemistry or soil
humidity but also of the economic circumstances under
which the land is cultivated; the condition of the market
in the early years of the twentieth century admitted of
more profitable cultivation of these relatively barren lands
than of much richer lands in the depressed period. Finally,
there were after 1890 still more supplies of rich land in
Canada, which farmers from the United States did not
hesitate to occupy. In 1914, Canadian officials estimated
that 925,000 Americans had moved, chiefly during the
sixteen years past, across the border to the lands of Al-
berta and Saskatchewan.[9] Lavish opportunities to settle on
new lands or open new acres were still available after
1890,[1] and in fact much use was made of these opportunities during the nineties. In so far as farmers were
deterred from further settlement, it was not by the absence
of land but because the international agrarian depression
made the nineties a hazardous time to begin a farm.

The conception that the end of free or cheap land was
primarily responsible for precipitating discontent implies

51; cf. *Final Report of the Industrial Commission* (Washington, 1902),
Vol. XIX, pp. 58, 105–6; Benjamin H. Hibbard: *A History of the
Public Land Policies* (New York, 1924), pp. 396–8.
[9] Marcus L. Hansen and J. Bartlet Brebner: *The Mingling of the Canadian and American Peoples* (New York, 1940), pp. 219–35; Paul F.
Sharp: *The Agrarian Revolt in Western Canada* (Minneapolis, 1948),
pp. 1–8, 17.
[1] As late as 1913, when David F. Houston became Wilson's Secretary
of Agriculture, he found that "less than 60 per cent of our arable land
was under cultivation, and of the land under cultivation not more than
12 per cent was yielding reasonably full returns." *Eight Years with Wilson's Cabinet* (New York, 1926), Vol. I, p. 200. The largest number
of final entries under the Homestead Act came in 1913, almost a
quarter century after the alleged disappearance of the frontier. During
World War I it was still possible to expand crop acreages very substantially even within states long settled. See Lloyd P. Jorgensen: "Agricultural Expansion," *Agricultural History*, Vol., XXIII (January 1949),
pp. 30–40.

that the existence of such land had been effective in alle-
viating it, and suggests that the effects of the Homestead
Act up to about 1890 were what had been hoped for at
the time of its passage. But the Homestead Act had never
been successful in creating the inland freehold empire
that agrarian reformers had dreamed of. Its maladministration and its circumvention by speculators and railroads
is by now well known. From 1860 to 1900, for every
free farm entered and kept by a bona fide farmer under
the act there were about nine bought from railroads or
speculators or from the government itself.[2] Speculators, en-
grossing immense tracts of land under the privilege of unrestricted "entry," which was not abolished until 1888,
did far more damage to rural society in the West than
merely transmitting "free" land to farmers at substantial
prices. They drove immigrants to remote parts of the
frontier; they created "speculators' deserts"—large tracts
of uncultivated absentee-owned land—and thus added to
the dispersal of the population, making the operation of
roads and railroads far more costly than necessary; they refused to pay taxes, thus damaging local government
finances and limiting local improvements; they added to
all the characteristic evils of our rural culture while they
built up land prices and kept a large portion of the farm
population in a state of tenancy.[3]

The promise of free Homestead land or cheap land was
self-defeating. The Homestead Act itself, which required
five years of residence before title to a free farm was
granted, was based upon the assumption that settlement
would take place in a gradual and stable way, after the
manner of the mythical yeoman. It made no allowance

---

[2] Fred A. Shannon: *The Farmer's Last Frontier* (New York, 1945), pp.
51, 55. Shannon estimates that about 400,000 farms were alienated
under Homestead terms during a period in which 3,730,000 new farms
were created.

[3] Paul Wallace Gates: "Land Policy and Tenancy in the Prairie States,"
Journal of Economic History, Vol. I (May 1941), pp. 60–82; see also
his "The Homestead Act in an Incongruous Land System," *American
Historical Review*, Vol. XLI (July 1936), pp. 652–81.

for the mobile habits of the American farmer.[4] The number of forfeited entries under the Homestead Act was extraordinary. What effect the Homestead Act *might* have had if the West had been gradually settled by yeoman farmers protected from speculators and living after the fashion of the myth seems no more than a utopian conjecture. As it worked out, the Homestead Act was a triumph for speculative and capitalistic forces, and it translated cheap or free land into a stimulus for more discontent than it could quiet. The promise of the Homestead Act was a lure for over-rapid settlement in regions where most settlers found, instead of the agrarian utopia, a wilderness of high costs, low returns, and mortgages.

The self-defeating tendency of relatively cheap land in a speculative society is perfectly illustrated in an intensive contemporary study of a Nebraska township by Arthur F. Bentley. This township was first settled in 1871–2. In the early days when land prices were low, there was a prosperous period of rapid settlement, and the farmer's rate of profit was high whenever he had good crops; this encouraged him to buy and work more land than he could properly manage. The rapid appreciation of the price of land led him to try to realize his gains in advance by mortgaging. As fast as he could increase his loan he would do so, using the funds either to pay temporary losses or for further investment or speculation. "It is true," Bentley observed, "the farmer may often have suffered from excessive interest and grasping creditors; but it was less frequently the avarice of the lender that got him into trouble than the fact that he was too sanguine and too prone to believe that he could safely go into debt, on the assumption that crops and prices in the future would equal those in the present." [5] At any rate, the typical farmer soon

---

[4] Malin: "Mobility and History," pp. 181–2. For the maladministration of the Homestead Act, see Roy M. Robbins: *Our Landed Heritage* (Princeton, 1942), part III.

[5] Arthur F. Bentley: *The Condition of the Western Farmer as Illustrated by the Economic History of a Nebraska Township* (Baltimore, 1893), p. 46; for substantial evidence that the speculative and risk-ridden

found himself in such a vulnerable position that one bad
crop year or a brief temporary cessation of increase in
land values, such as that of 1890–1, would put him on the
verge of failure. Those farmers who came in early and
took government land, who managed with some skill and
got clear of heavy debt, made out well; those who came
later, took railroad land, and made the usual errors of
management were in straits.[6] By 1892, when Bentley made
his study, he concluded that a would-be purchaser who
did not have enough capital to buy his farm outright and
to hold it over subsequent periods of hard times "had almost better throw his money away than invest it in farming operations in Nebraska at the current prices of land
and under the present agricultural conditions; unless, he
be possessed of unusual energy and ability." [7]

It is evident that Western Populism was, among other
things, the outgrowth of a period of incredible expansion,
one of the greatest in the world history of agriculture.
From 1870 to 1900 more new farm land was taken up
than in all previous American history.[8] By the mid-eighties
a feverish land boom was under way, and it is the collapse
of this boom that provides the immediate background of
Western Populism. We may take the experience of Kansas
as illustrative. The boom, originally based on the high
prices of farm produce, had reached the point of artificial
inflation by 1885. It had swept not only the country,
where the rapid advance in prices had caused latecomers
to buy and mortgage at hopelessly inflated values, but
also the rising towns, which were all "bonded to the limit
for public improvements [and] public utilities." [9] As a

character of Western settlement could be as important as "the avarice
of the lender," see Allan G. Bogue: "The Land Mortgage Company in
the Early Plains States," *Agricultural History*, Vol. XXV (January 1951),
pp. 20–33.
[6] Bentley, op. cit., pp. 46, 68, 76, 79, 80.
[7] Ibid., pp. 69–70.
[8] Land in farms rose from 407,735,000 acres in 1870 to 838,592,000 in
1900.
[9] William Allen White: *Autobiography* (New York, 1946), p. 187.

state official later remarked, "Most of us crossed the Mississippi or Missouri with no money but with a vast wealth of hope and courage. . . . Haste to get rich has made us borrowers, and the borrower has made booms, and booms made men wild, and Kansas became a vast insane asylum covering 80,000 square miles." [1] In the winter of 1887–8 this boom, which had been encouraged by railroads, newspapers, and public officials, abruptly collapsed—in part because of drought in the western third of the state, in part because farm prices had stopped going up, and in part because the self-created confidence upon which the fever fed had broken.

The fathers of the Homestead Act and the fee-simple empire had acted upon a number of assumptions stemming from the agrarian myth which were out of date even before the act was passed. They trusted to the beneficence of nature, to permanent and yeomanlike nonspeculative settlement; they expected that the land really would pass without cost into the hands of the great majority of settlers; and they took it for granted that the native strength of the farmer would continue to rest upon the abundance produced on and for the farm. These assumptions were incongruous with the Industrial Revolution that was already well under way by 1862 and with the Communications Revolution that was soon to come; they were incongruous even with the natural character of the plains, with their winds, sandstorms, droughts, and grasshoppers. And the farmer, caught in the toils of cash-crop commercial farming, did not, and could not, reckon his prosperity by the abundance produced on the farm but rather by the exchange value of his products as measured by the supplies and services they could buy. His standard of living, as well as the security of his home, became dependent upon

[1] Quoted in Raymond C. Miller: *The Populist Party in Kansas*, ms. Ph.D. dissertation, University of Chicago, 1928, p. 22; cf. Miller's article: "The Background of Populism in Kansas," *Mississippi Valley Historical Review*, Vol. II (March 1925), pp. 474–85; Hicks, op. cit., chapter i, has a good brief account of the speculative background.

his commercial position, which in turn was dependent upon the vicissitudes of the world market.[2]

In pointing to the farmer's commercial role I am not trying to deny the difficulties of his position or the reality and seriousness of his grievances: the appreciation of debts through deflation, the high cost of credit, inequitable tax burdens, discriminatory railroad rates,[3] unreasonable elevator and storage charges. Populism can best be understood, however, not as a product of the frontier inheritance, but as another episode in the well-established tradition of American entrepreneurial radicalism, which goes back at least to the Jacksonian era.[4] It was an effort on the part of a few important segments of a highly heterogeneous capitalistic agriculture to restore profits in the face of much exploitation and under unfavorable market and price

---

[2] The farmer himself was not content to be told that his living standards had improved, because he looked to his commercial welfare as well. Disappointments are relative to expectations. While enduring the short-lived rigors of frontier existence, the farmer lived on expectation and hope, accepting present sacrifices in the interest of a future that seemed rosy to the mind of the boomer. Once this stage was passed, he assumed that his living standards would rise materially and was irritated at the very suggestion that this alone should satisfy him. Cf. Bentley, op. cit., p. 87; Henrietta M. Larson: *The Wheat Market and the Farmer in Minnesota, 1858–1900* (New York, 1926), p. 167.

[3] Concerning the place of freight rates in the background of the farmer's situation, Theodore Saloutos has reinforced a reservation advanced much earlier by Charles F. Adams, Jr.: "Historians have repeatedly attributed the plight of the farmers, at least in part, to high freight rates, yet available figures show conclusively that the rates dropped drastically during the last half of the nineteenth century, while the farmers' returns failed to show anything commensurate with the drop in rates. Many farmers attributed the sagging prices to these alleged extortionate rates, but by doing so they overlooked the fact that it was these lower rates that had made it possible for them to reach markets which were formerly considered incredible . . . rates that in many other countries would have been considered incredibly low." See the rest of the argument in Saloutos's astute article: "The Agricultural Problem and Nineteenth-Century Industrialism," *Agricultural History*, Vol. XXI (July 1948), p. 167. On this issue, however, see Shannon: *The Farmer's Last Frontier*, pp. 295–302.

[4] For the entrepreneurial interpretation of Jacksonian democracy see the review by Bray Hammond, *Journal of Economic History*, Vol. VI (May 1946), pp. 78–84, and Richard Hofstadter: *The American Political Tradition* (New York, 1948), chapter iii.

conditions. It arose as a part of a transitional stage in the history of American agriculture, in which the commercial farmer was beginning to cast off habits of thought and action created almost as much by the persistence of the agrarian myth as by the realities of his position. He had long since taken from business society its acquisitive goals and its speculative temper, but he was still practicing the competitive individualism that the most advanced sectors of industry and finance had outgrown. He had not yet learned much from business about its marketing devices, strategies of combination, or skills of self-defense and self-advancement through pressure politics. His dual identity itself was not yet resolved. He entered the twentieth century still affected by his yeoman inheritance but with a growing awareness of the businesslike character of his future.

CHAPTER II
THE FOLKLORE OF POPULISM

❁

1 · *The Two Nations*

For a generation after the Civil War, a time of great
economic exploitation and waste, grave social corruption
and ugliness, the dominant note in American political life
was complacency. Although dissenting minorities were
always present, they were submerged by the overwhelming
realities of industrial growth and continental settlement.
The agitation of the Populists, which brought back to
American public life a capacity for effective political indignation, marks the beginning of the end of this epoch.
In the short run the Populists did not get what they wanted,
but they released the flow of protest and criticism that
swept through American political affairs from the 1890's
to the beginning of the first World War.

Where contemporary intellectuals gave the Populists a
perfunctory and disdainful hearing, later historians have
freely recognized their achievements and frequently overlooked their limitations. Modern liberals, finding the Populists' grievances valid, their programs suggestive, their motives creditable, have usually spoken of the Populist episode
in the spirit of Vachel Lindsay's bombastic rhetoric:

Prairie avenger, mountain lion,
Bryan, Bryan, Bryan, Bryan,
Gigantic troubadour, speaking like a siege gun,
Smashing Plymouth Rock with his boulders from the West.

There is indeed much that is good and usable in our Populist past. While the Populist tradition had defects that have been too much neglected, it does not follow that the virtues claimed for it are all fictitious. Populism was the first modern political movement of practical importance in the United States to insist that the federal government has some responsibility for the common weal; indeed, it was the first such movement to attack seriously the problems created by industrialism. The complaints and demands and prophetic denunciations of the Populists stirred the latent liberalism in many Americans and startled many conservatives into a new flexibility. Most of the "radical" reforms in the Populist program proved in later years to be either harmless or useful. In at least one important area of American life a few Populist leaders in the South attempted something profoundly radical and humane—to build a popular movement that would cut across the old barriers of race—until persistent use of the Negro bogy distracted their following. To discuss the broad ideology of the Populist does them some injustice, for it was in their concrete programs that they added most constructively to our political life, and in their more general picture of the world that they were most credulous and vulnerable. Moreover, any account of the fallibility of Populist thinking that does not acknowledge the stress and suffering out of which that thinking emerged will be seriously remiss. But anyone who enlarges our portrait of the Populist tradition is likely to bring out some unseen blemishes. In the books that have been written about the Populist movement, only passing mention has been made of its significant provincialism; little has been said of its relations with nativism and nationalism; nothing has been said of its tincture of anti-Semitism.

The Populist impulse expressed itself in a set of notions that represent what I have called the "soft" side of agrarianism. These notions, which appeared with regularity in the political literature, must be examined if we are to re-create for ourselves the Populist spirit. To extract them

from the full context of the polemical writings in which
they appeared is undoubtedly to oversimplify them; even
to name them in any language that comes readily to the
historian of ideas is perhaps to suggest that they had a
formality and coherence that in reality they clearly lacked.
But since it is less feasible to have no labels than to have
somewhat too facile ones, we may enumerate the dominant themes in Populist ideology as these: the idea of a
golden age; the concept of natural harmonies; the dualistic
version of social struggles; the conspiracy theory of history;
and the doctrine of the primacy of money. The last of
these I will touch upon in connection with the free-silver
issue. Here I propose to analyze the others, and to show
how they were nurtured by the traditions of the agrarian
myth.

The utopia of the Populists was in the past, not the
future. According to the agrarian myth, the health of the
state was proportionate to the degree to which it was
dominated by the agricultural class, and this assumption
pointed to the superiority of an earlier age. The Populists
looked backward with longing to the lost agrarian Eden,
to the republican America of the early years of the nineteenth century in which there were few millionaires and, as
they saw it, no beggars, when the laborer had excellent
prospects and the farmer had abundance, when statesmen
still responded to the mood of the people and there was no
such thing as the money power.[1] What they meant—
though they did not express themselves in such terms—
was that they would like to restore the conditions prevailing before the development of industrialism and the commercialization of agriculture. It should not be surprising
that they inherited the traditions of Jacksonian democracy,

[1] Thomas E. Watson: *The Life and Times of Andrew Jackson* (Thomson, Ga., 1912), p. 325: "All the histories and all the statesmen agree
that during the first half-century of our national existence, we had no
poor. A pauper class was unthought of: a beggar, or a tramp never
seen." Cf. Mrs. S. E. V. Emery: *Seven Financial Conspiracies Which
Have Enslaved the American People* (Lansing, ed. 1896), pp. 10–11.

that they revived the old Jacksonian cry: "Equal Rights for All, Special Privileges for None," or that most of the slogans of 1896 echoed the battle cries of 1836.[2] General James B. Weaver, the Populist candidate for the presidency in 1892, was an old Democrat and Free-Soiler, born during the days of Jackson's battle with the United States Bank, who drifted into the Greenback movement after a short spell as a Republican, and from there to Populism. His book, *A Call to Action*, published in 1892, drew up an indictment of the business corporation which reads like a Jacksonian polemic. Even in those hopeful early days of the People's Party, Weaver projected no grandiose plans for the future, but lamented the course of recent history, the growth of economic oppression, and the emergence of great contrasts of wealth and poverty, and called upon his readers to do "All in [their] power to arrest the alarming tendencies of our times."[3]

Nature, as the agrarian tradition had it, was beneficent. The United States was abundantly endowed with rich land and rich resources, and the "natural" consequence of such an endowment should be the prosperity of the people. If the people failed to enjoy prosperity, it must be because of a harsh and arbitrary intrusion of human greed and error. "Hard times, then," said one popular writer, "as well as the bankruptcies, enforced idleness, starvation, and the crime, misery, and moral degradation growing out of conditions like the present, being unnatural, not in accordance with, or the result of any natural law, must be attributed to that kind of unwise and pernicious legislation which history proves to have produced similar results in all ages of the world. It is the mission of the age to correct these errors in human legislation, to adopt and establish policies and systems, in accord with, rather than in opposition to divine law."[4] In assuming a lush natural order whose workings were being deranged by human

---

[2] Note for instance the affectionate treatment of Jacksonian ideas in Watson, op. cit., pp. 343–4.
[3] James B. Weaver: *A Call to Action* (Des Moines, 1892), pp. 377–8.
[4] B. S. Heath: *Labor and Finance Revolution* (Chicago, 1892), p. 5.

laws, Populist writers were again drawing on the Jacksonian tradition, whose spokesmen also had pleaded for a
proper obedience to "natural" laws as a prerequisite of
social justice.[5]

Somewhat akin to the notion of the beneficence of nature
was the idea of a natural harmony of interests among the
productive classes. To the Populist mind there was no
fundamental conflict between the farmer and the worker,
between the toiling people and the small businessman.
While there might be corrupt individuals in any group,
the underlying interests of the productive majority were
the same; predatory behavior existed only because it was
initiated and underwritten by a small parasitic minority
in the highest places of power. As opposed to the idea
that society consists of a number of different and frequently
clashing interests—the social pluralism expressed, for instance, by Madison in the *Federalist*—the Populists adhered, less formally to be sure, but quite persistently, to
a kind of social dualism: although they knew perfectly
well that society was composed of a number of classes,
for all practical purposes only one simple division need
be considered. There were two nations. "It is a struggle,"
said Sockless Jerry Simpson, "between the robbers and
the robbed."[6] "There are but two sides in the conflict
that is being waged in this country today," declared a
Populist manifesto. "On the one side are the allied hosts of
monopolies, the money power, great trusts and railroad
corporations, who seek the enactment of laws to benefit
them and impoverish the people. On the other are the
farmers, laborers, merchants, and all other people who
produce wealth and bear the burdens of taxation. . . .
Between these two there is no middle ground."[7] "On

[5] For this strain in Jacksonian thought, see Richard Hofstadter: "William Leggett, Spokesman of Jacksonian Democracy," *Political Science
Quarterly*, Vol. XLVIII (December 1943), pp. 581–94, and *The American Political Tradition*, pp. 60–1.
[6] Elizabeth N. Barr: "The Populist Uprising," in William E. Connelley,
ed.: *A Standard History of Kansas and Kansans*, Vol. II, p. 1170.
[7] Ray Allen Billington: *Westward Expansion* (New York, 1949), p. 741.

the one side," said Bryan in his famous speech against the repeal of the Sherman Silver Purchase Act, "stand the corporate interests of the United States, the moneyed interests, aggregated wealth and capital, imperious, arrogant, compassionless. . . . On the other side stand an unnumbered throng, those who gave to the Democratic party a name and for whom it has assumed to speak." [8] The people versus the interests, the public versus the plutocrats, the toiling multitude versus the money power —in various phrases this central antagonism was expressed. From this simple social classification it seemed to follow that once the techniques of misleading the people were exposed, victory over the money power ought to be easily accomplished, for in sheer numbers the people were overwhelming. "There is no power on earth that can defeat us," said General Weaver during the optimistic days of the campaign of 1892. "It is a fight between labor and capital, and labor is in the vast majority." [9]

The problems that faced the Populists assumed a delusive simplicity: the victory over injustice, the solution for all social ills, was concentrated in the crusade against a single, relatively small but immensely strong interest, the money power. "With the destruction of the money power," said Senator Peffer, "the death knell of gambling in grain and other commodities will be sounded; for the business of the worst men on earth will have been broken up, and the mainstay of the gamblers removed. It will be an easy matter, after the greater spoilsmen have been shorn of their power, to clip the wings of the little ones.

[8] Allan Nevins: *Grover Cleveland* (New York, 1933), p. 540; Heath, op. cit., p. 27: "The world has always contained two classes of people, one that lived by honest labor and the other that lived off of honest labor." Cf. Governor Lewelling of Kansas: "Two great forces are forming in battle line: the same under different form and guise that have long been in deadly antagonism, represented in master and slave, lord and vassal, king and peasant, despot and serf, landlord and tenant, lender and borrower, organized avarice and the necessities of the divided and helpless poor." James A. Barnes: *John G. Carlisle* (New York, 1931), pp. 254–5.

[9] George H. Knoles: *The Presidential Campaign and Election of 1892* (Stanford, 1942), p. 179.

Once get rid of the men who hold the country by the throat, the parasites can be easily removed." [1] Since the old political parties were the pirmary means by which the people were kept wandering in the wilderness, the People's Party advocates insisted, only a new and independent political party could do this essential job.[2] As the silver question became more prominent and the idea of a third party faded, the need for a monolithic solution became transmuted into another form: there was only one *issue* upon which the money power could really be beaten and this was the money issue. "When we have restored the money of the Constitution," said Bryan in his Cross of Gold speech, "all other necessary reforms will be possible; but . . . until this is done there is no other reform that can be accomplished."

While the conditions of victory were thus made to appear simple, they did not always appear easy, and it would be misleading to imply that the tone of Populistic thinking was uniformly optimistic. Often, indeed, a deep-lying vein of anxiety showed through. The very sharpness of the struggle, as the Populists experienced it, the alleged absence of compromise solutions and of intermediate groups in the body politic, the brutality and desperation that were imputed to the plutocracy—all these suggested that failure of the people to win the final contest peacefully could result only in a total victory for the plutocrats and total extinction of democratic institutions, possibly after a period of bloodshed and anarchy. "We are nearing a serious crisis," declared Weaver. "If the present strained relations between wealth owners and wealth producers continue much longer they will ripen into frightful disaster. This universal discontent must be quickly interpreted and its causes removed." [3] "We meet," said the Populist platform of 1892, "in the midst of a nation brought to the verge of moral, political, and material ruin. Corruption

---

[1] William A. Peffer: *The Farmer's Side* (New York, 1891), p. 273.
[2] Ibid., pp. 148–50.
[3] Weaver, op. cit., p. 5.

dominates the ballot-box, the Legislatures, the Congress, and touches even the ermine of the bench. The people are demoralized. . . . The newspapers are largely subsidized or muzzled, public opinion silenced, business prostrated, homes covered with mortgages, labor impoverished, and the land concentrating in the hands of the capitalists. The urban workmen are denied the right to organize for self-protection, imported pauperized labor beats down their wages, a hireling standing army, unrecognized by our laws, is established to shoot them down, and they are rapidly degenerating into European conditions. The fruits of the toil of millions are boldly stolen to build up colossal fortunes for a few, unprecedented in the history of mankind; and the possessors of these, in turn, despise the Republic and endanger liberty." Such conditions foreboded "the destruction of civilization, or the establishment of an absolute despotism."

The common fear of an impending apocalypse had its most striking articulation in Ignatius Donnelly's fantastic novel *Cæsar's Column.* This book, published under a pseudonym, was a piece of visionary writing, possibly inspired by the success a few years earlier of Bellamy's utopian romance *Looking Backward,* which called forth a spate of imitators during the last decade of the century.[4] Praised by leading members of the Populist movement and by persons as diverse as Cardinal Gibbons, George Cary Eggleston, Frances E. Willard, and Julian Hawthorne,[5] *Cæsar's Column* became one of the most widely read books of the early nineties. Donnelly's was different from the other utopias. Although in its anticlimactic conclusion it did describe a utopia in a remote spot of Africa, the main story portrayed a sadistic anti-utopia arrived at, as it were, by standing Bellamy on his head. The idea seems to have occurred to Donnelly in a moment of great discouragement at the close of the unu-

---

[4] See Allyn B. Forbes: "The Literary Quest for Utopia," *Social Forces,* Vol. VI (1927), pp. 178–9.
[5] E. W. Fish: *Donnelliana* (Chicago, 1892), pp. 121–2.

sually corrupt Minnesota legislative session of 1889,[6] when he was struck with the thought of what might come to be if the worst tendencies of current society were projected a century into the future. The story takes place in the year 1988, missing by four years the date of the more recent anti-utopia of George Orwell, with which it invites comparison, though not on literary grounds.

Donnelly's hero and narrator is a stranger, a shepherd of Swiss extraction living in the state of Uganda, Africa, who visits New York and reports his adventures in a series of letters. New York is a center of technological marvels much like Bellamy's. The stranger approaches it in an airship, finds it lit so brightly that its life goes on both night and day. Its streets are covered with roofs of glass; underneath them is the city's subway system, with smokeless and noiseless electric trains to which passengers are lowered by electric elevators. Its air-conditioned hotels are capped by roof-top restaurants serving incredible luxuries, where "star-eyed maidens . . . wander half seen amid the foliage, like the houris in the Mohammedan's heaven." [7]

This sybaritic life is supported at the cost of great mass suffering, and conceals a fierce social struggle. The world of 1988 is governed by an inner council of plutocratic leaders who stop at nothing to crush potential opposition. They keep in their hire a fleet of "Demons," operators of dirigibles carrying poison-gas bombs, whose aid they are ready to use at any sign of popular opposition. The people themselves have become equally ruthless—"brutality above had produced brutality below." The farmers are "no longer the honest yeomanry who had filled, in the old time, the armies of Washington, and Jackson, and Grant, and Sherman . . . but their brutalized descendants— fierce serfs—cruel and bloodthirsty peasants." [8] The brunt of the social struggle, however, is borne by the urban

---

[6] Ibid., pp. 119–20.
[7] Cæsar's Column (Chicago, 1891), p. 327.
[8] Ibid.

laborers, a polyglot, silent mass of sullen, underfed humanity. The traveler from Uganda learns in a conversation (documented by Donnelly with real articles from current magazines) that as early as 1889 many writers had warned against the potentialities of this state of affairs. It was not an inevitable development, but greed and stupidity had kept the ruling classes from heeding such prophets of disaster. Rapacious business methods, the bribery of voters, the exploitation of workers and farmers by the plutocracy, had gone unchecked until the end of the nineteenth century, when the proletariat had rebelled. The rebellion had been put down by the farmers, not yet completely expelled by mortgage foreclosures from their position as property-owners and businessmen. Now that the farmers too are destroyed as a prop of the existing order, the rulers rely solely upon the bomb, the dirigible, and a mercenary army.

The convolutions of Donnelly's plot, which includes two tasteless love stories, do little more than entitle the book to be called a novel, and the work is full of a kind of suppressed lasciviousness that one finds often in popular writing of the period. At the climax of the story, the secret revolutionary organization, the Brotherhood of Destruction, after buying off the "Demons," revolts and begins an incredible round of looting and massacre which may have been modeled on the French Revolutionary Terror but makes it seem pale and bloodless in comparison. Some members of the governing class are forced to build a pyre on which they are then burned. There is so much carnage that the disposal of the bodies becomes an immense sanitary problem. Cæsar, one of the three leaders (who is himself beheaded in the end), commands that the corpses be piled up and covered with cement to form a gigantic pyramidal column as a monument to the uprising. The city is finally burned, but a saving remnant of decent folk escapes in a dirigible to the African mountains, where under the guidance of an elite of intellectuals they form a Christian socialist state in which the Populist program for land, transportation, and finance becomes a reality and interest is illegal.

Doubtless this fantasy was meant to say what would happen if the warnings of the reformers and the discontents of the people went unheard and unalleviated. Far more ominous, however, than any of the vivid and hideous predictions of the book is the sadistic and nihilistic spirit in which it was written. It is perhaps a childish book, but in the middle of the twentieth century it seems anything but laughable: it affords a frightening glimpse into the ugly potential of frustrated popular revolt. When *Cæsar's Column* appeared, the reform movement in America had not yet made a dent upon the torments and oppressions that were felt by a large portion of the people. In some men the situation fostered a feeling of desperation, and Donnelly's was a desperate work. It came at a moment when the threat of a social apocalypse seemed to many people not at all remote, and it remains even now a nettlesome if distinctly minor prophetic book.

II · *History as Conspiracy*

Both sides of Donnelly's struggle, the Council of governing plutocrats and the Brotherhood of Destruction, are significantly portrayed as secret organizations—this despite the fact that the Brotherhood has millions of members. There was something about the Populist imagination that loved the secret plot and the conspiratorial meeting. There was in fact a widespread Populist idea that all American history since the Civil War could be understood as a sustained conspiracy of the international money power.

The pervasiveness of this way of looking at things may be attributed to the common feeling that farmers and workers were not simply oppressed but oppressed deliberately, consciously, continuously, and with wanton malice by "the interests." It would of course be misleading to imply that the Populists stand alone in thinking of the events of their time as the results of a conspiracy.

This kind of thinking frequently occurs when political and social antagonisms are sharp. Certain audiences are especially susceptible to it—particularly, I believe, those who have attained only a low level of education, whose access to information is poor,[9] and who are so completely shut out from access to the centers of power that they feel themselves completely deprived of self-defense and subjected to unlimited manipulation by those who wield power. There are, moreover, certain types of popular movements of dissent that offer special opportunities to agitators with paranoid tendencies, who are able to make a vocational asset out of their psychic disturbances.[1] Such persons have an opportunity to impose their own style of thought upon the movements they lead. It would of course be misleading to imply that there are no such things as conspiracies in history. Anything that partakes of political strategy may need, for a time at least, an element of secrecy, and is thus vulnerable to being dubbed conspiratorial. Corruption itself has the character of conspiracy. In this sense the Crédit Mobilier was a conspiracy, as was the Teapot Dome affair. If we tend to be too condescending to the Populists at this point, it may be necessary to remind ourselves that they had seen so much bribery and corruption, particularly on the part of the railroads, that they had before them a convincing model of the management of affairs through conspiratorial behavior. Indeed, what makes conspiracy theories so widely acceptable is that they usually contain a germ of truth. But there is a great difference between locating conspiracies *in* history and saying that history *is*, in effect, a conspiracy, between singling out those conspiratorial acts that do on occasion occur and weaving a vast fabric of social explanation out of nothing but skeins of evil plots.

---

[9] In this respect it is worth pointing out that in later years, when facilities for realistic exposure became more adequate, popular attacks on "the money power" showed fewer elements of fantasy and more of reality.
[1] See, for instance, the remarks about a mysterious series of international assassinations with which Mary E. Lease opens her book *The Problem of Civilization Solved* (Chicago, 1895).

When conspiracies do not exist it is necessary for those who think in this fashion to invent them. Among the most celebrated instances in modern history are the forgery of the Protocols of the Elders of Zion and the grandiose fabrication under Stalin's regime of the Trotzkyite-Buk-harinite-Zinovievite center. These inventions were cynical. In the history of American political controversy there is a tradition of conspiratorial accusations which seem to have been sincerely believed. Jefferson appears really to have believed, at one time, that the Federalists were conspiring to re-establish monarchy. Some Federalists believed that the Jeffersonians were conspiring to subvert Christianity. The movement to annex Texas and the war with Mexico were alleged by many Northerners to be a slaveholders' conspiracy. The early Republican leaders, including Lincoln, charged that there was a conspiracy on the part of Stephen A. Douglas to make slavery a nationwide institution. Such pre-Civil War parties as the Know-Nothing and Anti-Masonic movements were based almost entirely upon conspiratorial ideology. The Nye Committee, years ago, tried to prove that our entry into the first World War was the work of a conspiracy of bankers and munitions-makers. And now not only our entry into the second World War, but the entire history of the past twenty years or so is being given the color of conspiracy by the cranks and political fakirs of our own age.[2]

---

[2] One by-product of this conspiratorial mania is the myth that the recognition of Russia in 1933 was the result of a plot by the New Dealers. Paul Boller, Jr., in a highly amusing article, "The 'Great Conspiracy' of 1933: a Study in Short Memories," Southwest Review, Vol. XXXIX (Spring, 1954), pp. 97–112, shows that some of the same persons who have indulged in the conspiracy cry were advocates of recognition before 1933.

In reading the excellent study by Leo Lowenthal and Norbert Guterman, Prophets of Deceit (New York, 1949), a study of recent authoritarian agitators, I am impressed by certain similarities in the style of thought displayed by their subjects and that of a certain type of Populist writer represented by Mrs. Emery, "Coin" Harvey, Donnelly, and Mrs. Lease. There seem to be certain persistent themes in popular agitation of this sort that transcend particular historical eras. Among the themes delineated by Lowenthal and Guterman that one finds in Populist literature as well as among their agitators are the following: the con-

Nevertheless, when these qualifications have been taken into account, it remains true that Populist thought showed an unusually strong tendency to account for relatively impersonal events in highly personal terms. An overwhelming sense of grievance does not find satisfactory expression in impersonal explanations, except among those with a well-developed tradition of intellectualism. It is the city, after all, that is the home of intellectual complexity. The farmer lived in isolation from the great world in which his fate was actually decided. He was accused of being unusually suspicious,[s] and certainly his situation, trying as it was, made thinking in impersonal terms difficult. Perhaps the rural middle-class leaders of Populism (this was a movement of farmers, but it was not led by farmers) had more to do than the farmer himself with the cast of Populist thinking. At any rate, Populist thought often carries one into a world in which the simple virtues and unmitigated villainies of a rural melodrama have been projected on a national and even an international scale. In Populist thought the farmer is not a speculating businessman, victimized by the risk economy of which he is a part, but rather a wounded yeoman, preyed upon by those who are alien to the life of folkish virtue. A villain was needed, marked with the unmistakable stigmata of the villains of melodrama, and the more remote he was from the familiar scene, the more plausibly his villainies could be exaggerated.

---

ception of history as conspiracy; an obsessive concern with the fabulous enjoyments deemed to be the lot of the plutocrats; cynicism about the two-party system; the notion that the world is moving toward an immense apocalypse; the exclusive attention to the greed and other personal vices of bankers and other selected plutocrats, as opposed to a structural analysis of the social system; anti-Semitism and xenophobia; the appeal to the native simplicity and virtue of the folk. There are, of course, other themes singled out by Lowenthal and Guterman that seem more peculiar to the conditions of our own time and lack cognates in the literature of Populism.

[s] Frederick L. Paxson: "The Agricultural Surplus: a Problem in History," *Agricultural History*, Vol. VI (April 1932), p. 58; cf. the observations of Lord Bryce in *The American Commonwealth* (New York, ed. 1897), Vol. II, pp. 294–5.

It was not enough to say that a conspiracy of the money power against the common people was going on. It had been going on ever since the Civil War. It was not enough to say that it stemmed from Wall Street. It was international: it stemmed from Lombard Street. In his preamble to the People's Party platform of 1892, a succinct, official expression of Populist views, Ignatius Donnelly asserted: "A vast conspiracy against mankind has been organized on two continents, and it is rapidly taking possession of the world. If not met and overthrown at once it forebodes terrible social convulsions, the destruction of civilization, or the establishment of an absolute despotism." A manifesto of 1895, signed by fifteen outstanding leaders of the People's Party, declared: "As early as 1865–66 a conspiracy was entered into between the gold gamblers of Europe and America. . . . For nearly thirty years these conspirators have kept the people quarreling over less important matters while they have pursued with unrelenting zeal their one central purpose. . . . Every device of treachery, every resource of statecraft, and every artifice known to the secret cabals of the international gold ring are being made use of to deal a blow to the prosperity of the people and the financial and commercial independence of the country." [4]

The financial argument behind the conspiracy theory was simple enough. Those who owned bonds wanted to be paid not in a common currency but in gold, which was at a premium; those who lived by lending money wanted as high a premium as possible to be put on their commodity by increasing its scarcity. The panics, depressions, and bankruptcies caused by their policies only added to their wealth; such catastrophes offered opportunities to engross the wealth of others through business consolidations and foreclosures. Hence the interests actually relished and encouraged hard times. The Greenbackers had long since popularized this argument, insisting that an adequate

─────────────

[4] Frank L. McVey: *The Populist Movement* (New York, 1896), pp. 201–2.

legal-tender currency would break the monopoly of the
"Shylocks." Their demand for $50 of circulating medium
per capita, still in the air when the People's Party arose,
was rapidly replaced by the less "radical" demand for free
coinage of silver. But what both the Greenbackers and
free-silverites held in common was the idea that the contraction of currency was a deliberate squeeze, the result
of a long-range plot of the "Anglo-American Gold Trust."
Wherever one turns in the Populist literature of the
nineties one can find this conspiracy theory expressed. It
is in the Populist newspapers, the proceedings of the
silver conventions, the immense pamphlet literature broad-
cast by the American Bimetallic League, the Congressional
debates over money; it is elaborated in such popular books
as Mrs. S. E. V. Emery's *Seven Financial Conspiracies
Which Have Enslaved the American People* or Gordon
Clark's *Shylock: as Banker, Bondholder, Corruptionist,
Conspirator.*

Mrs. Emery's book, first published in 1887, and dedicated to "the enslaved people of a dying republic,"
achieved great circulation, especially among the Kansas
Populists. According to Mrs. Emery, the United States
had been an economic Garden of Eden in the period before
the Civil War. The fall of man had dated from the war
itself, when "the money kings of Wall Street" determined
that they could take advantage of the wartime necessities
of their fellow men by manipulating the currency. "Controlling it, they could inflate or depress the business of
the country at pleasure, they could send the warm life
current through the channels of trade, dispensing peace,
happiness, and prosperity, or they could check its flow,
and completely paralyze the industries of the country." [5]
With this great power for good in their hands, the Wall
Street men preferred to do evil. Lincoln's war policy of
issuing greenbacks presented them with the dire threat
of an adequate supply of currency. So the Shylocks
gathered in convention and "perfected" a conspiracy to

---
[5] Emery, op. cit., p. 13.

create a demand for their gold.[6] The remainder of the
book was a recital of a series of seven measures passed
between 1862 and 1875 which were alleged to be a part
of this continuing conspiracy, the total effect of which was
to contract the currency of the country further and further
until finally it squeezed the industry of the country like
a hoop of steel.[7]

Mrs. Emery's rhetoric left no doubt of the sustained
purposefulness of this scheme—described as "villainous
robbery," and as having been "secured through the most
soulless strategy."[8] She was most explicit about the
so-called "crime of 1873," the demonetization of silver, giving a fairly full statement of the standard greenback-
silverite myth concerning that event. As they had it, an
agent of the Bank of England, Ernest Seyd by name, had
come to the United States in 1872 with $500,000 with
which he had bought enough support in Congress to
secure the passage of the demonetization measure. This
measure was supposed to have greatly increased the value
of American four per cent bonds held by British capitalists
by making it necessary to pay them in gold only. To it
Mrs. Emery attributed the panic of 1873, its bankruptcies,
and its train of human disasters: "Murder, insanity,
suicide, divorce, drunkenness and all forms of immorality
and crime have increased from that day to this in the
most appalling ratio."[9]

"Coin" Harvey, the author of the most popular single
document of the whole currency controversy, *Coin's
Financial School*, also published a novel, *A Tale of Two
Nations*, in which the conspiracy theory of history was in-

---

[6] Ibid., pp. 14–18.
[7] The measures were: the "exception clause" of 1862; the National Bank
Act of 1863; the retirement of the greenbacks, beginning in 1866; the
"credit-strengthening act" of March 18, 1869; the refunding of the
national debt in 1870; the demonetization of silver in 1873; and the
destruction of fractional paper currency in 1875.
[8] Ibid., pp. 25, 43.
[9] Ibid., pp. 54–5. For a more elaborate statement of this story see
Gordon Clark: *Shylock: as Banker, Bondholder, Corruptionist, Conspirator* (Washington, 1894), pp. 88–99.

corporated into a melodramatic tale. In this story the powerful English banker Baron Rothe plans to bring about the demonetization of silver in the United States, in part for his own aggrandizement but also to prevent the power of the United States from outstripping that of England. He persuades an American Senator (probably John Sherman, the *bête noire* of the silverites) to co-operate in using British gold in a campaign against silver. To be sure that the work is successful, he also sends to the United States a relative and ally, one Rogasner, who stalks through the story like the villains in the plays of Dion Boucicault, muttering to himself such remarks as "I am here to destroy the United States—Cornwallis could not have done more. For the wrongs and insults, for the glory of my own country, I will bury the knife deep into the heart of this nation." [1] Against the plausibly drawn background of the corruption of the Grant administration, Rogasner proceeds to buy up the American Congress and suborn American professors of economics to testify for gold. He also falls in love with a proud American beauty, but his designs on her are foiled because she loves a handsome young silver Congressman from Nebraska who bears a striking resemblance to William Jennings Bryan!

One feature of the Populist conspiracy theory that has been generally overlooked is its frequent link with a kind of rhetorical anti-Semitism. The slight current of anti-Semitism that existed in the United States before the 1890's had been associated with problems of money and credit.[2] During the closing years of the century it grew

---

[1] W. H. Harvey: *A Tale of Two Nations* (Chicago, 1894), p. 69.

[2] Anti-Semitism as a kind of rhetorical flourish seems to have had a long underground history in the United States. During the panic of 1837, when many states defaulted on their obligations, many of which were held by foreigners, we find Governor McNutt of Mississippi defending the practice by baiting Baron Rothschild: "The blood of Judas and Shylock flows in his veins, and he unites the qualities of both his countrymen. . . ." Quoted by George W. Edwards: *The Evolution of Finance Capitalism* (New York, 1938), p. 149. Similarly we find Thaddeus Stevens assailing "the Rothschilds, Goldsmiths, and other large

noticeably.[3] While the jocose and rather heavy-handed anti-Semitism that can be found in Henry Adams's letters of the 1890's shows that this prejudice existed outside Populist literature, it was chiefly Populist writers who expressed that identification of the Jew with the usurer and the "international gold ring" which was the central theme of the American anti-Semitism of the age. The omnipresent symbol of Shylock can hardly be taken in itself as evidence of anti-Semitism, but the frequent references to the House of Rothschild make it clear that for many silverites the Jew was an organic part of the conspiracy theory of history. Coin Harvey's Baron Rothe was clearly meant to be Rothschild; his Rogasner (Ernest Seyd?) was a dark figure out of the coarsest anti-Semitic tradition. "You are very wise in your way," Rogasner is told at the climax of the tale, "the commercial way, inbred through generations. The politic, scheming, devious way, inbred through generations also."[4] One of the cartoons in the effectively illustrated *Coin's Financial School* showed a map of the world dominated by the tentacles of an octopus at the site of the British Isles, labeled: "Rothschilds."[5] In Populist demonology, anti-Semitism and Anglophobia went hand in hand.

The note of anti-Semitism was often sounded openly in the campaign for silver. A representative of the New Jersey Grange, for instance, did not hesitate to warn the members of the Second National Silver Convention of 1892 to watch out for political candidates who represented

money dealers" during his early appeals for greenbacks. See James A. Woodburn: *The Life of Thaddeus Stevens* (Indianapolis, 1913), pp. 576, 579.

[3] See Oscar Handlin: "American Views of the Jew at the Opening of the Twentieth Century," *Publications of the American Jewish Historical Society*, no. 40 (June 1951), pp. 323–44.

[4] Harvey: *A Tale of Two Nations*, p. 289; cf. also p. 265: "Did not our ancestors . . . take whatever women of whatever race most pleased their fancy?"

[5] Harvey: *Coin's Financial School* (Chicago, 1894), p. 124; for a notable polemic against the Jews, see James B. Goode: *The Modern Banker* (Chicago, 1896), chapter xii.

"Wall Street, and the Jews of Europe." [6] Mary E. Lease described Grover Cleveland as "the agent of Jewish bankers and British gold." [7] Donnelly represented the leader of the governing Council of plutocrats in *Cæsar's Column,* one Prince Cabano, as a powerful Jew, born Jacob Isaacs; one of the triumvirate who lead the Brotherhood of Destruction is also an exiled Russian Jew, who flees from the apocalyptic carnage with a hundred million dollars which he intends to use to "revive the ancient splendors of the Jewish race, in the midst of the ruins of the world." [8] One of the more elaborate documents of the conspiracy school traced the power of the Rothschilds over America to a transaction between Hugh McCulloch, Secretary of the Treasury under Lincoln and Johnson, and Baron James Rothschild. "The most direful part of this business between Rothschild and the United States Treasury was not the loss of money, even by hundreds of millions. It was the resignation of the country itself INTO THE HANDS OF ENGLAND, as England had long been resigned into the hands of HER JEWS." [9]

Such rhetoric, which became common currency in the

---

[6] *Proceedings of the Second National Silver Convention* (Washington, 1892), p. 48.
[7] Mary E. Lease: *The Problem of Civilization Solved,* pp. 319–20; cf. p. 291.
[8] Donnelly, op. cit., pp. 147, 172, 331.
[9] Gordon Clark, op. cit., pp. 59–60; for the linkage between anti-Semitism and the conspiracy theme, see pp. 2, 4, 8, 39, 55–8, 102–3, 112–13, 117. There was a somewhat self-conscious and apologetic note in populistic anti-Semitism. Remarking that "the aristocracy of the world is now almost altogether of Hebrew origin," one of Donnelly's characters explains that the terrible persecutions to which the Jews had been subjected for centuries heightened the selective process among them, leaving "only the strong of body, the cunning of brain, the long-headed, the persistent . . . and now the Christian world is paying, in tears and blood, for the sufferings inflicted by their bigoted and ignorant ancestors upon a noble race. When the time came for liberty and fair play the Jew was master in the contest with the Gentile, who hated and feared him." *Cæsar's Column,* p. 37. In another fanciful tale Donnelly made amends to the Jews by restoring Palestine to them and making it very prosperous. *The Golden Bottle* (New York and St. Paul, 1892), pp. 280–1.

movement, later passed beyond Populism into the larger
stream of political protest. By the time the campaign of
1896 arrived, an Associated Press reporter noticed as "one
of the striking things" about the Populist convention at St.
Louis "the extraordinary hatred of the Jewish race. It is
not possible to go into any hotel in the city without hearing the most bitter denunciation of the Jews as a class and
of the particular Jews who happen to have prospered in
the world." [1] This report may have been somewhat over-
done, but the identification of the silver cause with anti-
Semitism did become close enough for Bryan to have to
pause in the midst of his campaign to explain to the
Jewish Democrats of Chicago that in denouncing the
policies of the Rothschilds he and his silver friends were
"not attacking a race; we are attacking greed and avarice
which know no race or religion." [2]

It would be easy to misstate the character of Populist
anti-Semitism or to exaggerate its intensity. For Populist
anti-Semitism was entirely verbal. It was a mode of expression, a rhetorical style, not a tactic or a program. It
did not lead to exclusion laws, much less to riots or po-
groms. There were, after all, relatively few Jews in the
United States in the late 1880's and early 1890's, most
of them remote from the areas of Populist strength. It is
one thing, however, to say that this prejudice did not go
beyond a certain symbolic usage, quite another to say
that a people's choice of symbols is of no significance.
Populist anti-Semitism does have its importance—chiefly
as a symptom of a certain ominous credulity in the Populist mind. It is not too much to say that the Greenback-
Populist tradition activated most of what we have of
modern popular anti-Semitism in the United States. [3] From

[1] Quoted by Edward Flower: *Anti-Semitism in the Free Silver and Populist Movements and the Election of 1896*, unpublished M.A. thesis, Columbia University, 1952, p. 27; this essay is illuminating on the de-velopment of anti-Semitism in this period and on the reaction of some of the Jewish press.
[2] William Jennings Bryan: *The First Battle* (Chicago, 1897), p. 581.
[3] I distinguish here between popular anti-Semitism, which is linked with political issues, and upper-class anti-Semitism, which is a variety of snob-

Thaddeus Stevens and Coin Harvey to Father Coughlin, and from Brooks and Henry Adams to Ezra Pound, there has been a curiously persistent linkage between anti-Semitism and money and credit obsessions. A full history of modern anti-Semitism in the United States would reveal, I believe, its substantial Populist lineage, but it may be sufficient to point out here that neither the informal connection between Bryan and the Klan in the twenties nor Thomas E. Watson's conduct in the Leo Frank case were altogether fortuitous.[4] And Henry Ford's notorious anti-Semitism of the 1920's, along with his hatred of "Wall Street," were the foibles of a Michigan farm boy who had been liberally exposed to Populist notions.[5]

---

bery. It is characteristic of the indulgence which Populism has received on this count that Carey McWilliams in his *A Mask for Privilege: Anti-Semitism in America* (Boston, 1948) deals with early American anti-Semitism simply as an upper-class phenomenon. In his historical account of the rise of anti-Semitism he does not mention the Greenback-Populist tradition. Daniel Bell: "The Grass Roots of American Jew Hatred," *Jewish Frontier*, Vol. XI (June 1944), pp. 15–20, is one of the few writers who has perceived that there is any relation between latter-day anti-Semites and the earlier Populist tradition. See also Handlin, op. cit. Arnold Rose has pointed out that much of American anti-Semitism is intimately linked to the agrarian myth and to resentment of the ascendancy of the city. The Jew is made a symbol of both capitalism and urbanism, which are themselves too abstract to be satisfactory objects of animosity. *Commentary*, Vol. VI (October 1948), pp. 374–78.
[4] For the latter see Woodward: *Tom Watson*, chapter xxiii.
[5] Keith Sward: *The Legend of Henry Ford* (New York, 1948), pp. 83–4, 113–14, 119–20, 132, 143–60. Cf. especially pp. 145–6: "Ford could fuse the theory of Populism and the practice of capitalism easily enough for the reason that what he carried forward from the old platforms of agrarian revolt, in the main, were the planks that were most innocent and least radical. Like many a greenbacker of an earlier day, the publisher of the Dearborn *Independent* was haunted by the will-o'-the-wisp of 'money' and the bogy of 'race.' It was these superstitions that lay at the very marrow of his political thinking." For further illustration of the effects of the Populist tradition on a Mountain State Senator, see Oscar Handlin's astute remarks on Senator Pat McCarran in "The Immigration Fight Has Only Begun," *Commentary*, Vol. XIV (July 1952), pp. 3–4.

III · The Spirit Militant

The conspiratorial theory and the associated Anglophobic and Judophobic feelings were part of a larger complex of fear and suspicion of the stranger that haunted, and still tragically haunts, the nativist American mind. This feeling, though hardly confined to Populists and Bryanites, was none the less exhibited by them in a particularly virulent form. Everyone remote and alien was distrusted and hated—even Americans, if they happened to be city people. The old agrarian conception of the city as the home of moral corruption reached a new pitch. Chicago was bad; New York, which housed the Wall Street bankers, was farther away and worse; London was still farther away and still worse. This traditional distrust grew stronger as the cities grew larger, and as they were filled with immigrant aliens. As early as 1885 the Kansas preacher Josiah Strong had published *Our Country*, a book widely read in the West, in which the cities were discussed as a great problem of the future, much as though they were some kind of monstrous malignant growths on the body politic.[6] Hamlin Garland recalled that when he first visited Chicago, in the late 1880's, having never seen a town larger than Rockford, Illinois, he naturally assumed that it swarmed with thieves. "If the city is miles across," he wondered, "how am I to get from the railway station to my hotel without being assaulted?" While such extreme fears could be quieted by some contact with the city, others were actually confirmed—especially when the farmers were confronted with city prices.[7] Nativist prejudices were equally aroused by immigration, for which urban manufacturers, with their insatiable demand for labor, were blamed. "We have be-

---

[6] Josiah Strong: *Our Country* (New York, 1885), chapter x; for the impact of the city, see Arthur M. Schlesinger: *The Rise of the City* (New York, 1933).

[7] Hamlin Garland: *A Son of the Middle Border* (New York, ed. 1923), pp. 269, 295.

come the world's melting pot," wrote Thomas E. Watson. "The scum of creation has been dumped on us. Some of our principal cities are more foreign than American. The most dangerous and corrupting hordes of the Old World have invaded us. The vice and crime which they have planted in our midst are sickening and terrifying. What brought these Goths and Vandals to our shores? The manufacturers are mainly to blame. They wanted cheap labor: and they didn't care a curse how much harm to our future might be the consequence of their heartless policy." [8]

Anglo-Saxons, whether Populist or patrician, found it difficult to accept other peoples on terms of equality or trust. Others were objects to be manipulated—benevolently, it was often said, but none the less firmly. Mary E. Lease, that authentic voice of inland Populism who became famous for advising farmers to "raise less corn and more hell," wrote a book in 1895 under the ingratiating title: *The Problem of Civilization Solved,* in which this ethnic condescension was rather ingenuously displayed. According to Mrs. Lease, Europe and America stood on the brink of one of two immense catastrophes—a universal reign of anarchistic terror or the establishment of a worldwide Russian despotism. The only hope of averting catastrophe was, as she put it, "the most stupendous migration of races the world has ever known, and thereby relieve the congested centers of the world's population of half their inhabitants and provide Free Homes for half of mankind." [9] She proposed a vast reshuffling of peoples in which the tropics in both hemispheres be taken over by white planters with Negroes and Orientals as "tillers of the soil." "Through all the vicissitudes of time, the Caucasian has arisen to the moral and intellectual supremacy of the world, until now this favored race is fitted for the

---

[8] Watson: *Andrew Jackson,* p. 326; cf. *Cæsar's Column,* p. 131: "The silly ancestors of the Americans called it 'national development' when they imported millions of foreigners to take up the public lands and left nothing for their own children."

[9] Lease, op. cit., p. 17.

*Stewardship of the Earth and Emancipation from Manual
Labor."* [1] This stewardship, far from being an imposition
on the lesser breeds without the law, would be an act of
mercy; it would take the starved and miserable ryots and
coolies of the world and by giving them management and
supervision provide them with the means of life, as well
as rescue them from paganism. Such a change they would
"hail with joy." [2]

The proposal for colonization under government supervision and with governmental subsidies was supplemented
by a grand plan for what Mrs. Lease candidly called the
partitioning of the world, in which the Germanic and
Latin peoples would be united into two racial confedera-
tions, and the British and Russian empires checked and
neutralized by other powerful states. The role of the
United States in this world was to be the head of the
federated American republics. Canada should be annexed
—so also Cuba, Haiti, Santo Domingo, and Hawaii. The
Latin republics would be fertile fields for colonization by
the surplus population of the United States—which no
longer had a public domain to give its citizens—and the
North Americans would import "vast swarms of Asiatics as
laborers for the plantations." Mrs. Lease felt that the
Latins, like the Asiatics, would certainly benefit from this
and that they ought to like it. Moreover, they owed the
United States a debt of gratitude: "We stand, and have
stood for. years, ready to extend our blood and treasure
in defense of Latin America against European aggression.
Can they not *reciprocate* by giving us the leadership on
this continent? If not, we should take it! We should follow
the example of European nations and annex all we can
and establish protectorates wherever possible in America." [3]

Mrs. Lease's book, the work of a naïve but imaginative
mind driven to the pitch of its powers by an extraordinary

---

[1] Loc. cit.
[2] Ibid., pp. 31–2, 34, 35.
[3] Ibid., pp. 177–8.

capacity for suspicion, was hardly as representative or popular as *Coin's Financial School* or *Cæsar's Column*, though its author was one of the indigenous products of Populist political culture. Mrs. Lease's peculiar ideas of *Weltpolitik*, her particular views on tropical colonization, were not common currency in Populist thinking. But other assumptions in her book could be found among the Populists with great frequency—the smug assumption of Anglo-Saxon superiority and benevolence, the sense of a need for some new area of expansion, the hatred of England, the fear of Russia,[4] the anxiety over the urban masses as a potential source of anarchy.

The nationalist fervor of Mrs. Lease's book also represents one side of a curiously ambiguous aspect of Populism. On the surface there was a strong note of anti-militarism and anti-imperialism in the Populist movement and Bryan democracy. Populists were opposed to large standing armies and large naval establishments; most of them supported Bryan's resistance to the acquisition of the Philippines. They looked upon the military as a threat to democracy, upon imperialist acquisitions as gains only to financiers and "monarchists," not to the people.[5] But what they chiefly objected to was institutional militarism rather than war itself, imperialism rather than jingoism. Under a patina of pacifist rhetoric they were profoundly nationalistic and bellicose. What the nativist mind most resolutely opposed was not so much war itself as co-operation with European governments for any ends at all.[6]

---

[4] Since this was a commonplace in the nineteenth century, it would be too much to ascribe to Mrs. Lease any special prophetic stature.

[5] See W. H. Harvey: *Coin on Money, Trusts, and Imperialism* (Chicago, 1900), for an expression of popular feelings on these and other issues.

[6] The best illustration was the American bimetallist movement. It was only during the 1870's that the international gold standard can be said to have come into existence, and it did so on the eve of the long price decline of the "Great Depression." The desire of the silver interests in various parts of the world, together with those groups that sought in silver a means of raising the general level of prices, gave rise almost from the beginning to bimetallic movements nearly everywhere in western Europe. Even in England, the commercial center and the

Those who have been puzzled in our own time by the anti-European attitudes of men like Senator Taft and General MacArthur, and by their alternating espousal of dangerously aggressive and near-pacifistic (or anti-militarist) policies, will find in the Populist mentality a suggestive precedent.

The Populists distinguished between wars for humanity and wars of conquest. The first of these they considered legitimate, but naturally they had difficulty in discriminating between the two, and they were quite ready to be ballyhooed into a righteous war, as the Cuban situation was to show. During the early nineteenth century popular sentiment in the United States, especially within the democratic camp, had been strong for the republican movements in Europe and Latin America. With the coming of the nineties and the great revulsion against the outside world, the emphasis was somewhat changed; where sympathy with oppressed and revolutionary peoples had been the dominant sentiment in the past, the dominant sentiment now seemed rather to be hatred of their governments. That there must always be such an opposition between peoples and governments the Populist mind did not like to question, and even the most demo-

---

creditor nation which did not relish being paid its debts in depreciated currency, there were eminent statesmen who favored bimetallism; and the two greatest economists of the era, Jevons and Marshall, considered it seriously. But everywhere except in the United States the bimetallic movements looked to international action as the method of establishing a bimetallic standard; in the United States alone the silver interests adhered to the possibility of unilateral action. The constant expectation that the United States would act alone to maintain the price of silver was an impediment to action elsewhere. From the 1870's onward conservative American statesmen who sought to initiate action that would lead to an international bimetallic standard had been caught between the difficulty of lining up the other nations and the sharp impatience of domestic silver interests, which insisted with growing asperity as the years went by that reluctance to go it alone was treasonable. See J. B. Condliffe: *The Commerce of Nations* (New York, 1950), chapter xii, "The International Gold Standard"; Jeannette P. Nichols: "Silver Diplomacy," *Political Science Quarterly*, Vol. XXXVIII (December 1933), pp. 565–88. On the relation between silverism and isolationism, see Ray Allen Billington: "The Origins of Middle Western Isolationism," *Political Science Quarterly*, Vol. LX (March 1945), esp. pp. 50–2.

cratic governments of Europe were persistently looked upon as though they were nothing but reactionary monarchies.[7]

After the success of *Cæsar's Column*, Donnelly wrote another fantasy called *The Golden Bottle*, in which this antagonism had a vivid expression. The first part of the story need not detain us: it deals with the life of one Ephraim Benezet of Kansas who is given a bottle that empowers him to turn iron into gold, a windfall which not surprisingly makes it possible for him to solve his own and the country's financial problems. Before long he is elected President, and after foiling a plot to kill him and checking a bankers' conspiracy to start a civil war, he delivers an extraordinary inaugural message. The one thing that prevents the American people, he tells them, from rising "to still higher levels of greatness and happiness" is the Old World. America is "united by a ligament to a corpse—Europe!" This begins an appeal to close the gates against further wretched immigrants from Europe who will be used by American capitalists to beat down the wages of American workingmen. "We could, by wise laws and just conditions, lift up the toilers of our own country to the level of the middle classes, but a vast multitude of the miserable of other lands clung to their skirts and dragged them down. Our country was the safety-valve which permitted the discontent of the Old World to escape. If that vent was closed, every throne in Europe would be blown up in twenty years. . . . For the people of the Old World, having to choose between death by starvation and resistance to tyrants, would turn upon their oppressors and tear them to pieces." There follows an appeal to the peoples of Europe to revolt against their rulers. The countries of Europe respond by declaring war, and in the great international conflict that follows, the United States comes to Europe as an invading liberator. President Benezet wins, of course, and frees even the Russians simply by making them literate. He

[7] See Harvey's *Coin on Money, Trusts, and Imperialism, passim.*

also establishes a world government to keep the peace.[8]

It is no coincidence, then, that Populism and jingoism grew concurrently in the United States during the 1890's. The rising mood of intolerant nationalism was a nationwide thing, certainly not confined to the regions of Populist strength; but among no stratum of the population was it stronger than among the Populists. Moreover it was on jingoist issues that the Populist and Bryanite sections of the country, with the aid of the yellow press and many political leaders, achieved that rapport with the masses of the cities which they never succeeded in getting on economic issues. Even conservative politicians sensed that, whatever other grounds of harmony were lacking between themselves and the populace of the hinterland, grounds for unity could be found in war.

The first, and for the Populists the preferred, enemy would have been England, the center of the gold power. *Coin's Financial School* closed with a better philippic against England: "If it is claimed we must adopt for our money the metal England selects, and can have no independent choice in the matter, let us make the test and find out if it is true. It is not American to give up without trying. If it is true, let us attach England to the United States and blot her name out from among the nations of the earth. A war with England would be the most popular ever waged on the face of the earth . . . the most just war ever waged by man." [9] Some leaders of the Republican Party, which had attempted to appease the powerful silver sentiment in 1890 by passing the Sherman Silver Purchase Act, made a strategic move in the troubled year of 1894 to capture Western sentiment. On May 2 there opened in London an unofficial bimetallic

---

[8] Ignatius Donnelly: *The Golden Bottle*, pp. 202 ff. "I would be sorry," said Donnelly in his preface, "if any one should be so foolish as to argue that the triumph of the People's Party means a declaration of war against the whole world." What concerns us here, however, is not the Populists' intentions in this sphere, which were doubtless innocent enough, but the emotions laid bare by Donnelly's fantasy.

[9] *Coin's Financial School*, pp. 131–2.

conference in which American bimetallists were represented by Brooks Adams and Senator Wolcott of Colorado;
fifteen prominent Senators, including outstanding Republicans, cabled their endorsement of international
bimetallism. Senator Lodge proposed in the Senate to
blackmail Britain by passing a discriminatory tariff against
her if she did not consent to a bimetallic plan, a scheme
nicely calculated to hold in line some of the Western
silverite jingoes and Anglophobes.[1]

This proposal was defeated by the Cleveland Democrats,
but the Democratic Party's turn to make capital out of
jingo sentiment came the next year with the excessively
belligerent conduct of the Venezuela affair, one of the
few really popular moves of the Cleveland administration.[2]
A west-coast newspaper spoke for many Americans when
it said: "We are at the mercy of England, as far as our
finances go, and [war] is our only way out." [3] "War
would be a good thing even if we got whipped," declared
the silver Senator from Nevada, William M. Stewart,
"for it would rid us of English bank rule." [4] And a
Congressman from a strong Populist state wrote to con-
gratulate Secretary of State Olney for having spiked the
guns of Populism and anarchism with his vigorous
diplomacy.[5] Olney was also urged by the American con-
sul in Havana to identify the administration and the
sound-money Democrats with a strong policy of mediation
or intervention in the war in Cuba; it would either get
credit for stopping the atrocities, for buying Cuba, if
that was the outcome, or for "fighting a successful war,
if war there be. In the latter case, the enthusiasm, the
applications for service, the employment of many of the

[1] Nevins, op. cit., pp. 608–9.
[2] On domestic pressures behind this incident, see Nelson M. Blake: "Background of Cleveland's Venezuela Policy," *American Historical Review*, Vol. XLVII (January 1942), pp. 259–77.
[3] James A. Barnes: *John G. Carlisle* (New York, 1931), p. 410.
[4] Nevins, op. cit., p. 641.
[5] Alfred Vagts: *Deutschland und die Vereinigten Staaten in der Weltpolitik* (New York, 1935), Vol. I, p. 511.

unemployed, might do much towards directing the minds of the people from imaginary ills, the relief of which is erroneously supposed to be reached by 'Free Silver.'"[6]

When the Venezuela matter was settled, the attention of jingoes turned toward Cuba. The situation of the oppressed Cubans was one with which the Populist elements in the country could readily identify themselves, and they added their voice to the general cry throughout the country for an active policy of intervention. After the defeat of Bryan, popular frustration in the silver areas, blocked on domestic issues, seemed to find expression in the Cuban question. Here at last was a point at which the goldbugs could be vanquished. Neither the big business and banking community nor the Cleveland and McKinley administrations had much sympathy with the crusading fever that pervaded the country at large, and there were bitter mutual recriminations between conservative and Populist papers. Wall Street was accused of a characteristic indifference to the interests of humanity; the Populists in return were charged with favoring war as a cover under which they could smuggle in an inflationary policy. One thing seems clear: "most of the leading Congressional backers of intervention in Cuba represented southern and western states where Populism and silver were strongest." [7] And it appears that one of the reasons why McKinley was advised by many influential Republicans to yield to the popular demand for war was the common fear, still meaningful in 1898, that the Democrats would go into the next presidential election with the irresistible slogan of Free Silver and Free Cuba as its battle cry.[8] Jingoism was confined to no class, section, or party; but the Populist areas stood in the vanguard,

[6] Ibid., Vol. II, p. 1266 n.

[7] J. E. Wisan: *The Cuban Crisis as Reflected in the New York Press* (New York, 1934), p. 455; for the relation of this crisis to the public temper of the nineties, see Richard Hofstadter: "Manifest Destiny and the Philippines," in Daniel Aaron, ed.: *America in Crisis* (New York, 1952).

[8] Vagts, op. cit., Vol. II, p. 1308 n.

and their pressure went far to bring about a needless war. When the war was over, the economic and emotional climate in which their movement had grown no longer existed, and their forces were scattered and confused. A majority of them, after favoring war, attempted honorably to spurn the fruits of war by taking up the cause of anti-imperialism. Thomas E. Watson, one of the few Populists who had consistently opposed the war, later insisted that "The Spanish War finished us. The blare of the bugle drowned the voice of the reformer." [9] The cause of reform was, in fact, too resilient to be permanently crushed by a short war; but, for the moment, Free Cuba had displaced Free Silver in public interest, and when reform raised its head again, it had a new face.

As we review these aspects of Populist emotion, an odd parallel obtrudes itself. Where else in American thought during this period do we find this militancy and nationalism, these apocalyptic forebodings and drafts of world-political strategies, this hatred of big businessmen, bankers, and trusts, these fears of immigrants and urban workmen, even this occasional toying with anti-Semitic rhetoric? We find them, curiously enough, most conspicuous among a group of men who are in all obvious respects the antithesis of the Populists. During the late 1880's and the '90's there emerged in the eastern United States a small imperialist elite representing, in general, the same type that had once been Mugwumps, whose spokesmen were such solid and respectable gentlemen as Henry and Brooks Adams, Theodore Roosevelt, Henry Cabot Lodge, John Hay, and Albert J. Beveridge. While the silverites were raging openly and earnestly against the bankers and the Jews, Brooks and Henry Adams were expressing in their sardonic and morosely cynical private correspondence the same feelings, and acknowledging with bemused irony their kinship at this point with the mob. While Populist Congressmen and newspapers called for war with England or Spain, Roosevelt and Lodge did

[9] Woodward: *Tom Watson*, p. 334.

the same, and while Mrs. Lease projected her grandiose
schemes of world partition and tropical colonization,
men like Roosevelt, Lodge, Beveridge, and Mahan projected more realistic plans for the conquest of markets
and the annexation of territory. While Populist readers
were pondering over Donnelly's apocalyptic fantasies,
Brooks and Henry Adams were also bemoaning the approaching end of their type of civilization, and even the
characteristically optimistic T. R. could share at moments
in "Brooks Adams' gloomiest anticipations of our gold-
ridden, capitalist-bestridden, usurer-mastered future." Not
long after Mrs. Lease wrote that "we need a Napoleon in
the industrial world who, by agitation and education,
will lead the people to a realizing sense of their condition
and the remedies," [1] Roosevelt and Brooks Adams talked
about the threat of the eight-hour movement and the
danger that the country would be "enslaved" by the
organizers of the trusts, and played with the idea that
Roosevelt might eventually lead "some great outburst of
the emotional classes which should at least temporarily
crush the Economic Man." [2]

Not only were the gentlemen of this imperialist elite

---

[1] Lease, op. cit., p. 7. Thomas E. Watson wrote in 1902 a lengthy
biography: Napoleon, a Sketch of His Life, Character, Struggles, and
Achievements, in which Napoleon, "the moneyless lad from despised
Corsica, who stormed the high places of the world, and by his own
colossal strength of character, genius, and industry took them," is calmly
described as "the great Democratic despot." Elsewhere Watson wrote:
"There is not a railway king of the present day, not a single self-made
man who has risen from the ranks to become chief in the vast movement of capital and labor, who will not recognize in Napoleon traits of
his own character; the same unflagging purpose, tireless persistence,
silent plotting, pitiless rush to victory . . ."—which caused Watson's
biographer to ask what a Populist was doing celebrating the virtues of
railroad kings and erecting an image of capitalist acquisitiveness for his
people to worship. "Could it be that the Israelites worshipped the
same gods as the Philistines? Could it be that the only quarrel between
the two camps was over a singular disparity in the favors won?" Woodward, op. cit., pp. 340–2.
[2] Matthew Josephson: The President Makers (New York, 1940), p. 98.
See the first three chapters of Josephson's volume for a penetrating
account of the imperialist elite. Daniel Aaron has an illuminating
analysis of Brooks Adams in his Men of Good Hope (New York, 1951).

better read and better fed than the Populists, but they despised them. This strange convergence of unlike social elements on similar ideas has its explanation, I believe, in this: both the imperialist elite and the Populists had been bypassed and humiliated by the advance of industrialism, and both were rebelling against the domination of the country by industrial and financial capitalists. The gentlemen wanted the power and status they felt due them, which had been taken away from their class and type by the *arriviste* manufacturers and railroaders and the all-too-potent banking houses. The Populists wanted a restoration of agrarian profits and popular government. Both elements found themselves impotent and deprived in an industrial culture and balked by a common enemy. On innumerable matters they disagreed, but both were strongly nationalistic, and amid the despairs and anxieties of the nineties both became ready for war if that would unseat or even embarrass the moneyed powers, or better still if it would topple the established political structure and open new opportunities for the leaders of disinherited farmers or for ambitious gentlemen. But if there seems to be in this situation any suggestion of a forerunner or analogue of modern authoritarian movements, it should by no means be exaggerated. The age was more innocent and more fortunate than ours, and by comparison with the grimmer realities of the twentieth century many of the events of the nineties take on a comic-opera quality. What came in the end was only a small war and a quick victory; when the farmers and the gentlemen finally did coalesce in politics, they produced only the genial reforms of Progressivism; and the man on the white horse turned out to be just a graduate of the Harvard boxing squad, equipped with an immense bag of platitudes, and quite willing to play the democratic game.

CHAPTER III

FROM PATHOS TO PARITY

1 · Success Through Failure

A paradox pervades modern interpretations of the agrarian revolt of the nineties. On one hand the failure of the revolt has been described again and again as the final defeat of the American farmer. John Hicks, in his history of the movement, speaks of the Populists as having begun "the last phase of a long and perhaps a losing struggle —the struggle to save agricultural America from the devouring jaws of industrial America," while another historian calls Populism "the last united stand of the country's agricultural interest . . . the final attempt made by the farmers of the land to beat back an industrial civilization whose forces had all but vanquished them already." [1] On the other hand, it has been equally common to enumerate, as evidence of the long-range power of Populism, the substantial list of once derided Populist proposals that were enacted within less than twenty years after the defeat of Bryan, and to assign to the agrarian agitations of the Populist era an important influence on the golden age of Progressive reform.[2] How can a movement whose program was in the long run so generally successful be identified with such a final and disastrous defeat for the class it was supposed to represent?

---

[1] *The Populist Revolt*, p. 237; Louis Hacker in Hacker and Kendrick: *The United States since 1865* (New York, ed. 1949), p. 253. For a similar view see Woodward: *Tom Watson*, p. 330.
[2] Hicks: *The Populist Revolt*, chapter xv; Hacker and Kendrick, op. cit., pp. 257, 352–3.

There is something valid in both these views. Populism and Bryanism were the last attempt to incorporate what I have called the "soft" side of the farmer's dual character into a national mass movement. But the further conclusion that the eclipse of this sort of reform represents the total and final defeat of agriculture is no more than the modern liberal's obeisance to the pathos of agrarian rhetoric. After the defeat of Populism and Bryanism and the failure of the agrarian catchwords, the "hard" side of the farmers' movements, based upon the commercial realities of agriculture, developed more forcefully and prosperously than ever. It was during the twenty years after McKinley routed Bryan that American agriculture enjoyed its greatest prosperity under modern peacetime conditions, prior to 1945–55; and it was the same twenty years that saw agriculture make the greatest gains it had ever made in the sphere of national legislation.

The failure of a political movement based upon the old phrases of agrarian ideology must not be identified with the failure of commercial agriculture as an economic interest. Certainly no one would maintain that even a victory for Bryan in 1896 could have seriously delayed the industrialization of the country and the relative shrinkage of the rural farm population. But it can be said that the Populist movement, despite its defeat, activated a stream of agrarian organization and protest that subsequently carried point after point. Before these victories could be won it was necessary that both the market situation of agriculture and the political climate of the country should change. The attempt to make agrarianism into a mass movement based upon third-party ideological politics also had to be supplanted by the modern methods of pressure politics and lobbying within the framework of the existing party system. Populism was the expression of a transitional stage in the development of our agrarian politics: while it reasserted for the last time some old ways of thought, it was also a harbinger of the new. American agricultural leaders were spurred by its achievements and

educated by its failures. Far from being the final defeat
of the farmer, it was the first uncertain step in the development of effective agrarian organization.

Agrarian organization in the United States has veered
back and forth between two kinds of programs: those
based primarily upon local and regional problems and
carried out chiefly through nonpartisan action, and those
based upon broader and more comprehensive goals and
tending toward third-party action. The Granger movement of the 1870's had emphasized action within the states,
and only in 1875 and 1876, when it was already declining
in numbers and prestige, did it hesitantly reach out toward
national legislation.[3] The various Farmers' Alliances, which
mark the beginnings of the Populist Party, also began as
business, educational, and social organizations, often quite
explicitly nonpartisan. Unlike the Granges, they moved
rapidly and decisively toward political action, and as
farmers flocked into the Alliance movement in the late
1880's, the possibility of third-party action became more
and more real. After an imposing original success in the
state and Congressional elections of 1890, the Populists
proceeded with much enthusiasm to organize for the
presidential election of 1892. In the South the Alliancemen had worked chiefly through the Democratic Party;
but the nomination of Grover Cleveland by the Democrats in 1892, which showed that both major parties were
in the hands of conservatives unsympathetic to the
farmers, clinched the drive for a nationwide third-party
movement.

The move toward third-party politics seems to have
been a realistic way of dramatizing the aims of the
Alliancemen. The forces they were fighting, the problems
they were trying to solve, were too powerful, too complex
for any agency weaker or less inclusive than the federal
government, and the two major parties had been dis-
couragingly indifferent to their demands. The agrarian

---

[3] Solon J. Buck: *The Granger Movement* (Cambridge, 1933), p. 122.

myth, which taught them that any government was a failure that did not foster the interests of the agricultural class, liberated the farm leaders from allegiance to the prevailing notions of *laissez faire* and left them without inhibitions about advocating whatever federal measure seemed likely to aid the farmers, whether it was government ownership of transportation or government warehousing.

But third-party leaders in the United States must look for success in terms different from those that apply to the major parties, for in those terms third parties always fail. No third party has ever won possession of the government or replaced one of the major parties. (Even the Republican Party came into existence as a new major party, created out of sections of the old ones, not as a third party grown to major-party strength.) Third parties have often played an important role in our politics, but it is different in kind from the role of the governing parties.[4] Major parties have lived more for patronage than for principles; their goal has been to bind together a sufficiently large coalition of diverse interests to get into power; and once in power, to arrange sufficiently satisfactory compromises of interests to remain there. Minor parties have been attached to some special idea or interest, and they have generally expressed their positions through firm and identifiable programs and principles. Their function has not been to win or govern, but to agitate, educate, generate new ideas, and supply the dynamic element in our political life. When a third party's demands become popular enough, they are appropriated by one or both of the major parties and the third party disappears. Third parties are like bees: once they have stung, they die.

If third parties are judged by the adoption of their

[4] See the astute essay by John D. Hicks: "The Third Party Tradition in American Politics," *Mississippi Valley Historical Review*, Vol. XX (June 1933), pp. 3–28; cf. also Arthur N. Holcombe: *The Political Parties of Today* (New York, 1924), chapter xi; on the types of minor parties, see Arthur M. Schlesinger: *The American as Reformer* (Cambridge, 1950), pp. 54 ff.

principles, their history records some notable successes. Even the obscure Anti-Masonic Party brought the national convention into our political system in place of the party caucus. The Liberty and Free-Soil parties of the pre-Civil War era were notoriously successful in forcing the slavery issue into the center of politics. The moral and intellectual leverage exerted by the Socialist Party and Socialist ideas in the Progressive era has never been sufficiently recognized. The People's—or Populist—Party is a striking case of the exertion of broad influence by a relatively small force through third-party action.

If third-party leaders always accepted the premise that third parties are destined to this peculiar kind of failure-in-success, they might not have the courage and initiative to start their crusades. What the founders of the People's Party thought they were trying to do is not altogether clear, but they seem to have been misled by the early local successes of the movement and by the more than one million votes cast for General Weaver in the presidential election of 1892 into believing that they had a major-party future. What most impresses the historian, however, is the negligible chance they had to replace a major party. In 1892 General Weaver had 8.5 per cent of the total vote—and it may help to gauge the dimensions of his support if we remember that this was much closer, say, to Debs's 5.9 per cent in 1912 than it was to La Follette's 16.6 per cent in 1924. The sharp sectional confinement of Populist support is also worth noting. Weaver was strong in a few plains and mountain states and a half-dozen states of the South. But throughout a great range of states which controlled over 55 per cent of the electoral college, including, in the West, Iowa, Wisconsin, and Illinois, and ranging eastward through all the Middle Atlantic and New England states and southward to Virginia, the Populist Party was almost invisible, receiving everywhere less than 5 per cent of the total vote. There were only nine states, several of them sparsely populated, in which Weaver got the vote of more than one third of the electorate. Plainly the Populists had shown strength enough to influence the local character of the major parties in several states, or to form a small bloc in the Senate, but little more.

These limitations upon the appeal of the People's Party are not hard to understand. As a third-party movement, it was confined to the areas of the most acute agricultural discontent where one-crop cash staple farming, heavily dependent upon the export market, was found in combination with exceptional transportation problems or a high rate of mortgaged indebtedness. It was feeble everywhere else, except in the thinly populated mountain states. The middle classes, which often took seriously the hysterical literature describing the Populists as anarchists or socialists, either ridiculed or feared them. Workingmen did not vote consciously as a class; and between the Knights of Labor, which was dying, and the American Federation of Labor, which was in its infancy, there was hardly a labor movement to speak of.[5] Eastern farmers who had acute problems and discontents of their own looked upon Western farmers as competitors and enemies, and realized that the Populist proposals were not designed to meet their needs.[6] But what was perhaps most decisive in the sectional confinement of Populism was its failure to gain a following in the farm-belt states of the old Northwest that only ten or fifteen years before had been leading centers of disaffection. By 1892, states like Iowa, Illinois, and Wisconsin

---

[5] The experience of Illinois suggested that when labor became class-conscious enough to play an independent political role, it tended toward collectivist programs that were incompatible with the usual Populist outlook. Cf. Chester McA. Destler: *American Radicalism, 1865–1901* (New London, 1946), chapters viii, ix, xi. Cf. Daniel M. Feins: *Labor's Role in the Populist Movement, 1890–96*, unpublished M.A. thesis, Columbia University, 1939.

[6] Lee Benson: *The New York Farmers' Rejection of Populism: the Background*, unpublished M.A. thesis, Columbia University, 1948. American farmers had much in common ideologically, but such was the heterogeneity of American agriculture that their concrete interests often conflicted head-on. For an account of some of these differences see Herman C. Nixon: "The Cleavage within the Farmers' Alliance Movement," *Mississippi Valley Historical Review*, Vol. XV (June 1928), pp. 22–33.

had long since passed the period of their most intense
speculative development; they had reckoned with their
railroads and middlemen during the Granger era, and
their grievances were much less acute than those in the
regions farther west. Above all, the prosperous and ready-
cash industry of dairying and the more stable corn-hog
complex—neither of which was as dependent upon exports and the world market as wheat or cotton—had replaced wheat in a great many areas.[7] A substantial local
urban market had grown up in these states, and agriculture generally was more prosperous. Not only did Weaver
lose these states in 1892, but even Bryan, running under
a major-party label during a severe depression four years
later, lost Illinois, Iowa, Minnesota, and Wisconsin, and
with them enough electoral support to lose the election.
In these states the steady advance of the cow and the
hog had done at least as much as Mark Hanna's slush
fund to temper the force of the agrarian crusade.

In the Congressional and state elections of 1894 the
Populists reached their maximum strength, but there was
evidence that the movement had already passed its peak
as a third-party force. While the two major parties were

---

[7] There was in fact an almost direct relation in the West between the
prevalence of the wheat crop and the centers of third-party action. For
an excellent account of the stabilizing effects of diversification and the
development of dairying and corn-hog farming, see Chester McA.
Destler: "Agricultural Readjustment and Agrarian Unrest in Illinois,
1880–1896," Agricultural History, Vol. XXI (April 1947), pp. 104–
16. See Benton H. Wilcox: "An Historical Definition of Northwestern
Radicalism," Mississippi Valley Historical Review, Vol. XXVI (December 1939), pp. 377–94 and the same author's A Reconsideration of
the Character and Economic Basis of Northwestern Radicalism, unpublished Ph.D. dissertation, University of Wisconsin, 1933, pp. 56–
8 and passim for an illuminating discussion of Northwestern regional
differentiation. Clyde O. Ruggles: "The Economic Basis of the Greenback Movement in Iowa and Wisconsin," Mississippi Valley Historical
Association Proceedings, Vol. VI (1912–13), pp. 142–65, esp. pp. 154–
7, shows how the development of diversification and dairying had in
earlier years cramped the support of Greenbackism as later it was
to do to Populism. For the situation in prosperous Iowa see Herman
C. Nixon: "The Populist Movement in Iowa," Iowa Journal of History
and Politics, Vol. XXIV (January 1926), esp. pp. 3–45, 68–70, 99–
100, 103–7.

both still nationally controlled by conservatives, they were flexible enough at the local level, in areas where Populists were strong, to head off the movement. In Kansas, where the Populist victory in 1892 had been decisive enough for solid control of the legislature, the Populists had been lured by the Republicans into a futile "legislative war" and had failed to enact any important legislation.[8] Experience elsewhere—in Minnesota, for example, and Nebraska—made it clear that where the Populists had programs designed to cope with major local grievances of the farmers, their issues were either appropriated by the major parties in sufficient measure to drain off their strength or incorporated by the Populists in faulty legislation that did not stand the test of the hostile conservative courts.[9] In the South the Negro question was used effectively to divert attention from reform. Populists were driven, after 1893, to look more searchingly for a general issue that would give them a broad national appeal, unite their sectional fragments, and constitute a challenge to the relatively inflexible national leadership of the major parties.

Here it is necessary to consider the nature of Populist leadership. Farmers had never drawn their political leaders from their own ranks, but rather from a ragged elite of professional men, rural editors, third-party veterans, and professional reformers—men who had had much experience in agitation but little or no experience with responsibility or power.[1] It is significant that the leader-

---

[8] Elizabeth N. Barr, in William E. Connelley: *A Standard History of Kansas and Kansans*, Vol. II (Chicago, 1918), pp. 1167 ff.

[9] Hicks: *The Populist Revolt*, chapter x; on the situation in Minnesota see Hicks: "The People's Party in Minnesota," *Minnesota History Bulletin*, Vol. V (November 1924), pp. 547 ff.

[1] Even Iowa, with its substantial farmers, sent to Congress between 1844 and 1938 only 15 farmers out of a total of 419 elected Congressmen. Other representatives were from the professions (309 were lawyers) and business. Of the 15 farmers, 12 were elected between 1844 and 1890 and 3 between 1932 and 1938—not one during the years from 1890 to 1932. Johnstone: "Old Ideals versus New Ideas," pp. 156-7. On the problem of leadership see also Hicks: *The Populist Revolt*, pp. 151-2.

An exploration of the Donnelly papers suggests that in the organiza-

ship of this "radical" movement included a surprisingly
large number of old men born in the Jackson era, gray-
haired veterans of innumerable Granger, Greenback, and
antimonopoly campaigns. Many, like General Weaver,
were men with a deep passion for justice; some were
cranks or careerists who had failed to find a place for
themselves within the established political machines.
Many had been subsisting for long years upon a monoto-
nous diet of failure, and to them it appeared that with
the crisis of the nineties the time had at last come for
one of the third-party movements to succeed. They
hungered for success as major-party leaders knew it, and
this left them open to temptation: they could, without too
much difficulty, be persuaded to give up a large part of
their program if they felt that this was the way to win.

The Populist leaders, moreover, had been confronted
all along with a besetting weakness that was hardly any
fault of their own: lack of funds. It has been too little
understood that because of the small sums of money
available to the Populists their movement was almost from
the beginning—and out of necessity, not out of corruption
—for sale cheap. It found its takers in the silver interests.
Farmers, it should be remembered, were often generous
with enthusiasm but could rarely afford to be generous
with cash. It was difficult to get many poverty-ridden
farmers to part, literally, with a nickel, and the Farmers'
Alliance, the People's Party, the innumerable little newspapers that were the organs of the movement, were all
shoestring operations. For instance, the treasurer's report

tion of the Alliance in Minnesota the rural middle class played a
crucial part. Farmers were too busy to be available for lecturing or
organizing, but men whose farming was overshadowed by their other
business interests—small merchants who sold to farmers and were dependent upon their prosperity, for instance—were able to undertake
such tasks. For them it was possible to combine the functions of
agitation and salesmanship. This need of the movement for leaders
also gave an opportunity for country cranks to find a pleasant vocational outlet for their notions. For this reason one cannot always be
sure to what extent the more extreme manifestations of Populist
thinking were representative of the farmers themselves rather than of
such rural agitators.

of the Alliance for 1890—a year when the organization claimed more than one million affiliated farmers—showed receipts from membership fees of only $11,231. At five cents each the membership should have been able to provide $50,000! [2] When the Populists of Iowa were engaged in their state campaign of 1895, repeated pleas for campaign funds had to be supplemented by a five-cent assessment—which yielded $317.[3] Sometimes substantial farmers were willing and eager to help but almost completely unable to do so because they were land-poor. One of them wrote to Ignatius Donnelly: "The . . . effort I have made for existence since August 29, 1881 places me in a position unable to advance a dollar for the most Riteous Cause on earth. Onely upon one condition, and that is if you can send me a man who will put up $35. per acre for 240 acres ($8400) with crops. I will advance $800. . . . I not onely will advance this 800 but will put on the harness and work till victory is ours." [4] The meager amounts with which political campaigns were conducted in the early days of the Populist Party were indeed pathetic. Some of its leaders believed in 1891 that they could elect their entire state ticket in Kentucky if they had a few thousand dollars to spend.[5] By early August of the following year they had collected only $400 for their state ticket in Minnesota, though pledged sums uncollected were far greater.[6] In 1892 they were hoping to raise $2,000 for their campaign in the three states of Arkansas, Georgia, and Florida.[7]

---

[2] Orville M. Kile: *The Farm Bureau Movement* (New York, 1921), p. 28.
[3] Nixon: "The Populist Movement in Iowa," p. 81; cf. the lament recorded on p. 82.
[4] A. L. D. Austin to Ignatius Donnelly, June 19, 1896, Donnelly Papers.
[5] H. E. Taubeneck to Donnelly, July 2, 1891.
[6] Donnelly to K. Halvorson, August 5, 1892.
[7] Taubeneck to Donnelly, July 27, August 4, 1892. The same difficulty had attended the organization of the Alliance itself. "The most serious obstruction in my way of organizing Alliances is the absence of the fifty cents," wrote one organizer to Donnelly. Another: ". . . in some places money was so scarce it was hard to get 7 men who had 50

Between 1889 and 1893, three things happened that gave an immense impetus to the silver movement. In 1889–90 six new Western states with strong silver movements—Idaho, Montana, North Dakota, South Dakota, Washington, and Wyoming—were admitted to the Union, expanding considerably the silver bloc in the Senate. In 1893 the depression broke, bringing hard times to many regions that had been spared some of the worst consequences of the price decline, and arousing interest in old panaceas. In the same year the federal fiscal crisis and the repeal of the Sherman Silver Purchase Act at the instance of Grover Cleveland further angered the silver inflationists and spurred the silver-mining interests of the West to action.

Free coinage of silver was not distinctively a People's Party idea, nor was it considered one of the more "radical" planks in the People's Party program. The Kansas Republicans, for instance, had regularly included free silver in their platforms for years, and there was a large silver bloc in both major parties in Congress. Almost half the Democrats in the House of Representatives had voted for an unsuccessful free-coinage amendment to the bill repealing the Silver Purchase Act. Gold monometallism, after all, had been American policy only since the 1870's, and it was still possible in the early 1890's for a man to stand for free silver as a return to an old policy rather than as a drastic innovation. Free silver inherited the old banners of American monetary inflationism that had been kept waving since the Civil War by the Greenbackers. And while free silver has been much ridiculed, and rightly so, as the single cure-all of the popular thought of the nineties, it is worth remembering that from the debtor's

---

cents each." A farmer wrote: "We farmers are poor but I think we can surely contribute 10¢ apiece." Letters to Donnelly, June 10, 11, 1890, July 18, 1891. The Donnelly Papers are full of such evidence. Unable to provide Alliance lectures with salaries, the leaders tried to meet the problem by giving them a sales agency for hail and crop insurance. In Minnesota this precipitated a fight over the control of such insurance companies.

standpoint silver inflation, however inadequate, was not
a totally unfitting expedient.

To the most steadfast Populist radicals, however—
among them men like Henry Demarest Lloyd, who hoped
to make of Populism the first step in an American social-
democratic movement—free silver was a snare and a de-
lusion. The original Populist program had embraced a
number of reforms aimed to meet the central problems of
land, transportation, and finance; those who stood for this
balanced platform, with its demand for government ownership of communications and government aid to farm
credits, felt that free silver was a dangerous obsession
that threatened to distract attention from the full scope
of the reform movement.[8] The majority, however, of the
"practical," success-hungry leaders of the People's Party,
like General Weaver and its permanent national chairman,
Herman Taubeneck of Illinois, saw in free silver the one
issue by which the third-party movement could broaden
its base among the electorate. The party became a battle-
ground between a minority who wished to adhere to the
original and "pure" Populist program, including those
planks that were considered ultraradical and collectivist,
and a majority who hoped to succeed through silver.

In making their decision to go all the way with silver,
the leaders gambled everything on one premise: that
neither the Republican Party of Mark Hanna nor the
Democratic Party of Grover Cleveland would accept free
silver by 1896. In this case it seemed reasonably certain
that the large silver factions in both parties would bolt
(as indeed the silver Republicans did). Then, it was expected, all the silver forces would unite in a new party,
which would actually have the stature of a major party
and in which the People's Party leaders would certainly
play a major role. These leaders were trying, in short, to
build the silver issue into a bridge that would connect
them with the silver forces in the major parties. They
did succeed in building the bridge, but as it turned out,

[8] Cf. Miller: *The Populist Party in Kansas*, pp. 144–7, 162.

the traffic that crossed it moved in the opposite direction from what they had hoped.

It was at this point that the role of the organized silver movement became crucial. No history of this movement has been written, and everything said about it here is based upon fragmentary evidence; but there is reason to believe that it turned out one of the best promotional jobs in our history. It did not have lavish funds at its disposal, even by the standards of the time. But it had the only substantial funds among the forces of dissent, and it used them to great effect. It subsidized editors, politicians, and pamphleteers; it organized annual silver conventions in several states of the Union; and through such agencies as the American Bimetallic League it spread everywhere among receptive audiences the notion that all the country's basic ills could be cured by the single expedient of free coinage of silver.

The problem confronting the People's Party leaders was whether to fight this effort of the silver forces to impose a single issue upon the reform movement or to go along with it and join the silver chorus. To accept silver meant to soft-pedal the other issues, not only because the dynamic of the free-silver panacea tended to displace them but also because accepting silver meant reaching out for conservative support (like that of the silver-mine owners) that frowned on other Populist issues. The practical leaders went along with silver. Many of them feared, as Taubeneck put it in a letter to Donnelly, that if they lost touch with the groundswell for silver, the People's Party, instead of being the new party of the left, would be merely "the forerunner of a great third party that is to be organized, as the Abolition Party was to the Republican party." [9]

It became clear, as the time approached for the 1896 Democratic convention in Chicago, that, contrary to Populist expectations, the silver forces predominated. When

---

[9] Taubeneck to Donnelly, January 29, 1894, Donnelly Papers.

the Democrats adopted the free-silver platform by a vote of better than two to one, the Populists considered nominating Senator Teller, the leader of the schismatic silver Republicans; but when Teller himself endorsed Bryan, they were left out on a limb. Their sole issue—silver—was in the hands of Bryan and the Democrats. If they nominated their own candidate and stressed their own platform, they were not only sure of losing most of their votes to Bryan but also—as they thought—in danger of drawing away from him just enough votes to defeat him and elect McKinley. If they endorsed Bryan, their identity as a party was surely at an end. The cry for victory carried the day, and after much chicanery on the part of the fusionists the Populist convention at St. Louis endorsed Bryan and committed suicide.[1] It was a bitter pill for the principled reformers in the party, who saw clearly the inadequacy of the free-silver panacea and above all for the Southern Populists who had built their party in the teeth of the stubbornest and often the most unscrupulous resistance by the Southern Democrats.

Henry Demarest Lloyd insisted that most Populists would privately admit that "they knew silver was only the most trifling installment of reform" and that "many—a great many did not conceal their belief that it was no reform at all." "The delegates," he complained, "knew perfectly well that the silver miners were spending a great deal of money and politics to get them to do just what they were doing," but he concluded that their will to insist upon their integrity and their full quota of reforms

---

[1] For the story of the strategy of the silver forces, see Elmer Ellis: *Henry Moore Teller* (Caldwell, 1941) and "The Silver Republicans in the Election of 1896," *Mississippi Valley Historical Review*, Vol. XVIII (March 1932), pp. 519–34. Much light is shed on the movement for silver and fusion by Hicks: *Populist Revolt*, chapters xi-xiv; Woodward: *Watson*, chapters xvi, xvii; Destler: *American Radicalism*, chapter xi; Nixon: "Populist Movement in Iowa," pp. 67–100; Fred E. Haynes: *James Baird Weaver* (Iowa City, 1919), chapter xvi; Hicks: "The People's Party in Minnesota," pp. 548–58; Barnes: *Carlisle*, pp. 263–4 and chapter xvii, esp. pp. 433, 448.

had been paralyzed by their desire for success and their
fear of disunity among the reform forces.[2] Privately he
admitted that the Populists had long since paved the way
for their own downfall by their acceptance of the silver
issue: "The masses have been taught by us that 'silver' is
the issue, and they will of course have the common sense
to give their votes to the most powerful of the parties
promising it." He saw clearly that the leadership of the
reform party had undergone a remarkable degree of concentration, though he seems not to have understood how
thoroughly in keeping this was with the history of the
agrarian movement: "Curious that the new party, the Reform party, the People's party, should be more boss-ridden,
ring-ruled, gang-gangrened than the two old parties of
monopoly. The party that makes itself the special cham-
pion of the Referendum and Initiative tricked out of its
very life and soul by a permanent National Chairman—
something no other party has! Our Initiative and Referendum had better begin, like charity, at home!"[3]

Those writers who have given their sympathy to the
Lloyds and the Watsons have implicitly or openly condemned the abandonment of their rounded and intelligible
set of reforms in favor of the will-o'-the-wisp of free
silver. As convincing evidence of the soundness of the
original program, they point to the Populist proposals that
eventually became law: railroad regulation, the income
tax, an expanded currency and credit structure, direct
election of Senators, the initiative and referendum, postal
savings banks, even the highly controversial subtreasury
plan. It is precisely the enactment of so much of this
program within a twenty-year period that gives us some
cause to feel that third-party action was reasonably successful after all. The People's Party seems to have fulfilled
its third-party function. It transformed one of the major
parties, had a sharp impact on the other, and in the not

---

[2] Henry Demarest Lloyd: "The Populists at St. Louis," *American Review of Reviews*, Vol. XIV (September 1896), p. 303.
[3] Caro Lloyd: *Henry Demarest Lloyd*, Vol. I, pp. 259–60; cf. chapter
xii, *passim*.

too long run saw most of its program become law. Who
succeeded—in the end? The silver miners did not get free
silver, and the bones of the Weavers, the Taubenecks, and
the Donnellys soon lay bleaching on the sands in silent
testimony to the sacrificial function of third-party leaders.
But the cause itself went marching on, and the "pure"
Populists had the satisfaction of seeing plank after plank
of their platforms made law by the parties whose leaders
had once dismissed them as lunatics. Forming a third
party was no way to win office, but given some patience,
it proved a good way of getting things done.[4]

n · *The Golden Age and After*

Only two years after McKinley and Hanna inflicted their
overwhelming defeat on the forces of agrarianism, the
American commercial farmer entered upon the longest
sustained period of peacetime prosperity he has ever
enjoyed. "There has never been a time," declared President
Theodore Roosevelt's Commission on Country Life in
1909," when the American farmer was as well off as he
is today, when we consider not only his earning power,
but the comforts and advantages he may secure." [5] Thus
the "final" victory of industrialism over the farmer was
ironically followed by the golden age of American agriculture, to which agricultural interests later looked back
nostalgically when they were defining a goal for the
nation's farm policy.

How did all this agricultural well-being come to be, at

---

[4] One of the circumstances that made the ultimate success of the People's Party possible was the fact that the two major parties were, and
had been for some years at the time of its formation, precariously balanced in popular strength. In the elections of 1880, 1884, and 1888,
the difference between their percentages of the total popular vote had
not been as much as one per cent, and in 1892 it was only a fraction
over three per cent. The balance in the electoral college was almost as
tenuous. Separated by such a precarious margin, the major parties could
not be complacent about losing the votes of any substantial element
in the population, and the capitulation of one of them at an early
date to the spirit of Populism was therefore highly probable.
[5] *Report of the Commission on Country Life* (1909; ed. Chapel Hill,
1944), p. 36.

a time when the agricultural population was shrinking before the advance of industrialism and urbanism? The answer is that the prosperity of the commercial farmers was achieved not only in spite of but in good part because of the rise of American industry and the American city. Not only this, but the political as well as the economic position of the farmer in the golden age of American agriculture became measurably stronger year by year as his numbers, relative to the urban sector, progressively grew smaller.

A vital part of the change came, of course, simply with the upturn in prices. The farmer's principal relief at first came from a detested source—gold. After 1897 the new international supplies of gold brought that inflationary movement which the farmers had tried to win with silver. The general price level, which had been sinking steadily for the thirty years before 1896, turned sharply upward in the closing years of the old century and continued to rise until the reaction after the first World War. In the United States wheat went from 72 cents a bushel in 1896 to 98 cents in 1909; corn from 21 cents to 57 cents; cotton from 6 cents to 14 cents a pound.

However, it was not only the gold inflation but the American city itself that saved the American farmer. During these very years of the golden age the farmer in most lines of production was rapidly losing a large part of his foreign market.[6] What sustained his prosperity was the very thing that has been cited as evidence of his political submergence—the great increase of the urban population. In 1890, 5,737,000 American farms were supplying a domestic urban population of 22,100,000. Thirty years later there were only 711,000 additional farms, but there were 32,000,000 additional urban consumers. Relatively fewer but larger, more efficient, and more mechanized farms produced an increasing part of their total produce for the home market, and less for the foreign market,

---

[6] See E. G. Nourse: *American Agriculture and the European Market* (New York, 1924).

under far stabler and more advantageous conditions of
transportation and finance than had prevailed in the past.
True, the farm community was not expanding nearly as
rapidly as it once had. But this slower and saner pace of
expansion was itself a factor in rural well-being. And the
surplus rural population found in the fast-growing cities an
expansive safety valve. Many sons of farmers who were
unable to accommodate themselves in the farm economy
moved to the cities to find work or carve out careers.[7]

The improved position of the commercial farmer led
to a drastic change in dominant conceptions among farm
organizations as to the methods of advancing their interests. The pre-war gold inflation of course put an end
to the primacy of the money question that had been so
characteristic of the agrarian thinking of the nineties.
Where Greenback, Populist, and Bryanite panaceas, arising from a fixation on the quantity of money, had fostered legislative programs aimed above all at increasing the
volume of currency, the new approach was aimed rather
at decreasing and controlling the volume of the farm
products themselves as a means of sustaining or raising
prices.

Farm technology and farm acreage had clearly outrun
the growth of the world's purchasing power. It was increasingly recognized, as the world market was found to
be oversupplied with agricultural products, that costs,
inefficiency, and wastes in distribution and marketing
were at the heart of the farm problem.[8] Two new farmers'

[7] For the first elaboration of the idea that the growth of the city acted
as a safety valve for agrarian discontent, see Fred A. Shannon: "A Post
Mortem on the Labor-Safety-Valve Theory," *Agricultural History*, Vol.
XIX (January 1945) and *The Farmer's Last Frontier*, pp. 356–9. The
conception seems to me to have great value, but I cannot follow Professor Shannon's conclusion that the agrarian distress of the 1890's can
be explained by the hypothesis that "the cities were approaching a
static condition" and that the urban safety valve was closing. On the
contrary, urban growth continued at a very high rate after 1890, and
this growth was in great part responsible for agricultural recovery.
[8] See the significant article by James C. Malin: "The Background of
the First Bills to Establish a Bureau of Markets, 1911–12," *Agricultural History*, Vol. VI (July 1932), pp. 107–29.

organizations formed in 1902, the American Society of
Equity and the Farmers' Union, began to point toward the
need of controlling the volume of the product and improving methods of distribution. Their leaders urged the
control of production and the withholding of surpluses
from the market through storage schemes.[9] These marketing plans are suggestive of later New Deal methods and
of the "ever normal granary" idea, except that the theorists
of these earlier movements hoped to do the job through
voluntary association rather than under government sponsorship.

Another approach to agricultural prices stemmed from
a new awareness of the exactions of middlemen that was
shared by farmers and urban Progressives who were concerned with the high cost of living. Urban leaders argued
that the farmer could produce more abundantly, sell more
cheaply to the consumer, and make ample profits, if the
exorbitant "take" of the middlemen could be cut. In 1911,
as a result of agitations along these lines led by the Farmers' Union, bills calling for the creation of a Bureau of
Markets in the Department of Agriculture won a great
deal of sympathetic attention in Congress. Finally in 1913
a separate Office of Markets was created (it was later
merged with the Bureau of Agricultural Economics), and
after that year, when David F. Houston became Secretary
of Agriculture, the work of that Department was changed
in response to the changing outlook of agrarian leadership;
hitherto devoted almost exclusively to teaching and helping farmers to increase their yield, the Department of
Agriculture now began to give them more and more information and guidance bearing on the distribution of their
produce.[1]

---

[9] Both organizations are discussed in Saloutos and Hicks: *Agricultural
Discontent in the Middle West, 1900–1939* (Madison, 1951), chapters v and viii. See also the manifesto of the founder of the American
Society of Equity, J. A. Everitt: *The Third Power* (Indianapolis, 1905).
[1] See John M. Gaus and Leon O. Wolcott: *Public Administration and
the United States Department of Agriculture* (Chicago, 1940), pp.
30–47; Edward Wiest: *Agricultural Organization in the United States*

A corollary of this concern with distribution was the development of farmers' co-operatives, which spread from such well-organized industries as dairying into other fields. Here, as in so many things, the decade of the nineties marked a turning-point and the following two decades a period of rapid fruition. Statistics are not entirely reliable, but of the 10,803 marketing and purchasing organizations listed by the Department of Agriculture in 1925, only 102 had been organized before 1890. There were probably more associations organized between 1890 and 1895 than in all previous years, and the number grew thereafter year by year at an accelerated pace until the early 1920's. In 1928 the total of all business organizations among farmers —including organizations for credit, mutual insurance, and public utilities, as well as marketing and purchasing co-operatives—was estimated at 58,000.[2]

The farmers, who had traditionally raged against trusts and monopolies, now found themselves (it was eloquent testimony of their coming-of-age as modern businessmen) afoul of the anti-trust laws. After generations in which no one would have doubted their anti-monopolist integrity, they were becoming, however unfairly, targets of the Sherman Act. From 1890 to 1910 many attempts were made to prosecute directors and officers of farm marketing co-operatives, and although none was convicted of price-fixing, the legal status of co-operatives remained in doubt until it was defined by statute in several of the states.[3] Under the terms of the Clayton Anti-Trust Act of 1914, farmer as well as labor organizations were specifically exempted from the national anti-trust laws. The Capper-Volstead Act of 1922 further clarified the legal status of co-operative marketing associations. But the real signifi-

(Lexington, Kentucky, 1923), pp. 175 ff. A. C. True: *A History of Agricultural Experimentation and Research in the United States* (Washington, 1937), pp. 213, 233–4.

[2] On the growth of co-operatives and other associations, see R. H. Elsworth: *Agricultural Cooperative Associations*, U.S. Department of Agriculture Technical Bulletin No. 40 (Washington, 1928), esp. pp. 2, 6–8.

[3] Saloutos and Hicks, op. cit., pp. 63–4, 288.

cance of the prosecutions lay in the fact that farm leadership was putting less emphasis upon the traditional fight against big-business organization and more upon building their own organizations on the business model.

Along with this concern for marketing and organization came a new respect among farmers for experts. From the passage of the Morrill Land Grant College Act in 1862 to the end of the century, farmers had remained persistently hostile to what they called "book farming," and agriculture students in the Morrill land-grant schools had been outnumbered often as much as five to one by engineering students.[4] Early in the twentieth century attitudes changed rapidly and applied science began to influence the thinking of many farmers. M. L. Wilson recalls: "When I went to Ames to study agriculture in 1902, I was not the first boy in my Iowa neighborhood to go to college, but I was the first boy from that neighborhood to go to an *agricultural* college. Ten or fifteen years later it was becoming an accepted thing for all who could afford it. A few farmers began to keep books, count costs, and calculate where profit came and loss occurred. Still more farmers began to feed their stock scientifically, following the advice from 'Feeders' Hints' Columns in farm journals. Alfalfa came in, and farmers became aware of nitrogen needs of the soil. Dairymen began building up new herds of high-producing Holsteins. Hardy and rust-resistant strains of wheat were eagerly accepted by more and more farmers. Hog men improved their stock and inoculated against cholera. And finally came the popular demand for county agents—for thoroughly trained men to bring to farmers the advantages of scientific training." [5] The long-standing indifference of the commercial farmer to the techniques of his business was coming to an end.

[4] I. L. Kandel: *Federal Aid for Vocational Education* (New York, 1917), pp. 98–106. For the early use of the Morrill grants by states, see Earle D. Ross: *Democracy's College* (Ames, Iowa, 1942), chapter iv.

[5] M. L. Wilson in O. E. Baker, R. Borsodi, and M. L. Wilson: *Agriculture in Modern Life* (New York, 1939), pp. 224–5. Wilson probably locates this change somewhat later than the facts warrant.

Changes in the market position and economic techniques of the farmer were matched by the changes in his political situation. The agrarian organizations of the 1890's had had to work in an unfriendly atmosphere, with no strong allies in other classes and sections. In the Progressive era their isolation was broken down, and a congenial political climate made it possible for a number of old agrarian reform proposals to be realized by the two major parties. Henceforth, except for those who supported the La Follette campaign in 1924, farmers have generally been cold to the idea of nationwide third-party action. (On a state or regional scale organizations like the Non-Partisan League and the Minnesota Farmer-Labor Party have attempted independent political activity, and have even propagated old Populist antagonisms and Populist rhetoric.)

With the passing of third-party action and the rise of urbanism came a fundamental change in the whole strategy of agrarianism. For over a century, when farmers were in a majority, the ideologists of agrarianism had appealed to majority rule and to the idea that there is an inherent and necessary relation between agrarianism and democracy.[6] The political efforts of farmers had been efforts to secure or underwrite broad popular democracy, and agrarian thinking had been infused with a strong suspicion of organized power. Now, as the agrarian sector of the economy shrank, farmers ceased to think of majority rule and began to rely increasingly upon minority action—indeed, in the end, upon minority rule. For minority rule was the salvation of the prosperous farmers. One of the most striking features of twentieth-century American politics has been the way in which the farm population has *gained* in political striking power with its relative losses in numbers, growing more cohesive, more vocal, more effectual almost in proportion as it has been progressively

---

[6] On this theme and on modern agrarian politics see Grant McConnell: *The Decline of Agrarian Democracy* (Berkeley, 1953), chapter i.

more outnumbered.[7] In 1870, 53 per cent of the nation's gainfully employed population earned its living from agriculture, and in 1945 only 15 per cent; yet in the latter year the upper strata among the farmers had more political weight as a class than they had had in 1870.

The rise of agrarian strength was based upon the fall in agrarian numbers. The same "relentless" advance of industrialism and urbanism that, as the pathos of agrarian rhetoric has it, "crushed" the farmer in the lasting defeat of 1896 has actually provided him with greater and greater over-representation in our legislative bodies year by year. The legislative process in the United States takes place within the framework of a constricting rotten-borough system that perennially confronts urban constituencies, both in the states and in the nation, with a rural stranglehold. Even American cities are prevented from managing their own affairs by legislatures dominated by rural representatives. In the Connecticut House of Representatives, for instance, Hartford, which has a population of 166,000, and Colebrook, which has a population of 547, both have two members. The 4,125,000 urban residents of Los Angeles County have one senator in the California legislature, while the 13,560 rural inhabitants of Inyo County have one also. Such inequities are repeated on a nationwide scale in Congress. An Ohio district with 908,-403 residents has one Congressman; so does a South

---

[7] Thus Theodore Saloutos remarks, apropos of the Farm Bloc: "Curiously enough . . . the farmers found themselves at political flood-tide when their numbers had reached the lowest point in history." Saloutos and Hicks, op. cit., p. 341. It is worth remarking that Populism had served as a school for leadership for many of the later agrarian leaders. Populism not only taught them what could not be done, but also turned their attention to the possibilities of legislative action. Men who had been aroused and seasoned by the Populist movement played an important part in such later organizations as the Farmers' Union, the Society of Equity, and the Non-Partisan League. Ibid., chapter ii, and pp. 117, 221; Edward Wiest, op. cit., p. 475. On later farm leaders with Populist backgrounds see Gilbert C. Fite: "John A. Simpson," *Mississippi Valley Historical Review*, Vol. XXXV (March 1949), pp. 563–84, and Theodore Saloutos: "William A. Hirth," ibid., Vol. XXXVIII (September 1951), pp. 215–32

Dakota district with 148,147 residents. A Texas urban district with 802,000 people has the same Congressional strength as a rural district in the same state which has only 226,000 people. The Senate represents this inequity in its most extreme form. There, in 1940, the 25 smallest states, with a total population of 25,200,000, had 50 seats while the 23 largest states, with a total population of 106,500,000, had 46 seats. Thus 19 per cent of the population elected a majority of the Senate and the remaining 81 per cent were represented by a minority. The 24 states of the South Atlantic, East South Central, West South Central and Mountain regions—agrarian regions, generally—with 35 per cent of the country's population, had half the total membership of the Senate. When one considers also the rules of the Senate, which add to the power of determined minorities, one has a clearer grasp of the agrarian potential.[8] Much is said in our political discussions about the big-city machines and their role in politics. It is testimony to the grip of our agrarian traditions that relatively little attention is paid by the public to the exorbitant power of rural blocs.

My major concern here, however, is not with the consequences of rural legislative power for our own time, but rather with the way the farmers after 1896 found it possible to use their growing over-representation and their growing capacity for political and economic organization to win reforms that were, in fact, long overdue. What is most impressive is the contrast between the periods before

---

[8] There is, of course, a large literature on this aspect of our political system. I have taken my illustrations from two recent complaints: Richard L. Neuberger: "Rotten Boroughs and Our Lawless Lawmakers," *The Progressive*, December 1951, pp. 22–4, and Senator Paul Douglas's speech in the Senate: "The Surrender to the Filibuster," *Congressional Record* for March 17, 1949. See also the discussion by George A. Graham in *Morality in American Politics* (New York, 1952), pp. 96–109. In any discussion of the farm problem, it may be desirable to point out that with the growth of a substantial rural non-farm population, rural over-representation is not quite identical with over-representation of the farmer. The substantial rural non-farm population is also over-represented. Urban conservatives, it should be added, support the continuance of this over-representation.

and after 1900. During the long period of price decline
and persistent agrarian distress from 1865 to the turn of
the century, farmers had found little sympathy in the federal government and had won no great measures of legislative policy designed to give them relief.[9] But in the
early twentieth century, Theodore Roosevelt's Square Deal
and Woodrow Wilson's New Freedom produced much important farm legislation. One measure of the increasing
services of the federal government to farmers is the budget
of the Department of Agriculture, which in 1920 was
over thirty times as large as it had been in 1890.[1] Some
of the federal measures of value to the farmer, like the
beginning of effective railroad regulation with the Hepburn Act of 1906 and the passing of the income-tax amendment, were reminiscent of old Populist proposals.

The list of specifically agricultural measures is imposing.
Among the most important were measures whose goal was
to expand agricultural credits: the Federal Farm Loan
Act and the Warehouse Act of 1916 (the latter of which
embodied features of the Populist subtreasury scheme).
There were educational measures like the Smith-Lever
Act of 1914, which began the elaborate system of demonstration education for farmers, and the Smith-Hughes Act
of 1917, which gave subsidies to vocational education in
agriculture. There were measures bearing on the marketing and grading and standardization of agricultural prod-

---

[9] During the Civil War the Republican Party passed three measures:
the Homestead Act, the Morrill Land Grant College Act, and the act
creating the Department of Agriculture (not yet at Cabinet rank), all
of which manifested an interest in agrarian development. But from 1862,
the year in which all these were passed, to the end of the century,
the legislative field was quite barren. The most significant measure of
interest to agriculture was the Hatch Act (1887), creating a system of
agricultural experiment stations under the direction of the land-grant
colleges. In time this proved to have great significance. An act of 1889
also raised the Department of Agriculture to Cabinet rank. For a good
brief summary see Arthur P. Chew: *The Response of Government to
Agriculture* (Washington, 1937); cf. Donald Blaisdell: *Government
and Agriculture* (New York, 1940).
[1] Wiest, op. cit., pp. 31 ff., esp. p. 35; on the evolution of the Department's structure and functions see Gaus and Wolcott, op. cit., chapters i–v.

uce: the Pure Food and Drug Act (1906), the Meat
Inspection Act (1907), the Grain Standards Act (1916),
the Cotton Futures Act (1916), the Rural Post Roads
Act (1916).

In the 1920's, despite the powerful Farm Bloc and a
strong farm lobby, the two outstanding schemes for agricultural price-fixing, the equalization-fee and export-
debenture plans, were both defeated. The ability of the
farmers to command effective federal action slackened
chiefly because of stubborn vetoes by President Coolidge.
In the perspective of the 1950's this relatively lean legislative harvest of the 1920's appears to be no more than a
temporary check in the political capacity of agriculture.
By the end of the twenties the farmers had at least won
common acceptance of the idea that agriculture is "a
special national interest requiring a special public policy." [2]
Under the New Deal this recognition was institutionalized,
as the government itself stepped in to make possible what
private farm groups had failed to do—the nationwide
organization of farm producers to maintain prices.

The climactic achievement of the farm lobby was to establish, as a goal of national policy, the principle of parity
—the concept that it is a legitimate end of governmental
policy to guarantee to one interest in the country a price
level for its products that would yield a purchasing power
equal to what that class had had during its most prosperous period in modern times, the so-called "base period"
of 1909–14.[3] While it would be misleading to imply that
agricultural producers have invariably enjoyed a parity
income since the definition of the policy, it seems hardly
questionable that the agricultural bloc thus succeeded in
establishing for the commercial farmers a claim upon federal policy that no other single stratum of the population
can match. To gain the acceptance of such a principle, to

---

[2] Griswold, op. cit., p. 150.
[3] For a discussion of the implications of this concept see John D. Black,
Parity, Parity, Parity (Cambridge, 1942), and for its history chapter v
of that work.

get more than six million farmers on the government payroll collecting billions in the form of parity payments,
might be considered triumph enough for the agricultural
interest. But in 1942, during the war, the exacting power
of the Farm Bloc was shown in the most striking way
when Congress wrote into the Emergency Price Control
Act a clause prohibiting the OPA from imposing a price
ceiling of less than 110 per cent of parity on any farm
commodity. As a consequence many agricultural price
floors rose higher than the consumers' ceilings. Consumers
paid the ceiling prices and the government found itself
obliged to make up the differences by paying subsidies
to the producers. This exaction beyond the full measure
of parity itself, denounced by President Roosevelt as an
"act of favoritism for one particular group in the community," was a remarkable token of the political power
of American agriculture, which had developed, as A.
Whitney Griswold remarks, "from a ward of charity into
a political force capable of pursuing its own interests
even to the point of defying the head of the nation in
wartime." [4] Since the war, the parity issue has been one
which all administrations have had to handle with the
greatest care. Thus, a half century after the defeat of
Bryan, while the agrarian rhetoric portrays the farmer
as writhing in the "devouring jaws of industrial America,"
the selfsame industrial America goes on producing the
social surpluses out of which the commercial farmers are
subsidized.[5]

---

[4] Griswold, op. cit., p. 157; cf. Black, op. cit., chapters iv, xviii, and
passim.
[5] Here again the presence of a large industrial and a small agricultural
sector within the economy has worked to the farmers' advantage. Since
the urban sector is proportionately large, it can better afford to buy
off the upper strata of the farmers with subsidies than it could if there
were more farmers and fewer city people. This is one reason why the
farmers of western Canada are more radical than those of the United
States. A suggestive comparison may be found in Seymour M. Lipset:
Agrarian Socialism (Berkeley, 1950).

III · The Vanishing Hayseed

In the Populist era the dual identity of the American farmer, compounded of the soft agrarian traditions and his hard commercial role, had not yet been resolved. The economic, political, and social changes of the twentieth century tended to favor a candid acceptance by the farmer of his businesslike role. To be sure, the agrarian conceptions and the Populist rhetoric survived, and in some spots still survive, but they cover an increasingly solidified conservatism. One of the clearest symptoms of this conservatism was the rapid decline of the traditional identification with all laboring men, the growing tendency of substantial farmers to think of themselves as businessmen and employers. With the increasing mechanization of farming and the rise of berry, fruit, and vegetable crops relying more than ever upon migratory agricultural labor, substantial farmers thought of their workers less and less as familiar laborers and apprentice farmers. This process took place in different areas at different times, but the years around the turn of the century saw an accelerated change. "The old-fashioned term, 'help,' has been dropped," a Massachusetts farmer noticed in 1890, "and the word 'labor' used with a peculiar significance." [6] Farmers took a dim view of the new kind of agricultural labor, which was to them simply a disciplinary problem and a factor in the cost of production.[7] The Populists, with their belief in a single oppressed class of working folk in town and country, had identified themselves with all labor, agricultural or other. "Wealth belongs to him who creates it," said their 1892 platform. "The interests of rural and civic labor are the same; their enemies are identical." In the nineteenth-century farmer's lexicon the word "labor" applied to all work done by hand in city or country, and

---

[6] La Wanda F. Cox: "The American Agricultural Wage Earner, 1865–1900," *Agricultural History*, Vol. XXII (April 1948), p. 100.

[7] Johnstone: "Old Ideals versus New Ideas," pp. 147–52.

even as late as 1860 a Wisconsin farmer who owned 240
acres and cultivated 80 himself classified himself, when
interviewed by the census-taker, as a "farm laborer." [8]
This technical error bespoke a psychic bond that had not
yet been dissolved. The farmer had originally thought of
the city "mechanic" as a kind of craftsman-tradesman in
embryo, very much like the farmer himself, and as the
fellow victim of the aristocratic and exploiting classes.
The interest of the Knights of Labor in Populism showed
that this sympathy was reciprocated. In the twentieth
century, when stable trade-unionism developed among
workers, and when farmers adopted more businesslike techniques and became increasingly conscious of themselves
as employers of labor, this identification quickly disappeared.[9] Despite occasional local co-operation on specific
issues, a sharp tension emerged between labor and farmer
groups. Farmers, with their long hours, could not sympathize with the city workers' demand for a shorter working
day; and ignoring urban living costs, they often thought
labor's wage demands excessive. They were encouraged
by business propagandists and conservative leaders to
think of labor's wage gains chiefly as a factor contributing
to the high cost of the things they bought. And the more
powerful labor unions have become, the less has labor

---

[8] Joseph Schafer: *The Social History of American Agriculture* (New
York, 1936), pp. 199–200.
[9] The development of commercial employer-employee relations in modern agriculture has not put an end to attempts to portray even this
aspect of farm life in the light of the agrarian myth. In 1939 a Congressman gave this picture of labor relations on the farm: "The habits
and customs of agriculture of necessity have been different than those
of industry. The farmers and workers are thrown in close daily contact with one another. They, in many cases, eat at a common table.
Their children attend the same school. Their families bow together in
religious worship. They discuss together the common problems of our
economic and political life. The farmer, his family, and the laborers
work together as one unit. In the times of stress . . . the farmer
and laborer must stand shoulder to shoulder against the common enemy.
This develops a unity of interest which is not found in industry. This
unity is more effective to remove labor disturbances than any law can
be." Harry Schwartz: *Seasonal Farm Labor in the United States* (New
York, 1945), p. 4.

commanded the farmer's sympathy. As one student of farm mores has put it: "Whereas a century ago the American farmer was inclined to concentrate his suspicion of the city upon the wealthy and aristocratic, he now tends more and more to look upon the idleness of the unemployed and the tactics of industrial unions as the most prominent symbols of urban corruption." [1]

There has been, indeed, a certain hardening of the social sympathies among prosperous and organized farmers (and it is only the prosperous who are organized).[2] The Populists had appealed in a rather touching way to the principle of universality: they were working, they liked to think, for the interests of *all* toilers and certainly all farmers. In fact the diversity of interests among American farmers was such that even to them this could hardly apply; but the Populists' lip service to the idea was at least a tribute to their belief in the traditions of agrarian democracy. With the passing of Populism and with the frank twentieth-century commercialization of American agriculture, the tone of farmers' movements was completely transformed. The keynote was no longer the universality of labor or of the farming interest, but the special crop, the special skill, the special problem, the particular region, and above all a particular stratum of the farming population. The modern farmers' organizations—with the notable exception of the Farmers' Union—have shown no sympathy for, have often indeed shown much hostility to, the interests of those farmers who were dispossessed or bypassed or displaced by the processes of prosperity.[3]

---

[1] Ibid., p. 152; cf. Saloutos and Hicks, op. cit., pp. 258–61.

[2] See the table in McConnell, op. cit., p. 149, which shows that in all farm organizations, including the more "radical" Farmers' Union, membership is dominated by farmers of high economic status (and to a lesser degree of medium status) and that low-status farmers are a negligible part of the membership of all such organizations.

[3] The Farmers' Union, while carrying on much the same businesslike program as other modern farm organizations, has continued to express Populist sentiments and support liberal measures. For an excellent summary of its activities, see Carl C. Taylor: *The Farmers' Movement, 1620–1920* (New York, 1953), chapter xiv.

Farmers on marginal land, farmers bought out by the large-
scale units and unable to relocate, farmers handicapped
by credit difficulties, tenancy, race discrimination, political disfranchisement, the migratory farm workers who
wander with their families from place to place and crop
to crop, making possible the cultivation of seasonal fruit
and vegetable crops with a minimum of labor costs and a
minimum of employer responsibility—such. interests as
these have been spurned by the commercial farmers. Half
the American agricultural community, after all, has been
shut out from the characteristic material and social benefits of American life, and to this large stratum of the population the commercial farmers are consistently and ac-
tively unfriendly. The most significant organized effort to
do something about this problem—the work of the Re-
settlement Administration and the Farm Security Administration—met the implacable opposition of the lobbyists and wire-pullers of the Farm Bureau Federation, who
finally succeeded in destroying it.[4]

It was during the early years of the twentieth century
that American businessmen, disturbed by the anti-business
rhetoric of the agrarian movement and mindful of their
own stake in farm prosperity, began self-consciously to
woo the farmers and to build that rapport between the
two interests which is now so characteristic of American
politics. This tendency seems to have started on the local
level, chiefly in connection with the work of the agricultural reformer Seaman A. Knapp in popularizing demonstration education among the farmers. It was Knapp's
aim to interest farmers in the proper techniques of cultivation and the care of special crops and livestock. This
was an area in which most farmers were ultraconservative,
and Knapp found it necessary, in order to get a satisfactory hearing, to win the help of local businessmen,
merchants and bankers who had a business interest in
agricultural prosperity. These men practically forced
farmers into co-operating by threatening to withhold

[4] For this story see McConnell, op. cit., chapters viii, ix, x.

credit, and in this fashion a great many technologically reactionary husbandmen were dragooned into progressive agriculture. In time the railroads began to participate, arranging with the agricultural colleges to send farm trains with educational exhibits through rural areas. The bankers also became interested. The American Bankers' Association set up a Committee on Agricultural Development and Education to establish rapport between the farmer and the banker ("the banker has been misunderstood") and to assist in the work of promoting farm prosperity that would produce "a more contented and prosperous people." The bankers also began to put out a public-relations paper, the *Banker-Farmer.* They were followed by the producers of farm equipment, through the National Implement and Vehicle Association; and these in turn were followed by railroad, industrial, and merchants' organizations throughout the country. The Smith-Lever Act of 1914, which made a huge national institution of demonstration education in agriculture, was passed with the backing of a powerful business lobby.[5] American business, while contributing to agricultural prosperity through its support of agricultural technology and education, thus laid the foundations of a business-agrarian alliance that has never been broken.

Many farmers responded with enthusiasm to the attempt of business interests and the agricultural colleges to get them to adopt a businesslike outlook. While American business in general was beginning to turn its attention from enlarging its physical production and building new plants to techniques of marketing and salesmanship, consolidation, internal management, and the pooling of markets, a similar interest arose in agriculture. In 1907 a subscriber wrote to the editor of *Wallace's Farmer:* "Had you not better take up the subject of how to market our produce, rather than to tell us all the time how to produce more?" [6]

---

[5] McConnell, op. cit., pp. 29–33, has an excellent brief summary of this movement in the ranks of business. On the demonstration movement see Joseph C. Bailey: *Seaman A. Knapp* (New York, 1945), chapters ix–xii.

[6] Saloutos and Hicks, op. cit., p. 56.

Here lay the key to the new farm organizations, the new type of activity in the Department of Agriculture, and indeed of the "new day" in agriculture as a whole.

Toward the close of the nineteenth century much of the writing in farm journals and the work of farm organizations conformed with a dominant tendency to urge the farmer to think of himself as a businessman and to emulate the businessman in his methods of management and marketing. Such voices had been heard even before the Civil War on occasion; but now they rose to a steady and effectual chorus. "The time has come," declared a Southern farm journal as early as 1887, "when the farmer must be a businessman as well as an agriculturist. . . . He will have to keep farm accounts, know how much he spends, what his crops cost him, and how much the profit foots up"; and another writer in an article entitled "The Farmer as a Merchant" echoed: ". . . the one who sells best will have the best success. . . . Watch and study the markets, and the ways of marketmen, and dealers in all kinds of goods, and learn the art of 'selling well.' " [7] "Now the object of farming," declared a writer in the *Cornell Countryman* in 1904, "is not primarily to make a living, but it is to make money. To this end it is to be conducted on the same business basis as any other producing industry," and the same journal announced that the Farmers' Institute meeting held at the agricultural college was "a business meeting for businessmen." [8]

Leaders of the new farmers' organizations no longer spoke of the humble and exploited yeoman, but urged farmers to act like captains of industry, restrict production, withhold surpluses, control markets, and put farming, as the leader of the American Society of Equity expressed it, "on a safe profitable basis," with benefits "equalling those realized in other business undertakings." [9] In 1919

[7] Johnstone, op. cit., pp. 143, 145.
[8] Ibid., p. 145. Cf. Everett, op. cit., p. 42: "What the farmer wants to produce is not crops, but money."
[9] Saloutos and Hicks, op. cit., p. 114; cf. pp. 113–15.

the largest and most powerful of the farm organizations, the Farm Bureau Federation, was founded. This organization has expressed from the beginning the outlook of the most conservative and prosperous farmers and has been built upon quasi-official relations with the Department of Agriculture through its nationwide liaison with the Department's county agents. At the time of its founding, Henry C. Wallace, editor of *Wallace's Farmer* and later Secretary of Agriculture under Harding, delivered an influential address in which he urged: "This federation must get to work at once on a real business program if it is to justify its existence. *That doesn't mean turning the work over to committees of farmers, either. Every line of work must be in charge of experts.* The best qualified men in the United States should be hired to manage each of the various lines of work. This federation must not degenerate into an educational or social institution. It must be made the most powerful business institution in the country." [1] Like other businessmen, the members of the Federation were expected to hire experts; they have retained expensive leaders and able lobbyists at fat salaries, and have admitted into membership and influence men who are not farmers and whose primary interests lie outside farming.[2]

What has been true of the prosperous farmer's economic role has also been true of his social life, though the transition here has been perhaps less complete and less spectacular. I remarked earlier that the farmer of the nineteenth century, except in limited areas, had been deprived of the advantages of a folk culture and a folk community. The consequent physical, social, and cultural isolation was intensely felt by the farmers, and perhaps even more by

[1] Orville M. Kile: *The Farm Bureau Movement* (New York, 1921), p. 123.
[2] Saloutos and Hicks, op. cit., p. 273; for an account of the chief farm organizations, see DeWitt C. Wing: "Trends in National Farm Organizations," *Farmers in a Changing World*, pp. 941–79. Leaders of farm co-operatives, it should be added, are not so well paid as the outstanding national lobbyists.

their wives; it was one of the gaps in farm life that such
organizations as the Grange, the Alliance, and the Chautau-
quas tried to fill.[3] The social changes of the twentieth
century have gone far to wipe out some of the cultural
differences between the well-to-do farmer and urban
groups of comparable income. While the early farmer was
deprived of the satisfactions of a genuine folk culture,
his modern successor has had liberal access to modern
popular culture. In rapid succession, rural free delivery,
mail-order catalogues, improved roads, automobiles and
trucks, rural electrification, the telephone and radio, and
the movies have introduced him to the same entertain-
ments as middle-class city people. The old stereotype of
the farmer as the hayseed has become less meaningful, and
much less acceptable to the farmer himself. In 1921 a
journal for prosperous farmers ran a series of cartoons and
comments by nationally known cartoonists on the theme:
"What the Farmer Really Looks Like," in which they
generally agreed that the old cartoon figure of the lean,
bewhiskered rustic with a battered straw hat was no
longer accurate, and that the farmer looked just as much
like a businessman as anyone else.[4]

With these changes there has developed in the American countryside a disparity in living standards and outlook between the most affluent and the least privileged
that almost matches anything the city has to show. While

---

[3] It is noteworthy that the Chautauqua movement, which was a rural
institution, and which had flourished since the 1880's, went rapidly to
pieces in the mid-1920's when the farmer's isolation became a thing of
the past. See Victoria Case and Robert Ormond Case: We Called It
Culture (New York, 1948), and Henry F. Pringle: "Chautauqua in the
Jazz Age," American Mercury, Vol. XVI (January 1929), pp. 85–93.
[4] The series was started by Freeman Tilden's article: "What a Farmer
Really Looks Like," Country Gentleman, Vol. LXXXVI (July 2, 1921),
pp. 6–7, and was followed by cartoons in the subsequent issues to
December 17, 1921. Students of Americana can find in these cartoons
an interesting case in which the makers of stereotypes quite deliberately
and self-consciously lay one of their creations to rest. The willingness
of the cartoonists to abandon the old stereotype was not matched by
their ability to arrive at a new one. Their written comments made it
clear that one ancient notion was still widely shared: that the farmer
is, in effect, the moral center of the universe.

marginal farmers and migratory laborers live in desperate poverty and squalor, successful agriculturists have been able to respond to the canons of conspicuous consumption and the American love for luxurious gadgetry. Automobile manufacturers, advertising in farm journals, can describe their product as "a regally luxurious motor car . . . beautifully engineered, beautifully built—and stylish as the Rue de la Paix," and a farm reporter can say of a Farm Bureau Federation convention that "to watch . . . its milling thousands of farmers and their wives, prosperous-looking and often stylish, is often more like viewing a giant world fair or other amusement center." [5]

This seems a far cry from the atmosphere of the nineties, and still farther from the old picture of the yeoman. What it means for rural attitudes in the sphere of consumption may be illustrated by two quotations. In 1860 when Mary E. Lease, the future Kansas orator, was a little girl, a farm journal had satirized the imagined refinements and affectations of a city girl in the following picture: "Slowly [she] rises from her couch, the while yawning, for being compelled to rise so horrid early. Languidly she gains her feet, and oh! what vision of human perfection appears before us: Skinny, bony, sickly, hipless, thighless, formless, hairless, teethless. What a radiant belle! . . . The ceremony of enrobing commences. In goes the dentist's naturalization efforts; next the witching curls are fashioned to her 'classically molded head.' Then the womanly proportions are properly adjusted; hoops, bustles, and so forth, follow in succession, then a profuse quantity of whitewash, together with a 'permanent rose tint' is applied to a sallow complexion; and lastly the 'killing' wrapper is arranged on her systematical and matchless form." Compare with this the following beauty hints for farmers' wives from the *Idaho Farmer*, April 1935: "Hands should be soft enough to flatter the most delicate of the new fabrics. They must be carefully manicured, with none of

---

[5] Johnstone, op. cit., p. 162; William M. Blair in *New York Times*, December 16, 1951.

the hot, brilliant shades of nail polish. The lighter and
more delicate tones are in keeping with the spirit of fresh-
ness. Keep the tint of your fingertips friendly to the red
of your lips, and check both your powder and your rouge
to see that they best suit the tone of your skin in the bold
light of summer." [6]

While such advertisements do not tell us how many,
even among prosperous farmers' wives, found time to toy
with light and delicate tones of nail polish, neither the
advertiser, the journal, nor, we may assume, most farmers'
wives found it ludicrous that these things should be treated
in a farm magazine. The very presence of such an ideal
is significant. Would Mary Lease, who was accustomed
to address weary audiences of farm women in faded
calico dresses, turn over in her grave at the suggestion
of these rosy-tinted fingertips? I am not sure. What she
wanted to win for the farmers and their families was more
of the good things of life—the American standard of living
as it was known in her day. Standards have changed; and
it is hard to say exactly where the embattled farmers would
have chosen to stop. The dialectic of history is full of odd
and cunningly contrived ironies, and among these are re-
bellions waged only that the rebels might in the end be
converted into their opposites.

---

[6] For both quotations, Johnstone, op. cit., pp. 134, 162.

CHAPTER IV

THE STATUS REVOLUTION
AND PROGRESSIVE LEADERS

❂

1 · *The Plutocracy and the Mugwump Type*

Populism had been overwhelmingly rural and provincial.
The ferment of the Progressive era was urban, middle-
class, and nationwide. Above all, Progressivism differed
from Populism in the fact that the middle classes of the
cities not only joined the trend toward protest but took
over its leadership. While Bryan's old followers still kept
their interest in certain reforms, they now found themselves in the company of large numbers who had hitherto
violently opposed them. As the demand for reform spread
from the farmers to the middle class and from the Populist Party into the major parties, it became more powerful
and more highly regarded. It had been possible for their
enemies to brand the Populists as wild anarchists, especially since there were millions of Americans who had
never laid eyes on either a Populist or an anarchist. But
it was impossible to popularize such a distorted image of
the Progressives, who flourished in every section of the
country, everywhere visibly, palpably, almost pathetically
respectable.

William Allen White recalled in his *Autobiography*,
perhaps with some exaggeration, the atmosphere of the
Greenback and Populist conventions he had seen, first as a
boy, then as a young reporter. As a solid middle-class
citizen of the Middle West, he had concluded that "those
agrarian movements too often appealed to the ne'er-do-
wells, the misfits—farmers who had failed, lawyers and

doctors who were not orthodox, teachers who could not
make the grade, and neurotics full of hates and ebullient,
evanescent enthusiasms." Years later, when he surveyed
the membership of the Bull Moose movement of 1912, he
found it "in the main and in its heart of hearts *petit
bourgeois*": "a movement of little businessmen, professional
men, well-to-do farmers, skilled artisans from the upper
brackets of organized labor . . . the successful middle-
class country-town citizens, the farmer whose barn was
painted, the well-paid railroad engineer, and the country
editor." [1]

White saw himself as a case in point. In the nineties
he had been, in his own words, "a child of the governing
classes," and "a stouthearted young reactionary," who rallied with other young Kansas Republicans against the
Populists and won a national reputation with his fierce
anti-Populist diatribe: "What's the Matter with Kansas?"
In the Progressive era he became one of the outstanding
publicists of reform, a friend and associate of the famous
muckrakers, and an enthusiastic Bull Mooser. His change
of heart was also experienced by a large portion of that
comfortable society of which he was a typical and honored
spokesman, a society that had branded the Populists and
Bryan as madmen and then appropriated so much of the
Populist program, as White said of its political leaders,
that they "caught the Populists in swimming and stole all
of their clothing except the frayed underdrawers of free
silver." [2]

Clearly, the need for political and economic reform was
now felt more widely in the country at large. Another,
more obscure process, traceable to the flexibility and opportunism of the American party system, was also at work:
successful resistance to reform demands required a partial
incorporation of the reform program. As Bryan Democracy
had taken over much of the spirit and some of the program
of Populism, Theodore Roosevelt, in turn, persistently

---

[1] *Autobiography*, pp. 482–3.
[2] Quoted by Kenneth Hechler: *Insurgency* (New York, 1940), pp. 21–2.

blunted Bryan's appeal by appropriating Bryan's issues in modified form. In this way Progressivism became nation-wide and bipartisan, encompassing Democrats and Republicans, country and city, East, West, and South. A working coalition was forged between the old Bryan country and the new reform movement in the cities, without which the broad diffusion and strength of Progressivism would have been impossible. Its spirit spread so widely that by the time of the three-cornered presidential contest of 1912 President Taft, who was put in the position of the "conservative" candidate, got less than half the combined popular vote of the "Progressives," Wilson and Roosevelt.

After 1900 Populism and Progressivism merge, though a close student may find in the Progressive era two broad strains of thought, one influenced chiefly by the Populist inheritance, the other mainly a product of urban life. Certainly Progressivism was characterized by a fresh, more intimate and sympathetic concern with urban problems—labor and social welfare, municipal reform, the interest of the consumer. However, those achievements of the age that had a nationwide import and required Congressional action, such as tariff and financial legislation, railroad and trust regulation, and the like, were dependent upon the votes of the Senators from the agrarian regions and were shaped in such a way as would meet their demands.

While too sharp a distinction between Populist and Progressive thinking would distort reality, the growth of middle-class reform sentiment, the contributions of professionals and educated men, made Progressive thought more informed, more moderate, more complex than Populist thought had been. Progressivism, moreover, as the product of a more prosperous era, was less rancorous. With the exception of a few internally controversial issues of a highly pragmatic sort, the Populists had tended to be of one mind on most broad social issues, and that mind was rather narrow and predictable. The Progressives were

more likely to be aware of the complexities of social issues
and more divided among themselves. Indeed, the characteristic Progressive was often of two minds on many issues.
Concerning the great corporations, the Progressives felt
that they were a menace to society and that they were all
too often manipulated by unscrupulous men; on the other
hand, many Progressives were quite aware that the newer
organization of industry and finance was a product of
social evolution which had its beneficent side and that it
was here to stay. Concerning immigrants, they frequently
shared Populist prejudices and the Populist horror of ethnic mixture, but they were somewhat more disposed to
discipline their feelings with a sense of some obligation
to the immigrant and the recognition that his Americanization was a practical problem that must be met with a
humane and constructive program. As for labor, while
they felt, perhaps more acutely than most Populists of
the nineties, that the growth of union power posed a distinct problem, even a threat, to them, they also saw that
labor organization had arisen in response to a real need
among the urban masses that must in some way be satisfied. As for the bosses, the machines, the corruptions of
city life, they too found in these things grave evils; but
they were ready, perhaps all too ready, to admit that the
existence of such evils was in large measure their own
fault. Like the Populists the Progressives were full of
indignation, but their indignation was more qualified by a
sense of responsibility, often even of guilt, and it was supported by a greater capacity to organize, legislate, and
administer. But lest all this seem unfair to the Populists,
it should be added that the Progressives did not, as a rule,
have the daring or the originative force of the Populists
of the 1890's, and that a great deal of Progressive political
effort was spent enacting proposals that the Populists had
outlined fifteen or even twenty years earlier.

Curiously, the Progressive revolt—even when we have
made allowance for the brief panic of 1907 and the down-

ward turn in business in 1913—took place almost entirely during a period of sustained and general prosperity. The middle class, most of which had been content to accept the conservative leadership of Hanna and McKinley during the period of crisis in the mid-nineties, rallied to the support of Progressive leaders in both parties during the period of well-being that followed. This fact is a challenge to the historian. Why did the middle classes undergo this remarkable awakening at all, and why during this period of general prosperity in which most of them seem to have shared? What was the place of economic discontents in the Progressive movement? To what extent did reform originate in other considerations?

Of course Progressivism had the adherence of a heterogeneous public whose various segments responded to various needs. But I am concerned here with a large and strategic section of Progressive leadership, upon whose contributions the movement was politically and intellectually as well as financially dependent, and whose members did much to formulate its ideals. It is my thesis that men of this sort, who might be designated broadly as the Mugwump type, were Progressives not because of economic deprivations but primarily because they were victims of an upheaval in status that took place in the United States during the closing decades of the nineteenth and the early years of the twentieth century. Progressivism, in short, was to a very considerable extent led by men who suffered from the events of their time not through a shrinkage in their means but through the changed pattern in the distribution of deference and power.

Up to about 1870 the United States was a nation with a rather broad diffusion of wealth, status, and power, in which the man of moderate means, especially in the many small communities, could command much deference and exert much influence. The small merchant or manufacturer, the distinguished lawyer, editor, or preacher, was a person of local eminence in an age in which local eminence mattered a great deal. In the absence of very many nationwide sources of power and prestige, the pillars of the local communities were men of great importance in their own right. What Henry Adams remembered about his own bailiwick was, on the whole, true of the country at large: "Down to 1850, and even later, New England society was still directed by the professions. Lawyers, physicians, professors, merchants were classes, and acted not as individuals, but as though they were clergymen and each profession were a church." [3]

In the post-Civil War period all this was changed. The rapid development of the big cities, the building of a great industrial plant, the construction of the railroads, the emergence of the corporation as the dominant form of enterprise, transformed the old society and revolutionized the distribution of power and prestige. During the 1840's there were not twenty millionaires in the entire country; by 1910 there were probably more than twenty millionaires sitting in the United States Senate.[4] By the late 1880's this process had gone far enough to become the subject of frequent, anxious comment in the press. In 1891 the *Forum* published a much-discussed article on "The Coming Billionaire," by Thomas G. Shearman, who estimated that there were 120 men in the United States each of whom was worth over ten million dollars.[5] In 1892 the *New York Tribune*, inspired by growing popular criticism of the wealthy, published a list of 4,047 reputed millionaires, and in the following year a statistician of the Census Bureau published a study of the concentration of wealth in which he estimated that 9 per cent of the families of the nation owned 71 per cent of the wealth.[6]

---

[3] *The Education of Henry Adams* (New York, Modern Library ed., 1931), p. 32; cf. Tocqueville: *Democracy in America* (New York, 1912), Vol. I, pp. 40–1.
[4] Sidney Ratner: *American Taxation* (New York, 1942), pp. 136, 275.
[5] Thomas G. Shearman: "The Coming Billionaire," *Forum*, Vol. X (January 1891), pp. 546–57; cf. the same author's "The Owners of the United States," ibid., Vol. VIII (November 1889), pp. 262–73.
[6] Ratner, op. cit., p. 220. Sidney Ratner has published the *Tribune's* list and one compiled in 1902 by the *New York World Almanac*, together with a valuable introductory essay in his *New Light on the*

The newly rich, the grandiosely or corruptly rich, the masters of great corporations, were bypassing the men of the Mugwump type—the old gentry, the merchants of long standing, the small manufacturers, the established professional men, the civic leaders of an earlier era. In a score of cities and hundreds of towns, particularly in the East but also in the nation at large, the old-family, college-educated class that had deep ancestral roots in local communities and often owned family businesses, that had traditions of political leadership, belonged to the patriotic societies and the best clubs, staffed the governing boards of philanthropic and cultural institutions, and led the movements for civic betterment, were being overshadowed and edged aside in the making of basic political and economic decisions. In their personal careers, as in their community activities, they found themselves checked, hampered, and overridden by the agents of the new corporations, the corrupters of legislatures, the buyers of franchises, the allies of the political bosses. In this uneven struggle they found themselves limited by their own scruples, their regard for reputation, their social standing itself. To be sure, the America they knew did not lack opportunities, but it did seem to lack opportunities of the highest sort for men of the highest standards. In a strictly economic sense these men were not growing poorer as a class, but their wealth and power were being dwarfed by comparison with the new eminences of wealth and power. They were less important, and they knew it.

Against the tide of new wealth the less affluent and aris-

History of Great American Fortunes (New York, 1953). The *Tribune's* list was compiled chiefly to prove to the critics of the tariff that an overwhelming majority of the great fortunes had been made in businesses that were not beneficiaries of tariff protection. For an analysis of the *Tribune's* list, see G. P. Watkins: "The Growth of Large Fortunes," *Publications of the American Economic Association*, third series, Vol. VIII (1907), pp. 141–7. Out of the alarm of the period over the concentration of wealth arose the first American studies of national wealth and income. For a review of these studies, see C. L. Merwin: "American Studies of the Distribution of Wealth and Income by Size," in *Studies in Income and Wealth*, Vol. III (New York, 1939), pp. 3–84.

tocratic local gentry had almost no protection at all. The
richer and better-established among them found it still
possible, of course, to trade on their inherited money and
position, and their presence as window-dressing was an
asset for any kind of enterprise, in business or elsewhere,
to which they would lend their sponsorship. Often indeed
the new men sought to marry into their circles, or to buy
from them social position much as they bought from the
bosses legislation and franchises. But at best the gentry
could only make a static defense of themselves, holding
their own in absolute terms while relatively losing ground
year by year. Even this much they could do only in the
localities over which they had long presided and in which
they were well known. And when everyone could see that
the arena of prestige, like the market for commodities, had
been widened to embrace the entire nation, eminence in
mere localities ceased to be as important and satisfying as
once it had been. To face the insolence of the local boss
or traction magnate in a town where one's family had
long been prominent was galling enough;[7] it was still
harder to bear at a time when every fortune, every career,
every reputation, seemed smaller and less significant because it was measured against the Vanderbilts, Harrimans,
Goulds, Carnegies, Rockefellers, and Morgans.[8]

[7] In the West and South it was more often the absentee railroad or industrial corporation that was resented. In more recent times, such local
resentments have frequently taken a more harmful and less constructive form than the similar resentments of the Progressive era. Seymour
M. Lipset and Reinhard Bendix have pointed out that in small American cities dependent for their livelihood upon large national corporations, the local upper classes, who are upper class only in their own
community, resent their economic weakness and their loss of power to
the outsiders. "The small industrialist and business man of the nation
is caught in a struggle between big unionism and big industry, and
he feels threatened. This experience of the discrepancy between local
prominence and the decline of local economic power provides a fertile
ground for an ideology which attacks both big business and big unionism." "Social Status and Social Structure," British Journal of Sociology,
Vol. II (June 1951), p. 233.
[8] It may be significant that the era of the status revolution was also one
in which great numbers of patriotic societies were founded. Of 105
patriotic orders founded between 1783 and 1900, 34 originated before
1870 and 71 between 1870 and 1900. A high proportion of American

The first reaction of the Mugwump type to the conditions of the status revolution was quite different from that later to be displayed by their successors among the Progressives. All through the seventies, eighties, and nineties men from the upper ranks of business and professional life had expressed their distaste for machine politics, corruption, and the cruder forms of business intervention in political affairs. Such men were commonly Republicans, but independent enough to bolt if they felt their principles betrayed. They made their first organized appearance in the ill-fated Liberal Republican movement of 1872, but their most important moment came in 1884, when their bolt from the Republican Party after the nomination of James G. Blaine was widely believed to have helped tip the scales to Cleveland in a close election.

While men of the Mugwump type flourished during those decades most conspicuously about Boston, a center of seasoned wealth and seasoned conscience, where some of the most noteworthy names in Massachusetts were among them,[9] they were also prominent in a metropolis like New York and could be found in some strength in such Midwestern cities as Indianapolis and Chicago. None the less, one senses among them the prominence of the cultural ideals and traditions of New England, and beyond these of old England. Protestant and Anglo-Saxon for

patriotic societies is based upon descent and length of family residence in the United States, often specifically requiring family participation in some such national event as the American Revolution. The increase of patriotic and genealogical societies during the status revolution suggests that many old-family Americans, who were losing status in the present, may have found satisfying compensation in turning to family glories of the past. Of course, a large proportion of these orders were founded during the nationalistic outbursts of the nineties; but these too may have had their subtle psychological relation to status changes. Note the disdain of men like Theodore Roosevelt for the lack of patriotism and aggressive nationalism among men of great wealth. On the founding of patriotic societies, see Wallace E. Davies: *A History of American Veterans' and Hereditary Patriotic Societies, 1783–1900*, unpublished doctoral dissertation, Harvard University, 1944, Vol. II, pp. 441 ff.

[9] Notably Charles Francis Adams, Jr., Edward Atkinson, Moorfield Storey, Leverett Saltonstall, William Everett, Josiah Quincy, Thomas Wentworth Higginson.

the most part, they were very frequently of New England
ancestry; and even when they were not, they tended to
look to New England's history for literary, cultural, and
political models and for examples of moral idealism. Their
conception of statecraft was set by the high example of
the Founding Fathers, or by the great debating statesmen
of the silver age, Webster, Sumner, Everett, Clay, and
Calhoun. Their ideal leader was a well-to-do, well-edu-
cated, high-minded citizen, rich enough to be free from
motives of what they often called "crass materialism,"
whose family roots were deep not only in American history
but in his local community. Such a person, they thought,
would be just the sort to put the national interest, as
well as the interests of civic improvement, above personal
motives or political opportunism. And such a person was
just the sort, as Henry Adams never grew tired of complaining, for whom American political life was least likely
to find a place. To be sure, men of the Mugwump type
could and did find places in big industry, in the great
corporations, and they were sought out to add respectability to many forms of enterprise. But they tended to have
positions in which the initiative was not their own, or in
which they could not feel themselves acting in harmony
with their highest ideals. They no longer called the tune,
no longer commanded their old deference. They were expropriated, not so much economically as morally.

They imagined themselves to have been ousted almost
entirely by new men of the crudest sort. While in truth
the great business leaders of the Gilded Age were typically
men who started from comfortable or privileged beginnings
in life,[1] the Mugwump mind was most concerned with the

---

[1] See William Miller: "American Historians and the Business Elite,"
Journal of Economic History, Vol. IX (November 1949), pp. 184–208;
"The Recruitment of the American Business Elite," *Quarterly Journal of
Economics*, Vol. LXIV (May 1950), pp. 242–53. C. Wright Mills:
"The American Business Elite: a Collective Portrait," *Journal of Eco-
nomic History*, Vol. V (Supplemental issue, 1945), pp. 20–44. Frances
W. Gregory and Irene D. Neu: "The American Industrial Elite in the
1870's," in William Miller, ed.: *Men in Business* (Cambridge, 1952),
pp. 193–211.

newness and the rawness of the corporate magnates, and Mugwumps and reformers alike found satisfaction in a bitter caricature of the great businessman. One need only turn to the social novels of the "realists" who wrote about businessmen at the turn of the century—William Dean Howells, H. H. Boyesen, Henry Blake Fuller, and Robert Herrick, among others—to see the portrait of the captain of industry that dominated the Mugwump imagination. The industrialists were held to be uneducated and uncultivated, irresponsible, rootless and corrupt, devoid of refinement or of any sense of noblesse. "If our civilization is destroyed, as Macaulay predicted," wrote Henry Demarest Lloyd in an assessment of the robber barons, "it will not be by his barbarians from below. Our barbarians come from above. Our great money-makers have sprung in one generation into seats of power kings do not know. *The forces and the wealth are new, and have been the opportunity of new men. Without restraints of culture, experience, the pride, or even the inherited caution of class or rank,* these men, intoxicated, think they are the wave instead of the float, and that they have created the business which has created them. To them science is but a never-ending repertoire of investments stored up by nature for the syndicates, government but a fountain of franchises, the nations but customers in squads, and a million the unit of a new arithmetic of wealth written for them. They claim a power without control, exercised through forms which make it secret, anonymous, and perpetual. The possibilities of its gratification have been widening before them without interruption since they began, and even at a thousand millions they will feel no satiation and will see no place to stop." [2]

Unlike Lloyd, however, the typical Mugwump was a conservative in his economic and political views. He dis-

[2] Henry Demarest Lloyd: *Wealth against Commonwealth* (New York, 1894, ed. 1899), pp. 510–11; italics added. For some characteristic expressions on the plutocracy by other writers, see the lengthy quotations in Lloyd's article: "Plutocracy," in W. D. P. Bliss, ed.: *Encyclopedia of Social Reform* (New York, 1897), pp. 1012–16.

dained, to be sure, the most unscrupulous of the new men of wealth, as he did the opportunistic, boodling, tariff-mongering politicians who served them. But the most serious abuses of the unfolding economic order of the Gilded Age he either resolutely ignored or accepted complacently as an inevitable result of the struggle for existence or the improvidence and laziness of the masses.[3] As a rule, he was dogmatically committed to the prevailing theoretical economics of *laissez faire*. His economic program did not go much beyond tariff reform and sound money—both principles more easily acceptable to a group whose wealth was based more upon mercantile activities and the professions than upon manufacturing and new enterprises—and his political program rested upon the foundations of honest and efficient government and civil-service reform. He was a "liberal" in the classic sense. Tariff reform, he thought, would be the sovereign remedy for the huge business combinations that were arising. His pre-eminent journalist and philosopher was E. L. Godkin, the honorable old free-trading editor of the *Nation* and the New York *Evening Post*. His favorite statesman was Grover Cleveland, who described the tariff as the "mother of trusts." He imagined that most of the economic ills that were remediable at all could be remedied by free trade, just as he believed that the essence of government lay in honest dealing by honest and competent men.

Lord Bryce spoke of the Mugwump movement as being "made more important by the intelligence and social position of the men who composed it than by its voting power."[4] It was in fact intellect and social position, among other things, that insulated the Mugwump from the sources of voting power. If he was critical of the predatory capitalists and their political allies, he was even more contemptuously opposed to the "radical" agrarian movements

[3] For a cross-section of the views of this school, see Alan P. Grimes: *The Political Liberalism of the New York NATION, 1865–1932* (Chapel Hill, 1953), chapter ii.
[4] *The American Commonwealth*, Vol. II, p. 45; see pp. 45–50 for a brief characterization of the Mugwump type.

and the "demagogues" who led them, to the city workers when, led by "walking delegates," they rebelled against their employers, and to the urban immigrants and the "unscrupulous bosses" who introduced them to the mysteries of American civic life. He was an impeccable constitutionalist, but the fortunes of American politics had made him an equally firm aristocrat. He had his doubts, now that the returns were in, about the beneficence of universal suffrage.[5] The last thing he would have dreamed of was to appeal to the masses against the plutocracy, and to appeal to them against the local bosses was usually fruitless. The Mugwump was shut off from the people as much by his social reserve and his amateurism as by his candidly conservative views. In so far as he sought popular support, he sought it on aristocratic terms.

One of the changes that made Progressivism possible around the turn of the century was the end of this insulation of the Mugwump type from mass support. For reasons that it is in good part the task of these pages to explore, the old barriers melted away. How the Mugwump found a following is a complex story, but it must be said at once that this was impossible until the Mugwump type itself had been somewhat transformed. The sons and successors of the Mugwumps had to challenge their fathers' ideas, modify their doctrinaire commitment to *laissez faire,* replace their aristocratic preferences with a startling revival of enthusiasm for popular government, and develop greater flexibility in dealing with the demands of the discontented before they could launch the movement that came to dominate the political life of the Progressive era.

But if the philosophy and the spirit were new, the social type and the social grievance were much the same. The Mugwump had broadened his base. One need not be surprised, for instance, to find among the Progressive leaders in both major parties a large number of well-to-do men whose personal situation is reminiscent of the Mugwumps of an earlier generation. As Professor George Mowry has

[5] Grimes, op. cit., chapter iii.

remarked, "few reform movements in American history
have had the support of more wealthy men." [6] Such men
as George W. Perkins and Frank Munsey, who may perhaps be accused of joining the Progressive movement
primarily to blunt its edge, can be left out of account, and
such wealthy reformers as Charles R. Crane, Rudolph
Spreckels, E. A. Filene, the Pinchots, and William Kent
may be dismissed as exceptional. Still, in examining the
lives and backgrounds of the reformers of the era, one is
impressed by the number of those who had considerably
more than moderate means, and particularly by those who
had inherited their money. As yet no study has been made
of reform leaders in both major parties, but the systematic
information available on leaders of the Progressive Party
of 1912 is suggestive. Alfred D. Chandler, Jr., surveying
the backgrounds and careers of 260 Progressive Party
leaders throughout the country, has noted how overwhelmingly urban and middle-class they were. Almost entirely
native-born Protestants, they had an extraordinarily high
representation of professional men and college graduates.
The rest were businessmen, proprietors of fairly large enterprises. None was a farmer, only one was a labor-union
leader, and the white-collar classes and salaried managers
of large industrial or transportation enterprises were completely unrepresented. Not surprisingly, the chief previous
political experience of most of them was in local politics.
But on the whole, as Chandler observes, they "had had
little experience with any kind of institutional discipline.
In this sense, though they lived in the city, they were in
no way typical men of the city. With very rare exceptions,
all these men had been and continued to be their own
bosses. As lawyers, businessmen, and professional men,
they worked for themselves and had done so for most
of their lives. As individualists, unacquainted with institutional discipline or control, the Progressive leaders represented, in spite of their thoroughly urban backgrounds, the

---

[6] George Mowry: *Theodore Roosevelt and the Progressive Movement*
(Madison, 1946), p. 10.

ideas of the older, more rural America." [7] From the only
other comparable study, George Mowry's survey of the
California Progressives, substantially the same conclusions
emerge. The average California Progressive was "in the
jargon of his day, 'well fixed.' He was more often than not
a Mason, and almost invariably a member of his town's
chamber of commerce. . . . He apparently had been, at
least until 1900, a conservative Republican, satisfied with
McKinley and his Republican predecessors." [8]

While some of the wealthier reformers were self-made
men, like John P. Altgeld, Hazen Pingree, the Mayor of
Detroit and Governor of Michigan, and Samuel ("Golden
Rule") Jones, the crusading Mayor of Toledo, more were
men of the second and third generation of wealth or
(notably Tom Johnson and Joseph Fels) men who had
been declassed for a time and had recouped their fortunes.
Progressive ideology, at any rate, distinguished consistently
between "responsible" and "irresponsible" wealth—a distinction that seems intimately related to the antagonism

---

[7] Alfred D. Chandler, Jr.: "The Origins of Progressive Leadership," in
Elting Morison, ed.: *The Letters of Theodore Roosevelt*, Vol. VIII
(Cambridge, 1954), pp. 1462–5. Chandler found the 260 leaders
distributed as follows: business, 95; lawyers, 75; editors, 36; other
professional (college professors, authors, social workers, and a scattering
of others), 55. Chandler also found significant regional variations. In
the cities of the Northeast and the old Northwest, the role of the
intellectuals and professionals was large, while the businessmen were
chiefly those who managed old, established enterprises. In the South,
however, a rising social elite of aggressive new businessmen took part.
In the West and the rural areas, editors and lawyers dominated party
leadership, while the businessmen tended to be from businesses of
modest size, like cattle, real estate, lumber, publishing, small manufacturing.
[8] George Mowry: *The California Progressives* (Berkeley, 1951), pp.
88–9; see generally chapter iv, which contains an illuminating brief
account of 47 Progressive leaders. Three fourths of these were college-
educated. There were 17 lawyers, 14 journalists, 11 independent businessmen and real-estate operators, 3 doctors, 3 bankers. Of the ideology
of this group Mowry observed that they were opposed chiefly to "the
impersonal, concentrated, and supposedly privileged property represented by the behemoth corporation. Looking backward to an older
America [they] sought to recapture and reaffirm the older individualistic values in all the strata of political, economic, and social life."
Ibid., p. 89.

of those who had had money long enough to make temperate and judicious use of it for those who were rioting with newfound means.

A gifted contemporary of the Progressives, Walter Weyl, observed in his penetrating and now all but forgotten book *The New Democracy* that this distinction between types of wealth could often be seen in American cities: "As wealth accumulates, moreover, a cleavage of sentiment widens between the men who are getting rich and the men who *are* rich. The old Cincinnati distinction between the 'stick-'ems' (the actual pork-packers) and the rich 'stuck-'ems' is today reflected in the difference between the retired millionaires of New York and the millionaires, in process or hope, of Cleveland, Portland, Los Angeles, or Denver. The gilt-edged millionaire bondholder of a standard railroad has only a partial sympathy with timber thieves, though his own fortune may have originated a few generations ago in railroad-wrecking or the slave and Jamaica rum trade; while the cultured descendants of cotton manufacturers resent the advent into their society of the man who had made his 'pile' in the recent buying or selling of franchises. Once wealth is sanctified by hoary age . . . it tends to turn quite naturally against new and evil ways of wealth getting, the expedients of prospective social climbers. The old wealth is not a loyal ally in the battle for the plutocracy; it inclines, if not to democratic, at least to mildly reformatory, programs . . . the battle between the plutocracy and the democracy, which furiously wages in the cities where wealth is being actually fought for, becomes somewhat gentler in those cities where bodies of accumulated wealth exercise a moderating influence. Inheritance works in the same direction. Once wealth is separated from its original accumulator, it slackens its advocacy of its method of accumulation." [9]

Weyl realized, moreover, that so far as a great part of the dissenting public was concerned, the central grievance

---

[9] Walter Weyl: *The New Democracy* (New York, 1914), pp. 242–3.

against the American plutocracy was not that it despoiled
them economically but that it overshadowed them, that in
the still competitive arena of prestige derived from conspicuous consumption and the style of life, the new plutocracy had set standards of such extravagance and such
notoriety that everyone else felt humbled by comparison.
Not only was this true of the nation as a whole in respect
to the plutocracy, but there was an inner plutocracy in
every community and every profession that aroused the
same vague resentment: "The most curious factor," he
found, in the almost universal American antagonism toward the plutocracy, was "that an increasing bitterness
is felt by a majority which is not worse but better off than
before. This majority suffers not an absolute decline but
a relatively slower growth. It objects that the plutocracy
grows too fast; that in growing so rapidly it squeezes its
growing neighbors. Growth is right and proper, but there
is, it is alleged, a rate of growth which is positively immoral. . . . To a considerable extent the plutocracy is
hated not for what it does but for what it is. . . . It is
the mere existence of a plutocracy, the mere 'being' of our
wealthy contemporaries, that is the main offense. Our
over-moneyed neighbors cause a relative deflation of our
personalities. Of course, in the consumption of wealth,
as in its production, there exist 'non-competitive groups,'
and a two-thousand-dollar-a-year-man need not spend like
a Gould or a Guggenheim. Everywhere, however, we meet
the millionaire's good and evil works, and we seem to
resent the one as much as the other. Our jogging horses
are passed by their high-power automobiles. We are
obliged to take their dust.

"By setting the pace for a frantic competitive consumption, our infinite gradations in wealth (with which gradations the plutocracy is inevitably associated) increase the
general social friction and produce an acute social irritation. . . . We are developing new types of destitutes—
the automobileless, the yachtless, the Newport-cottageless.

The subtlest of luxuries become necessities, and their loss is bitterly resented. The discontent of today reaches very high in the social scale. . . .

"For this reason the plutocracy is charged with having ended our old-time equality. . . . Our industrial development (of which the trust is but one phase) has been towards a sharpening of the angle of progression. Our eminences have become higher and more dazzling; the goal has been raised and narrowed. Although lawyers, doctors, engineers, architects, and professional men generally, make larger salaries than ever before, the earning of one hundred thousand dollars a year by one lawyer impoverishes by comparison the thousands of lawyers who scrape along on a thousand a year. The widening of the competitive field has widened the variation and has sharpened the contrast between success and failure, with resulting inequality and discontent." [1]

II · *The Alienation of the Professionals*

Whenever an important change takes place in modern society, large sections of the intellectuals, the professional and opinion-making classes, see the drift of events and throw their weight on the side of what they feel is progress and reform. In few historical movements have these classes played a more striking role than in Progressivism. While those intellectuals and professional men who supported Progressive causes no doubt did so in part for reasons that they shared with other members of the middle classes, their view of things was also influenced by marked changes within the professions themselves and by changes in their social position brought about by the growing complexity of society and by the status revolution.

In the previous era, during the industrial and political conflicts of the 1870's and 1880's, the respectable opinion-making classes had given almost unqualified support to the extreme conservative position on most issues. The

---
[1] Ibid., pp. 244-8.

Protestant ministry, for instance, was "a massive, almost unbroken front in its defense of the status quo." [2] Most college professors preached the great truths of *laissez faire* and the conservative apologetics of social Darwinism, and thundered away at labor unions and social reformers. Lawyers, except for a rare small-town spokesman of agrarian unrest or little business, were complacent. And while an occasional newspaper editor launched an occasional crusade, usually on a local issue, the press was almost as unruffled.

Beginning slowly in the 1890's and increasingly in the next two decades, members of these professions deserted the standpat conservatism of the post-Civil War era to join the main stream of liberal dissent and to give it both moral and intellectual leadership. The reasons for this reversal are complex. But if the professional groups changed their ideas and took on new loyalties, it was not in simple response to changes in the nature of the country's problems—indeed, in many ways the problems of American life were actually less acute after 1897—but rather because they had become disposed to see things they had previously ignored and to agitate themselves about things that had previously left them unconcerned. What interests me here is not the changed external condition of American society, but the inward social and psychological position of the professionals themselves that made so many of them become the advisers and the gadflies of reform movements. The alienation of the professionals was in fact a product of many developments, but among these the effects of the status revolution must be given an important place. Conditions varied from profession to profession, but all groups with claims to learning and skill shared a common sense of humiliation and common grievances against the plutocracy.

The contrast between the attitude of the clergy in the 1870's and that of the 1890's measures the change. When

---

[2] Henry F. May: *Protestant Churches and Industrial America* (New York, 1949), p. 91.

the hard times following the panic of 1873 resulted in widespread labor unrest, culminating in the railway strikes of 1877, the Protestant religious press was bloodthirsty in its reaction. The laborers were described as "wild beasts" and "reckless desperadoes," and some of the religious papers suggested that if they could not be clubbed into submission they should be mowed down with cannon and Gatling guns. During the social conflicts of the 1880's, ministers expressed an attitude only slightly less hysterical. By the 1890's a liberal minority was beginning to express a far milder view of strikes, though the chief religious papers were still completely hostile, for instance, to the American Railway Union in the Pullman strike of 1894. By this time, however, a substantial reversal of opinion was under way, and the ideas of social Christianity and the social gospel had profoundly modified the outlook of many ministers in the major denominations. From 1895 through the Progressive era "the doctrines developed by the [early social-gospel] generation . . . increasingly dominated the most articulate sections of American Protestantism." [3]

The clergy were probably the most conspicuous losers from the status revolution. They not only lost ground in all the outward ways, as most middle-class elements did, but were also hard hit in their capacity as moral and intellectual leaders by the considerable secularization that took place in American society and intellectual life in the last three decades of the nineteenth century. On one hand, they were offended and at times antagonized by the attitudes of some of the rich men in their congregations.[4] On the other, they saw the churches losing the support of the working class on a large and ominous scale. Everywhere their judgments seemed to carry less weight. Religion itself seemed less important year by year, and even

---

[3] Ibid., pp. 202–3.
[4] An interesting but by no means representative case was the controversy between W. S. Rainsford, rector of St. George's (Episcopal) Church in New York City, and one of his vestrymen, J. Pierpont Morgan. See Rainsford: Story of a Varied Life (Garden City, 1924), p. 281.

in their capacity as moral and intellectual leaders of the community the ministers now had to share a place with the scientists and the social scientists. In the pre-Civil War days, for example, they had had a prominent place in the control of higher education. Now they were being replaced on boards of trustees by businessmen, bankers, and lawyers,[5] and the newer, more secular universities that were being founded with the money of the great business lords brought with them social scientists whose word began to appropriate some of the authority that the clergy had once held. University learning, in many fields, carried with it the fresh and growing authority of evolutionary science, while the ministers seemed to be preaching nothing but old creeds.

The general decline in deference to the ministerial role was shown nowhere more clearly than in the failure of the lay governors of Protestant congregations to maintain the standard of living of their pastors under the complex conditions of urban life and the rising price level of the period after 1897. Not only were the clergy less regarded as molders of opinion, but they were expected to carry on the arduous work of their pastorates with means that were increasingly inadequate and to defer meekly to far more affluent vestrymen.[6]

In the light of this situation, it may not be unfair to attribute the turning of the clergy toward reform and

---

[5] In 1860, clergymen comprised 39 per cent of the governing boards of Earl McGrath's sample of private institutions; in 1930, 7 per cent, McGrath: "The Control of Higher Education in America," *Educational Record*, Vol. XVII (April 1936), pp. 259–72. During the Progressive era clergymen were also beginning to be replaced with laymen in the college and university presidencies.

[6] In 1918 a *Literary Digest* survey showed that only 1,671 of the 170,-000 ministers in the United States paid taxes on incomes over $3,000. In 1920 a survey by the Interchurch World Movement found that the average annual pastoral income was $937. *Christian Advocate*, Vol. XCV (July 22, 1920), p. 985. Preachers were well aware that they had reached a point at which their wages were lower than those of many skilled workers, especially masons, plumbers, plasterers, and bricklayers. On preachers' salaries, see *Homiletic Review*, Vol. LXXXVI (December 1923), p. 437; Vol. LXXXVII (January 1924), p. 9.

social criticism not solely to their disinterested perception
of social problems and their earnest desire to improve the
world, but also to the fact that as men who were in their
own way suffering from the incidence of the status revolution they were able to understand and sympathize with
the problems of other disinherited groups. The increasingly
vigorous interest in the social gospel, so clearly manifested
by the clergy after 1890, was in many respects an attempt
to restore through secular leadership some of the spiritual
influence and authority and social prestige that clergymen had lost through the upheaval in the system of status
and the secularization of society.

That the liberal clergy succeeded in restoring some of
their prestige by making themselves a strong force in the
Progressive ranks no student of the history of American
social Christianity is likely to deny.[7] As practical participants and as ideologists and exhorters the clergy made
themselves prominent, and a great deal of the influence
of Progressivism as well as some of its facile optimism
and naïveté may be charged to their place in its councils.
Indeed, Progressivism can be considered from this standpoint as a phase in the history of the Protestant conscience,
a latter-day Protestant revival. Liberal politics as well
as liberal theology were both inherent in the response
of religion to the secularization of society. No other major
movement in American political history (unless one classi-
fies abolitionism or prohibitionism as a major movement)
had ever received so much clerical sanction. Jeffersonianism had taken the field against powerful clerical opposition; Jacksonianism had won its triumphs without benefit
of clergy; but the new-model army of Progressivism had its
full complement of chaplains.

The situation of the professors is in striking contrast
to that of the clergy—and yet the academic man arrived
by a different path at the same end as the cleric. While
the clergy were being in a considerable measure dis-

[7] May, op. cit., chapter iv, "The Social Gospel and American Progressivism."

possessed, the professors were rising. The challenge they made to the *status quo* around the turn of the century, especially in the social sciences, was a challenge offered by an advancing group, growing year by year in numbers, confidence, and professional standing. Modern students of social psychology have suggested that certain social-psychological tensions are heightened both in social groups that are rising in the social scale and in those that are falling; [8] and this may explain why two groups with fortunes as varied as the professoriat and the clergy gave so much common and similar support to reform ideologies.

Unlike the clergy, academic men in America before 1870 had had no broad public influence, no professional traditions nor self-awareness, hardly even any very serious professional standards. [9] The sudden emergence of the modern university, however, transformed American scholarship during the last three decades of the century. Where there had been only a number of denominational col-

---

[8] Cf. Joseph Greenbaum and Leonard I. Pearlin: "Vertical Mobility and Prejudice," in Reinhard Bendix and Seymour M. Lipset, eds.: *Class, Status and Power* (Glencoe, Illinois, 1953), pp. 480–91; Bruno Bettelheim and Morris Janowitz: "Ethnic Tolerance: a Function of Personal and Social Control," *American Journal of Sociology*, Vol. IV (1949), pp. 137–45.

An amusing parallel to the professoriat is provided by the architects. Nothing could be clearer than that the standards and status of this profession had been much improved in the years before the turn of the century, yet we find one of its older members complaining in 1902 that when he was a boy "an architect was somebody. . . . He ranked with the judge, the leading lawyer, the eminent physician—several pegs higher in the social rack than the merely successful merchant or broker." F. W. Fitzpatrick: "The Architects," *Inland Architect*, Vol. XXXIX (June 1902), pp. 38–9. What could have been responsible for this false consciousness of a decline in the position of the profession but the fact that the rise of the architect and the development of urban business had brought him into intimate contact with a plutocracy that made him feel small? He was unhappy not because he had actually lost out but because the "reference group" by which he measured his position was a different one. There were, of course, elements of alienation from the clients based on professional considerations. See Fitzpatrick: "Architect's Responsibilities," *ibid.*, Vol. L (October 1907), p. 41.

[9] Richard Hofstadter and Walter P. Metzger: *The Development of Academic Freedom in the United States* (New York, 1955), esp. chapters v, vi, ix.

leges, there were now large universities with adequate
libraries, laboratories, huge endowments, graduate schools,
professional schools, and advancing salaries. The professoriat was growing immensely in numbers, improving in
professional standards, gaining in compensation and security, and acquiring a measure of influence and prestige
in and out of the classroom that their predecessors of the
old college era would never have dreamed of. And yet
there was a pervasive discontent. To overestimate the
measure of radicalism in the academic community is a convention that has little truth. In the Progressive era the primary function of the academic community was still to
rationalize, uphold, and conserve the existing order of
things. But what was significant in that era was the presence of a large creative minority that set itself up as a
sort of informal brain trust to the Progressive movement.
To call the roll of the distinguished social scientists of the
Progressive era is to read a list of men prominent in their
criticism of vested interests or in their support for reform
causes—John R. Commons, Richard T. Ely, E. R. A.
Seligman, and Thorstein Veblen in economics, Charles
A. Beard, Arthur F. Bentley and J. Allen Smith in political
science, E. A. Ross and Lester Ward in sociology, John
Dewey in philosophy, and (for all his formal conservatism) Roscoe Pound in law. The professors had their intimate experience with and resentments of the plutocracy—
which illustrates Walter Weyl's apt remark that the bene-
factions of the millionaires aroused almost as much hostility as their evil works. Professors in America had always
had the status of hired men, but they had never had
enough professional pride to express anything more than
a rare momentary protest against this condition. Now,
even though their professional situation was improving,
they found in themselves the resources to complain against
their position; [1] not the least of their grievances was the

---

[1] Cf. the lament of John Dewey in 1902: "The old-fashioned college
faculty was pretty sure to be a thoro-going democracy in its way. Its
teachers were selected more often because of their marked individual

fact that their professional affairs were under the control of the plutocracy, since boards of trustees were often composed of those very businessmen who in other areas of life were becoming suspect for their predatory and immoral lives. Further, academic men in the social sciences found themselves under pressure to trim their sails ideologically; and caste self-consciousness was heightened by a series of academic-freedom cases involving in some instances the more eminent members of the emerging social sciences—Richard T. Ely, Edward A. Ross, J. Allen Smith, and others. In 1915 this rising self-consciousness found expression in the formation of the American Association of University Professors.

If the professors had motives of their own for social resentment, the social scientists among them had special reason for a positive interest in the reform movements. The development of regulative and humane · legislation required the skills of lawyers and economists, sociologists and political scientists, in the writing of laws and in the staffing of administrative and regulative bodies. Controversy over such issues created a new market for the books and magazine articles of the experts and engendered a new respect for their specialized knowledge. Reform brought with it the brain trust. In Wisconsin even before the turn of the century there was an intimate union between the La Follette regime and the state university at Madison that foreshadowed all later brain trusts. National recognition of the importance of the academic scholar came in 1918 under Woodrow Wilson, himself an ex-professor, when the President took with him as counselors to Paris that grand conclave of expert advisers from several fields of knowledge which was known to contemporaries as The Inquiry.

---

traits than because of pure scholarship. Each stood his own and for his own." "Academic Freedom," *Education Review*, Vol. XXIII (January 1902), p. 13. This very idealization of the professional past was a product of the rise of the profession. For the falseness of this idealization, see Hofstadter and Metzger, op. cit., chapters v and vi, and passim.

The legal profession, which stands in a more regular
and intimate relation with American politics than any
other profession or occupation, affords a good example of
the changing position of the middle-class professional in
the development of corporate society. The ambiguous situation of many lawyers, which often involved both profitable subservience to and personal alienation from corporate business, contributed significantly to the cast of
Progressive thought and the recruitment of Progressive
leaders. While many lawyers could participate in Progressive politics in the spirit of good counselors caring for
their constituents, many also felt the impact of the common demand for reform as a response to changes in their
own profession.

In the opening decades of the century the American
legal profession was troubled by an internal crisis, a crisis
in self-respect precipitated by the conflict between the
image of legal practice inherited from an earlier age of
more independent professionalism and the realities of
modern commercial practice. Historically the American
legal profession had had four outstanding characteristics.
Where it was practiced at its best in the most settled
communities, it had the position of a learned profession
with its own standards of inquiry and criticism, its own
body of ideas and ethics. A lawyer's reputation and fortune had been based upon courtroom advocacy, forensic
skill, learning, and presence. It was, secondly, a professional group of exceptional public influence and power.
Tocqueville's famous observation that in the absence of a
fixed and venerable class of rich men the closest thing
to an American aristocracy was to be found in the bench
and bar may have been somewhat exaggerated, but it
does justice to the mid-nineteenth-century position of this
professional group—the nursery of most American statesmen and of the rank and file of practicing politicians.
Thirdly, a sense of public responsibility had been present
in the moral and intellectual traditions of the bar—a feeling embodied in the notion that the lawyer was not simply

an agent of some litigant but also by nature an "officer of the court," a public servant. Finally, law had been, pre-eminently in the United States, one of the smoothest avenues along which a man who started with only moderate social advantages might, without capital, rise upward through the ranks to a position of wealth or power. Democratic access to the bar had been jealously protected—so much so that a peculiar notion of the "natural right" to practice law had developed and many professional leaders felt that the standards of admission to the profession had been set far too low.

At the turn of the century lawyers as a group were far less homogeneous than they had been fifty years before. The large, successful firms, which were beginning even then to be called "legal factories," were headed by the wealthy, influential, and normally very conservative minority of the profession that tended to be most conspicuous in the Bar Associations. In their firms were many talented young lawyers, serving their time as cheap labor. There was a second echelon of lawyers in small but well-established offices of the kind that flourished in smaller cities; lawyers of this sort, who were commonly attached to and often shared the outlook of new enterprisers or small businessmen, frequently staffed and conducted local politics. A third echelon, consisting for the most part of small partnerships or individual practitioners, usually carried on a catch-as-catch-can practice and eked out modest livings. As the situation of the independent practitioners deteriorated, they often drifted into ambulance-chasing and taking contingent fees. Much of the talk in Bar Associations about improving legal ethics represented the unsympathetic efforts of the richer lawyers with corporate connections to improve the reputation of the profession as a whole at the expense of their weaker colleagues.

A body of professional teachers of law, outside the ranks of practicing lawyers, was also developing as an independent force within the profession. The most effective type of legal education, then becoming dominant in

the best university law schools, was Langdell's case
method. It had been a part of Langdell's conception that
the proper training for the teaching of law was not law
practice but law study. As the part-time practicing lawyer
became less conspicuous in legal education and the full-
time *teaching* lawyer replaced him, the independent and
professional consciousness of the guild was once again
reinforced. Lawyers who were most attracted by the more
intellectual and professional aspects of their field tended
to go into teaching, just as those most interested in public
service went into politics or administration. Young Charles
Evans Hughes, for instance, temporarily deserted an extremely promising career in metropolitan practice for a
relatively ill-paid job as a professor in Cornell's law school.[2]
In the movement for broader conceptions of professional
service, for new legal concepts and procedural reforms,
for deeper professional responsibility, for criticism of the
courts, the teaching side of the profession now became
important. The teachers became the keepers of the professional conscience and helped implant a social view of
their functions in the young men who graduated from
good law schools.

With the rise of corporate industrialism and finance
capitalism, the law, particularly in the urban centers where
the most enviable prizes were to be had, was becoming
a captive profession. Lawyers kept saying that the law had
lost much of its distinctly professional character and had
become a business. Exactly how much truth lay in their
laments cannot be ascertained until we know more about
the history of the profession; but whether or not their
conclusions were founded upon a false sentimentalization
of an earlier era, many lawyers were convinced that their
profession had declined in its intellectual standards and
in its moral and social position. Around the turn of the
century, the professional talents of courtroom advocacy
and brief-making were referred to again and again as "lost

---

[2] Merlo Pusey: *Charles Evans Hughes* (New York, 1951), Vol. I,
pp. 95–104.

arts," as the occupation of the successful lawyer centered more and more upon counseling clients and offering business advice. General and versatile talent, less needed than in the old days, was replaced by specialized practice and the division of labor within law firms. The firms themselves grew larger; the process of concentration and combination in business, which limited profitable counseling to fewer and larger firms, engendered a like concentration in the law. Metropolitan law firms, as they grew larger and more profitable, moved into closer relationships with and became "house counsel" of the large investment houses, banks, or industrial firms that provided them with most of their business. But the relation that was the source of profit brought with it a loss of independence to the great practitioners. The smaller independent practitioner was affected in another, still more serious way: much of his work was taken from him by real-estate, trust, and insurance companies, collection agencies, and banks, which took upon themselves larger and larger amounts of what had once been entirely legal business.[8] A speaker at the meeting of the Baltimore Bar Association in 1911 estimated that 70 per cent of the members of the profession were not making a suitable living. "Corporations doing our business are working . . . to our detriment," he said. "Slowly, but with persistence, the corporations are pushing the lawyer to the wall. They advertise, solicit, and by their corporate influence and wealth monopolize the legal field."[4]

That the dignity and professional independence of the bar had been greatly impaired became a commonplace among lawyers and well-informed laymen. "How often we hear," declared an eminent lawyer in an address before the Chicago Bar Association in 1904, "that the profession is commercialized; that the lawyer today does not enjoy

[8] See Joseph Katz: *The American Legal Profession, 1890–1915*, unpublished M.A. thesis, Columbia University, 1953, for an illuminating discussion of trends in the profession during this period.
[4] "Corporate Monopoly in the Field of Law," 15 *Law Notes* (1911), p. 22.

the position and influence that belonged to the lawyer of seventy-five or a hundred years ago. . . ." He went on to deny—what many lawyers did not deny—that the alleged commercialization was serious; but he conceded that the lawyer had indeed suffered from what he called "the changed social and industrial conditions." These conditions, he observed, had "taken from the lawyer some of his eminence and influence in other than legal matters" and had also, for that matter, *"in the same way and in no less degree affected the other learned professions, and indeed all educated or exceptional men."* [5] Several years later another lawyer put it somewhat more sharply in an essay entitled "The Passing of the Legal Profession": "The lawyer's former place in society as an economical factor has been superseded by [the corporation] this artificial creature of his own genius, for whom he is now simply a clerk on a salary."[6]

Lord Bryce, in comparing the America of 1885 with the America of Tocqueville, had concluded that "the bar counts for less as a guiding and restraining power, tempering the crudity or haste of democracy by its attachment to rule and precedent, than it did." Shortly after the turn of the century he remarked that lawyers "are less than formerly the students of a particular kind of learning, the practitioners of a particular art. And they do not seem

[5] Lloyd W. Bowers: "The Lawyer Today," 38 *American Law Review* (1904), pp. 823, 829; italics added.
[6] George W. Bristol: "The Passing of the Legal Profession," 22 *Yale Law Journal* (1912–13), p. 590. For other discussions of this and similar issues, see George F. Shelton: "Law as a Business," 10 *Yale Law Journal* (1900), pp. 275–82; Robert Reat Platt: "The Decadence of Law as a Profession and Its Growth as a Business," 12 *Yale Law Journal* (1903), pp. 441–5; Newman W. Hoyles: "The Bar and Its Modern Development," 3 *Canadian Law Review* (1904), pp. 361–6; Henry Wynans Jessup: "The Professional Relations of the Lawyer to the Client, to the Court, and to the Community," 5 *Brief* (1904), pp. 145–68, 238–55, 335–45; Albert M. Kales: "The Economic Basis for a Society of Advocates in the City of Chicago," 9 *Illinois Law Review* (1915), pp. 478–88; Julius Henry Cohen: The Law: Business or Profession? (New York, 1916); John R. Dos Passos: The American Lawyer (New York, 1907); Willard Hurst: The Growth of American Law: the Law Makers (Boston, 1950), chapter xiii.

to be so much of a distinct professional class."[7] Commenting in 1905 on Bryce's observations, Louis D. Brandeis said that the lawyer no longer held as high a position with the people as he had held seventy-five or indeed fifty years before; but the reason, he asserted, was not lack of opportunity, but the failure to maintain an independent moral focus. "Instead of holding a position of independence, between the wealthy and the people, prepared to curb the excesses of either, able lawyers have, to a large extent, allowed themselves to become adjuncts of great corporations and have neglected the obligation to use their powers for the protection of the people. We hear much of the 'corporation lawyer,' and far too little of the 'people's lawyer.' "[8]

Thus internal conditions, as well as those outward events which any lawyer, as a citizen, could see, disposed a large portion of this politically decisive profession to understand the impulse toward change. That impecunious young or small-town lawyers or practitioners associated with small business, and academic teachers of law, should often have approached the problems of law and society from a standpoint critical of the great corporations is not too astonishing—though among these elements only one, the teacher, was consistently articulate. Somewhat more noteworthy is the occasional evidence of a mixed state of mind even among some of the outstanding corporation lawyers, for whom allegiance to the essentials of the *status quo* was qualified by a concern with its unremedied abuses and a feeling of irritation with its coarsest representatives. The top leaders of the law, in their strategic place as the source of indispensable policy advice to the captains

---

[7] Quoted by Louis D. Brandeis: *Business—a Profession* (Boston, 1927), pp. 333–4.

[8] ibid., p. 337; cf. Woodrow Wilson: "The Lawyer and the Community," *North American Review*, Vol. CXCII (November 1910), pp. 604–22. Brandeis's interest in having the lawyers play a mediating role between social classes may be compared with the comments of Tocqueville on this function of the profession: *Democracy in America*, Vol. I, chapter xvi.

of industry, probably enjoyed more wealth and as much
power as lawyers had ever had. But their influence was
of course no longer *independently* exercised; it was exerted
through the corporation, the bank, the business leader.
As A. A. Berle remarks, "responsible leadership in social
development passed from the lawyer to the business man,"
and the principal function of the legal profession became
that of "defending, legalizing, and maintaining this ex-
ploitative development."[9] The corporation lawyer lived in
frequent association with businessmen who were oppres-
sively richer, considerably less educated, and sometimes
less scrupulous than himself. By professional tradition and
training he saw things with much more disinterested eyes
than they did; and although it was his business to serve
and *advise* them, he sometimes recoiled. "About half
the practice of a decent lawyer," Elihu Root once said,
"consists in telling would-be clients that they are damned
fools and should stop."[1] "No amount of professional employment by corporations," he wrote to a correspondent
in 1898, "has blinded me to the political and social dangers which exist in their relations to government and
public affairs. . . ."[2] Such men turned to public service
with a sense of release. Root found that his work as Secretary of War under McKinley brought "a thousand new
interests" into his life and that his practice seemed futile
in comparison with his sense of accomplishment in Cabinet
work.[3] Similarly, Henry L. Stimson told his Yale class-
mates at their twentieth reunion, in 1908, that he had
never found the legal profession "thoroughly satisfactory

---

[9] A. A. Berle: "Modern Legal Profession," in *Encyclopedia of the Social Sciences.*
[1] Willard Hurst, op. cit., p. 345; there are many complexities in lawyer-
client relationships not dealt with here. On lawyer-client alienation, see
David Riesman: "Some Observations on Law and Psychology," *University of Chicago Law Review*, Vol. XIX (Autumn 1951), pp. 33–4,
and "Toward an Anthropological Science of Law and the Legal Profession," *American Journal of Sociology*, Vol. LVII (September 1951),
pp. 130–1.
[2] Hurst, op. cit., p. 369.
[3] Ibid., p. 369.

. . . simply because the life of the ordinary New York lawyer is primarily and essentially devoted to the making of money—and not always successfully so. . . . It has always seemed to me, in the law from what I have seen of it, that wherever the public interest has come into conflict with private interests, private interest was more adequately represented than the public interest." After the last three years of his private practice, which were concerned with the affairs of "the larger corporations of New York," he reported that when he did turn to federal service as a United States attorney (his important early cases were prosecutions for rebating), his "first feeling was that I had gotten out of the dark places where I had been wandering all my life, and got out where I could see the stars and get my bearings once more. . . . There has been an ethical side of it which has been of more interest to me, and I have felt that I could get a good deal closer to the problems of life than I ever did before, and felt that the work was a good deal more worth while. And one always feels better when he feels that he is working in a good cause." [4]

It may be objected that the progressivism espoused by corporation lawyers on a moral holiday would be a rather conservative sort of thing. In fact it was, but this was not out of harmony with the general tone of the Progressive movement, especially in the Eastern states, where this kind of leadership played an important role. There Progressivism was a mild and judicious movement, whose goal was not a sharp change in the social structure, but rather the formation of a responsible elite, which was to take charge of the popular impulse toward change and direct it into moderate and, as they would have said,

---

[4] Henry L. Stimson and McGeorge Bundy: *On Active Service in Peace and War* (New York, 1948), p. 17. Stimson's background provides an interesting insight into the moral atmosphere of the Mugwump type. His father, an old-family New Yorker, had been a banker and broker, After earning a modest fortune, he had quit business for the study and practice of medicine. He lived modestly and carried on his medical work in connection with philanthropic organizations. Ibid., p. xvii.

"constructive" channels—a leadership occupying, as Brandeis so aptly put it, "a position of independence between the wealthy and the people, prepared to curb the excesses of either."

III · From the Mugwump to the Progressive

What I have said thus far about the impact of the status revolution may help to explain the occurrence of the Progressive movement, but will not account for its location in time. A pertinent question remains to be answered: as the status revolution had been going on at least since the Civil War and was certainly well advanced by the 1890's, why did the really powerful outburst of protest and reform come only with the first fifteen years of the twentieth century? Why did our middle classes, after six years of civic anxieties and three years of acute and ominous depression, give Hanna and McKinley a strong vote of confidence in 1896? And then after this confidence seemed in fact to have been justified by the return of prosperity, when the nation's sense of security and power had been heightened by a quick victory in what John Hay called "our splendid little war," and when a mood of buoyant optimism had again become dominant, why should they have turned about and given ardent support to the forces that were raking American life with criticism?

First, it must be said that in some areas of American life those phenomena that we associate with the Progressive era were already much in evidence before 1900. In a limited and local way the Progressive movement had in fact begun around 1890. On the part of some business interests the movement for cheap transportation and against monopoly had already waxed strong enough to impel a reluctant Congress to pass the Interstate Commerce Act in 1887 and the Sherman Act in 1890.[5] Likewise the crusade for municipal reform was well under way in

---

[5] The traditional emphasis on agrarian discontent has diverted attention from the pressure from business for such measures. See Lee Benson: *New York Merchants and Farmers in the Communications Revolution*, unpublished Ph.D. dissertation, Cornell University, 1952.

the 1890's. A very large number of local organizations dedicated to good government and a variety of reforms had sprung into existence, and in some cities they had already achieved more than negligible changes.[6] Finally, the state legislatures had already begun to pass the sort of social legislation—regulation of hours and conditions of labor, for instance—that was later fostered more effectually by the Progressives.[7]

These were the timid beginnings of a movement that did not become nationwide until the years after 1901. One important thing that kept them from going further during the nineties was that the events of that decade frightened the middle classes so thoroughly that they did not dare dream of taking seriously ideas that seemed to involve a more fundamental challenge to established ways of doing things. The Progressive appeal was always directed very largely to people who felt that they did have something to lose. Populism, which was widely portrayed as "menacing socialism in the Western states," the Homestead and Pullman strikes with their violence and class bitterness, the march of Coxey's army, the disastrous slump in business activity, and the lengthening breadlines seemed like the beginnings of social revolution; and in the imagination of the timid bourgeois, Bryan, Altgeld, and Debs seemed like the Dantons, Robespierres, and Marats of the coming upheaval. Hence there was a disposition among the middle classes to put aside their own discontents and grievances until the time should come when it seemed safe to air them.[8]

---

[6] Clifford W. Patton: *The Battle for Municipal Reform* (Washington, 1940), chapter iv. William Howe Tolman: *Municipal Reform Movements in the United States* (New York, 1895) has a suggestive summary of over seventy such organizations.

[7] Legislation in this field before and after 1900 may be compared in Elizabeth Brandeis's treatment of the subject, John R. Commons, ed.: *History of Labor in the United States*, Vol. III (New York, 1935), pp. 399 ff. The chief fields that had been entered by state legislatures before 1900 were child labor, hours of women's labor, and employers' liability.

[8] There were, for instance, Eastern urban election districts, normally heavily Democratic, in which Bryan's support fell drastically in 1896 from its normal level both before and after.

More pertinent, perhaps, is the fact that the Progressive ferment was the work of the first generation that had been born and raised in the midst of the status revolution. In 1890 the governing generation still consisted of men born in the 1830's and 1840's, who through force of habit still looked upon events with the happier vision of the mid-nineteenth century. During the next twenty years the dominant new influence came from those who were still young enough in the nineties to have their thinking affected by the hard problems just emerging, problems for which the older generation, reared in the age of the great trans-continental settlement, had no precedents and no con-vincing answers. The crisis of the nineties was a searing experience. During the depression of 1893–7 it was clear that the country was being profoundly shaken, that men everywhere were beginning to envisage a turning-point in national development after which one could no longer live within the framework of the aspirations and expecta-tions that had governed American life for the century past. Americans had grown up with the placid assumption that the development of their country was so much unlike what had happened elsewhere that the social conflicts troubling other countries could never become a major problem here. By the close of the century, however, younger Americans began to feel that it would be their fate to live in a world subject to all the familiar hazards of European indus-trialism. "A generation ago," said one of the characters in Henry Blake Fuller's *With the Procession* (1895), "we thought . . . that our pacific processes showed social science in its fullest development. But today we have all the elements possessed by the old world itself, and we must take whatever they develop, as the old world does. We have the full working apparatus finally, with all its resultant noise, waste, stenches, stains, dangers, explo-sions." [9]

The generation that went Progressive was the genera-tion that came of age in the nineties. Contemporaries had

* Henry Blake Fuller: *With the Procession* (New York, 1895), p. 245.

often noticed how large a portion of the leaders at any Populist convention were the silver-haired veterans of old monetary reform crusades; Progressivism, however, passed into the hands of youth—William Allen White remembered them in his autobiography as the "hundreds of thousands of young men in their twenties, thirties, and early forties" whose "quickening sense of the inequities, injustices, and fundamental wrongs" of American society provided the motive power of reform.[1] The ascension of Theodore Roosevelt to the presidency, the youngest man ever to occupy the White House, was no more than symbolic of the coming-of-age of a generation whose perspectives were sharply demarcated from those of their fathers and who felt the need of a new philosophy and a new politics.[2] T. R. himself had been thirty-two in 1890, Bryan only thirty, La Follette thirty-five, Wilson thirty-four. Most of the Progressive leaders, as well as the muckraking journalists who did so much to form Progressive opinion, were, at the opening of that crucial *fin de siècle* decade, in their early thirties, or perhaps younger, and hence only around forty when the Progressive era got under way.[3]

The Progressive leaders were the spiritual sons of the Mugwumps, but they were sons who dropped much of the ideological baggage of their parents. Where the Mugwumps had been committed to aristocracy, in spirit if not in their formal theories of government, the Progressives spoke of returning government to the people; and where the Mugwumps had clung desperately to liberal economics and the clichés of *laissez faire*, the Progressives were pre-

---

[1] White: *Autobiography*, p. 367.

[2] As a consequence of the sharp difference in the viewpoint of the generations, family conflicts around the turn of the century tended to take on an ideological coloring. For the treatment of this theme in the works of the most popular Progressive novelist, see Richard and Beatrice Hofstadter: "Winston Churchill: a Study in the Popular Novel," *American Quarterly*, Vol. II (Spring 1950), pp. 12–28.

[3] Cf. Mowry: "Compositely, the California progressive leader was a young man, often less than forty years old. . . . In 1910 the average age of ten of the most prominent Progressives was thirty-eight." *The California Progressives*, pp. 87, 313.

pared to make use of state intervention wherever it suited
their purposes. The Mugwumps had lacked a consistent
and substantial support among the public at large. The
Progressives had an almost rabidly enthusiastic following.
The Mugwumps, except on sporadic occasions, were without allies among other sectors of the country. The Progressives had, on a substantial number of national issues, reliable allies in the very agrarian rebels for whom the
Mugwumps had had nothing but contempt. In many ways
the Mugwump type was refashioned into the Progressive
by the needs and demands of its own followers. The circumstances that awakened the public and provided the
Progressive leaders with large urban support are the
subject of the next two chapters. But I may anticipate here
at least one constellation of events that had vital importance, which centered on the reversal in the price trend.
The unorganized middle class now found itself in the
midst of a steady upward trend in the price cycle that was
linked with the growing organization of American industry
and labor. Prices, which began to go up after 1897, continued to go up steadily throughout the Progressive era,
and indeed even more steeply during the war that followed. In the years between 1897 and 1913 the cost of
living rose about 35 per cent. Those of us who have en-
dured the inflation of the past fifteen years may smile at
such a modest rise in prices; but the price movement of
1897–1913 was not accepted complacently by the generation that experienced it—particularly not by those who
lacked the means to defend themselves against it by aug-
menting their incomes or by those who found the growth
in their incomes largely eaten up by the higher cost of
living. Just as the falling prices of the period 1865–96 had
spurred agrarian discontents, so the rising prices of this
era added to the strength of the Progressive discontents.

Rising prices in themselves were trouble enough; but
the high cost of living took on added significance because
it was associated in the public mind with two other
unwelcome tendencies: the sudden development of a vig-

-orous, if small, labor movement, and an extraordinary acceleration in the trustification of American industry. Both of these took place with alarming suddenness in the years from 1898 to 1904. John Moody singles out 1898 as "the year in which the modern trust-forming period really dates its beginning." [4] General business prosperity, rising prices, and an active securities market spurred on this burst of trust formation. Of the 318 trusts listed by Moody in 1904, 82, with a total capitalization of $1,196,700,000, had been organized before 1898. But 234, with a capitalization of over $6,000,000,000, had been organized in the years between January 1, 1898, and January 1, 1904.[5] Thus in this short period almost three quarters of the trusts and almost six sevenths of the capital in trusts had come into existence. It was during the last years of McKinley's administration and the early years of Roosevelt's that such frighteningly large organizations as the United States Steel Corporation, Standard Oil, Consolidated Tobacco, Amalgamated Copper, International Mercantile Marine Company, and the American Smelting and Refining Company were incorporated. Major local consolidations simultaneously took place in the fields of the telephone, telegraph, gas, traction, and electric power and light.

Far less spectacular, but none the less nettlesome to the middle-class mentality, were the developments in labor organization. During the long price decline of 1865–96 the real wages of labor had been advancing steadily at the average rate of 4 per cent a year.[6] But beginning with the upward trend of prices in 1897, these automatic gains not only ceased but were turned into losses, as unorganized workers found themselves unable to keep abreast of the steady advance in commodity prices. While real annual wages rose slightly during the period 1900–14, real hourly

---

[4] John Moody: *The Truth about the Trusts* (New York, 1904), p. 486.
[5] Henry R. Seager and Charles A. Gulick, Jr.: *Trust and Corporation Problems* (New York, 1929), pp. 60–7.
[6] Black: *Parity, Parity, Parity*, p. 74.

wages remained almost stationary.[7] Under the spur of rising prices and the favorable auspices of good business conditions, the young A.F. of L. seized its opportunity to organize skilled workers. By 1911 the membership of all American trade unions was five times what it had been in 1897; that of the A.F. of L. was almost seven times as large. Total union membership had grown from 447,000 to 2,382,000,[8] and, as in the case of industry, most of this new organization was concentrated in a sharp organizing drive between 1897 and 1904, a drive marked by a large increase in the number of strikes.

The price rise after 1897 was a part of a world-wide trend, connected with the discovery of new gold supplies and new refining processes. How much of it can properly be laid to the growing organization of industry is a moot point. What is most relevant here, however, is that the restive consuming public was not content to attribute the high cost of living to such impersonal causes. The average middle-class citizen felt the pinch in his pocketbook.[9] On one side he saw the trusts mushrooming almost every day and assumed that they had something to do with it. On the other he saw an important segment of the working class organizing to protect itself, and in so doing also contributing, presumably, a bit more to higher prices. He saw himself as a member of a vast but unorganized and therefore helpless consuming public. He felt that he understood very well what Woodrow Wilson meant when he declared that "The high cost of living is arranged by private understanding,"[1] and he became indignant. The movement

---

[7] Paul H. Douglas: *Real Wages in the United States, 1890–1926* (Boston, 1930), p. 111.

[8] Leo Wolman: *The Growth of Trade Unionism* (New York, 1924), p. 33. Figures for all unions are estimates; they exclude the membership of company unions.

[9] Those portions of the middle classes that were on fixed salaries lost ground; notable among them were postal employees, many clerical workers, government employees, and ministers. Harold U. Faulkner: *The Decline of Laissez Faire* (New York, 1951), p. 252.

[1] *The Public Papers of Woodrow Wilson*, Vol. II (New York, 1925), p. 462. For a discussion of the cost-of-living issue by a contemporary, see Frederic C. Howe: *The High Cost of Living* (New York, 1917).

against the trusts took on new meaning and new power. To be sure, there had always been anti-trust sentiment, and the argument that the trusts would squeeze the consumers after they had eliminated their competitors had been familiar for more than a generation. So long, however, as prices were declining, this fear had lacked urgency. Now that prices were rising, it became a dominant motif in American life.[2]

It was in the Progressive era that the urban consumer first stepped forward as a serious and self-conscious factor in American social politics. "We hear a great deal about the class-consciousness of labor," wrote Walter Lippmann in 1914. "My own observation is that in America today consumers'-consciousness is growing very much faster." [3] Week after week the popular magazines ran articles of protest or speculations about the causes of the difficulty, in which the high protective tariff and the exactions of middlemen and distributors sometimes shared with the conspiratorial decisions of the trust executives as objects of denunciation. While such men as Theodore Roosevelt and E. A. Ross were decrying small families among the "best" family stocks and warning about the dangers of "race suicide," women writers in the magazines were asserting that the high cost of rent, food, and fuel made smaller families inevitable.[4]

---

[2] Cf. Walter Weyl, op. cit., p. 251: "The universality of the rise of prices has begun to affect the consumer as though he were attacked by a million gnats. The chief offense of the trust becomes its capacity to injure the consumer."
[3] Walter Lippmann: *Drift and Mastery* (New York, 1914), p. 73; cf. pp. 66–76.
[4] Christine T. Herrick: "Concerning Race Suicide," *North American Review*, Vol. CLXXXIV (February 15, 1907), p. 407, argued that it was impossible to raise large families and maintain an adequate standard of living, especially for clerks, clergymen, newspapermen, and writers, on whom she felt the inflation worked the greatest hardship.
In 1907 the *Independent* published an article by a New York City woman who reported that she had been forced to go to work to supplement her husband's income. After submitting a detailed analysis of the family budget, she closed with this stark manifesto: "Now, gentlemen, You Who Rule Us, we are your 'wage slaves.' . . . You Who Rule Us may take our savings and go to Europe with them, or do

Of the actual organization of consumers there was very little, for consumers' co-operation was a form of action that had no traditional roots in the United States. In the absence of organizations, consumers discontent tended to focus upon political issues. This itself marked a considerable change. In 1897, when Louis D. Brandeis had testified against the Dingley tariff before the House Ways and Means Committee as a representative of the consumers, he was greeted with jeers.[5] By 1906, when the Pure Food and Drug Act was being debated, it had become clear that consumer interests counted for something at least in politics. By 1909, when the Republican insurgents were waging their battle against the Payne-Aldrich tariff bill in the name of "the American housewife," the sophistries of Senator Aldrich at the expense of the consumers ("Who are the consumers? Is there any class except a very limited one that consumes and does not produce?")[6] were altogether out of tune with popular feeling. The Payne-Aldrich tariff was as important as any other mistake in bringing about the debacle of the Taft administration.[7]

Vague as it was, consumer consciousness became a thing of much significance because it was the lowest common political denominator among classes of people who had little else to unite them on concrete issues. A focus for the common interests of all classes that had to concern themselves over family budgets, it cut across occupational and class lines, and did a great deal to dissolve the old nineteenth-century American habit of viewing political issues solely from the standpoint of the producer. In the

sleight of hand tricks in insurance and railroading with them, so that we will not know where they are. You may raise our rent and the prices of our food steadily, as you have been doing for years back, without raising our wages to correspond. You can refuse us any certainty of work, wages, or provision for old age. We cannot help ourselves. But there is one thing you cannot do. You cannot ask me to breed food for your factories." "A Woman's Reason," *Independent* (April 4, 1904), pp. 780–4.
[6] Alpheus T. Mason: *Brandeis* (New York, 1946), pp. 91–2.
[6] Hechler, op. cit., p. 106.
   Cf. Henry F. Pringle: *The Life and Times of William Howard Taft* (New York, 1939), Vol. I, chapter xxiv.

discussion of many issues one now heard considerably less about their effects on the working class, the middle class, and the farmer, and a great deal more about "the plain people," "the common man," "the taxpayer," "the ultimate consumer," and "the man on the street." A token of a major shift in the American economy and American life from an absorbing concern with production to an equal concern with consumption as a sphere of life, this trend gave mass appeal and political force to many Progressive issues and provided the Progressive leaders with a broad avenue of access to the public.

CHAPTER V

THE PROGRESSIVE IMPULSE

1   *The Urban Scene*

From 1860 to 1910, towns and cities sprouted up with
miraculous rapidity all over the United States. Large
cities grew into great metropolises, small towns grew into
large cities, and new towns sprang into existence on vacant
land. While the rural population almost doubled during
this half century, the urban population multiplied almost
seven times. Places with more than 50,000 inhabitants
increased in number from 16 to 109.[1] The larger cities of
the Middle West grew wildly. Chicago more than doubled
its population in the single decade from 1880 to 1890,
while the Twin Cities trebled theirs, and others like Detroit, Milwaukee, Columbus, and Cleveland increased from
sixty to eighty per cent.[2]

The city, with its immense need for new facilities in
transportation, sanitation, policing, light, gas, and public
structures, offered a magnificent internal market for American business. And business looked for the sure thing, for
privileges, above all for profitable franchises and for

---

[1] I have followed recent census designations in defining "urban" population as that living in incorporated places having 2,500 inhabitants or
more. The rural population grew from 25,226,000 to 49,973,000 while
the urban grew from 6,216,000 to 41,998,000. The most rapid rate of
growth was shown in the very large cities of 100,000 or more. See
Historical Statistics of the United States, 1789–1945 (Washington,
1949), pp. 16, 25, 29.

[2] Arthur M. Schlesinger: *The Rise of the City* (New York, 1933), p.
64.

opportunities to evade as much as possible of the burden of taxation. The urban boss, a dealer in public privileges who could also command public support, became a more important and more powerful figure. With him came that train of evils which so much preoccupied the liberal muck-raking mind: the bartering of franchises, the building of tight urban political machines, the marshaling of hundreds of thousands of ignorant voters, the exacerbation of poverty and slums, the absence or excessive cost of municipal services, the co-operation between politics and "commercialized vice"—in short, the entire system of underground government and open squalor that provided such a rich field for the crusading journalists.

Even with the best traditions of public administration, the complex and constantly changing problems created by city growth would have been enormously difficult. Cities throughout the industrial world grew rapidly, almost as rapidly as those of the United States. But a great many of the European cities had histories stretching back hundreds of years before the founding of the first white village in North America, and therefore had traditions of government and administration that predated the age of unrestricted private enterprise. While they too were disfigured and brutalized by industrialism, they often managed to set examples of local administration and municipal planning that American students of municipal life envied and hoped to copy.[8] American cities, springing into life out of mere villages, often organized around nothing but the mill, the factory, or the railroad, peopled by a heterogeneous and mobile population, and drawing upon no settled governing classes for administrative experience, found the pace of their growth far out of proportion to their capacity for management. "The problem

---

[8] The works of the city reformer Frederic C. Howe are still worth study. See *The City: the Hope of Democracy* (New York, 1905); *The British City* (New York, 1907), esp. chapter xv; *European Cities at Work* (New York, 1913), esp. chapter xxi; and *The Modern City and Its Problems* (New York, 1915). On city development see also Lewis Mumford: *The Culture of Cities* (New York, 1938).

in America," said Seth Low, "has been to make a great
city in a few years out of nothing." [4]

The combination of underdeveloped traditions of management and mushroom growth put a premium on quick,
short-range improvisation and on action without regard
for considered rules—a situation ideal for the development of the city boss and informal government. The consequences were in truth dismal. Lord Bryce thought that
the government of cities was "the one conspicuous failure
of the United States." [5] Andrew D. White asserted in
1890 that "with very few exceptions, the city governments
of the United States are the worst in Christendom—the
most expensive, the most inefficient, and the most corrupt." [6]

One of the keys to the American mind at the end of
the old century and the beginning of the new was that
American cities were filling up in very considerable part
with small-town or rural people. The whole cast of American thinking in this period was deeply affected by the
experience of the rural mind confronted with the phenomena of urban life, its crowding, poverty, crime, corruption, impersonality, and ethnic chaos. To the rural
migrant, raised in respectable quietude and the high-toned
moral imperatives of evangelical Protestantism, the city
seemed not merely a new social form or way of life but a
strange threat to civilization itself. The age resounds with
the warnings of prophets like Josiah Strong that the city,
if not somehow tamed, would bring with it the downfall
of the nation. "The first city," wrote Strong, "was built
by the first murderer, and crime and vice and wretchedness
have festered in it ever since." [7]

In the city the native Yankee-Protestant American en-
countered the immigrant. Between the close of the Civil

---

[4] In the chapter on municipal government he wrote for Bryce's *American Commonwealth*, Vol. I, p. 652.
[5] Ibid., p. 637.
[6] *Forum*, Vol. X (December 1890), p. 25.
[7] Josiah Strong: *The Twentieth Century City* (New York, 1898), p.
181.

War and the outbreak of the first World War, the rise of American industry and the absence of restrictions drew a steady stream of immigrants, which reached its peak in 1907 when 1,285,000 immigrant entries were recorded. By 1910, 13,345,000 foreign-born persons were living in the United States, or almost one seventh of the total population. The country had long been accustomed to heavy immigration, but the native Yankee was not prepared for the great shift in the sources of immigration, especially noticeable after 1900, from the familiar English, Irish, Scandinavians, and Germans to the peasantry of southern and eastern Europe—swarms of Poles, Italians, Russians, eastern European Jews, Hungarians, Slovaks, and Czechs. The native was horrified by the conditions under which the new Americans lived—their slums, their crowding, their unsanitary misery, their alien tongues and religion— and he was resentful of the use the local machines made of the immigrant vote.[8] For it was the boss who saw the needs of the immigrant and made him the political instrument of the urban machine. The machine provided quick naturalization, jobs, social services, personal access to authority, release from the surveillance of the courts, deference to ethnic pride. In return it garnered votes, herding to the polls new citizens, grateful for services rendered and submissive to experienced leadership.

In many great cities the Yankee found himself outnumbered and overwhelmed. A city like Baltimore, where native children of native parents outnumbered immigrants and their children, was a rarity among the large cities. Far more characteristic of the East and Midwest were Boston, Chicago, Cleveland, New York, Philadelphia, Pittsburgh, and St. Louis, where the native stock was considerably outnumbered by the foreign-born and their

---

[8] "In those days educated citizens of cities said, and I think they believed—they certainly acted upon the theory—that it was the ignorant foreign riff-raff of the big congested towns that made municipal politics so bad." Lincoln Steffens: *Autobiography* (New York, 1931), p. 400.

children of the first generation.[9] Often the Yankee felt
himself pushed into his own ghetto, marked off perhaps
by its superior grooming but also by the political power-
lessness of its inhabitants.[1] The Irish politician—the established immigrant who knew how to manage—surveyed
the situation and found it good, but the Yankee brooded
over "the Irish conquest of our cities," and wondered if
it meant the beginning of the end of traditional American
democracy.[2] The Mugwump type, resentful of the failure
of both capitalist and immigrant to consider the public
good before personal welfare, had always been troubled
about the long-range consequences of unrestricted immigration and had begun to question universal suffrage out
of a fear that traditional democracy might be imperiled by
the decline of ethnic homogeneity.[3] Early civic reform was
strongly tainted with nativism.

Hostility to immigrants was probably most common
near the extreme ends of the political spectrum, among
ultraconservatives and among those Progressives whose

---

[9] See the charts in Frank Julian Warne: *The Immigrant Invasion* (New
York, 1913), facing pp. 118–19.

[1] Cf. Thomas Bailey Aldrich: "Kipling described exactly the government of every city and town in the . . . United States when he
described that of New York as being 'a despotism of the alien, by
the alien, for the alien, tempered with occasional insurrections of decent folk!'" Ferris Greenslet: *Life of Thomas Bailey Aldrich* (New
York, 1908), p. 169.

[2] Cf. John Paul Bocock: "The Irish Conquest of Our Cities," *Forum*,
Vol. XVII (April 1894), pp. 186–95, which lists a large roster of
cities ruled by the Irish minority. "Philadelphia, Boston, and New
York were once governed by the Quaker, the Puritan, and the Knicker-
bockers. Are they better governed now, since from the turbulence of
municipal politics the Irish American has plucked both wealth and
power? Surely those who are too scrupulous to contend with him for
those rewards should be the last to decry him for his success in securing them." Ibid., p. 195.

[3] See John Higham: "Origins of Immigration Restriction, 1882–1897:
a Social Analysis," *Mississippi Historical Review*, Vol. XXXIX (June
1952), pp. 77–88; and Barbara Miller Solomon: "The Intellectual
Background of the Immigration Restriction Movement in New England," *New England Quarterly*, Vol. XXV (March 1952), pp. 47–59.
For the views of historians see Edward Saveth: *American Historians
and European Immigrants* (New York, 1948).

views were most influenced by the Populist inheritance.[4]
The Populistic Progressives were frank to express their
dislike of the immigrant and to attack unrestricted immigration with arguments phrased in popular and "liberal"
language. Many labor leaders stood with them on this
issue,[5] and so did a number of academic scholars. Men
like Edward A. Ross, John R. Commons, and Edward
Bemis, all three of whom were considered radicals and
lost academic jobs on this ground, gave learned support
to the anti-immigrant sentiment.[6] Ross, formerly a Populist
and now one of the leading ideologues of Progressivism,
a stalwart member of the La Follette brain trust at the
University of Wisconsin, in 1914 wrote a tract on immigration, *The Old World in the New*, that expressed the
anti-immigrant case from the Anglo-Saxon Progressive
standpoint. Although he discussed the older immigrant
stocks with some indulgence, Ross was unsparing with the
currently most numerous immigrants from southern and
eastern Europe. Immigration, he said, was good for
the rich, the employing class, and a matter of indifference to the shortsighted professional classes with whom
immigrants could not compete, but it was disastrous
for native American workers. Immigrants were strike-
breakers and scabs, who lowered wage levels and reduced living standards toward their "pigsty mode of

---

[4] Thus in the election of 1912 the Taft Republicans adopted a platform that gestured vaguely toward immigration restriction while the
Bull Moosers spoke of the necessity to aid, protect, and Americanize
the immigrant. The Democratic Party, containing both the urban
machines and the more radical agrarians, who stood most sharply at
odds on this issue, straddled it by making no reference to the problem.

[5] Of course one reason why the immigrant held so fast to his ethnic
loyalties was that he could not develop any class loyalties because he
was excluded by the unions. Their attitude confirmed his feeling that
he was different. For Samuel Gompers's views on "racial purity," see
Arthur Mann's illuminating essay: "Gompers and the Irony of Racism,"
Antioch Review (Summer 1953), pp. 203–14.

[6] See, for instance, Commons's *Races and Immigrants in America*; cf.
Higham, op. cit., pp. 81, 85.

life," just as they brought social standards down to "their
brawls and their animal pleasures." They were unhygienic
and alcoholic, they raised the rate of illiteracy and insanity,
they fostered crime and bad morals; they lowered the
tone of politics by introducing ethnic considerations and
of journalism by providing readership for the poorest
newspapers, the yellow journals; they threatened the position of women with their "coarse peasant philosophy of
sex," and debased the educational system with parochial
schools; they spurred the monstrous overgrowth of cities,
and by selling their votes for protection and favors
increased the grip of the bosses upon city politics; they
bred in such numbers that they were increasingly dominant over the native stock and thus threatened to over-
whelm "American blood" and bastardize American civilization.[7]

Ross's book was an expression by an articulate and
educated man of feelings that were most common among
the uneducated and among those who were half ashamed
to articulate them. Hardly anyone devoted to the ways of
the predominantly Anglo-Saxon civilization and political
culture of the United States could help giving some
troubled thought to the consequences for its future of such
heavy immigration on the part of peoples whose ways
were so completely different. But more characteristic of
the educated Progressive than Ross's harsh judgments and
his studied appeal to what he called "pride of race" was
the attempt to meet the immigration problem with a pro-

---

[7] Edward A. Ross: *The Old World in the New* (New York, 1914),
passim, esp. pp. 219, 220, 226–7, 237, 272, 279–80, 286–7, 304, and
chapters vii, ix, x. Cf. some of the nonsense about "race" in William
Allen White's *The Old Order Changeth* (New York, 1910), pp. 128–
30, 197–9, 252, which, however, takes a more optimistic view of the
future. Ross's views should be compared with those of the racist, anti-
immigrant faction in the Socialist Party. Ira Kipnis: *The American
Socialist Movement, 1897–1912*, pp. 276–88. In 1936, when Ross
published his autobiography, he repudiated some of the racist implications of his earlier work. *Seventy Years of It* (New York, 1936), chapter xxvii.

gram of naturalization and Americanization.[8] Moderate conservatives and liberal-minded Progressives alike joined in the cause of Americanizing the immigrant by acquainting him with English and giving him education and civic instruction. One senses again and again in the best Progressive literature on immigration that the old nativist Mugwump prejudice is being held in check by a strenuous effort of mind and will, that the decent Anglo-Saxon liberals were forever reminding themselves of their own humane values, of the courage of the immigrant, the reality of his hardships, the poignancy of his deracination, the cultural achievements of his homeland, his ultimate potentialities as an American, and, above all, of the fact that the bulk of the hard and dirty work of American industry and urban life was his. Those Progressives who were engaged in practical politics in industrial communities also realized that they must appeal to the pride as well as to the interests of the immigrant if they were to have lasting success.

But the typical Progressive and the typical immigrant were immensely different, and the gulf between them was not usually bridged with much success in the Progressive era. The immigrant could not shear off his European identity with the rapidity demanded by the ideal of Americanization. He might be willing to take advantage of the practical benefits of night schools and English-language courses and to do what he could to take on a new nationality and learn about American ways. But even if he felt no hostility, he could hardly fail to sense the note of condescension in the efforts of those who tried to help him.[9]

---

[8] Edward G. Hartmann: *The Movement to Americanize the Immigrant* (New York, 1948). The Populists who accused businessmen of being indifferent to the immigrant's status in American life were not altogether correct. Such organizations as the North American Civic League for Immigrants received much support from businessmen who were interested in introducing immigrants to American life and keeping them clear of agitators.

[9] For a spirited statement of the immigrant reaction, see Bagdasar K. Baghdigian: *Americanism in Americanization* (Kansas City, Mo., 1921).

More often than not, he rebuffed the settlement worker or
the agent of Americanization, and looked elsewhere for
his primary contacts with American political and civic life.
He turned, instead, to the political boss, who accepted
him for what he was and asked no questions.

In politics, then, the immigrant was usually at odds with
the reform aspirations of the American Progressive. Together with the native conservative and the politically indifferent, the immigrants formed a potent mass that
limited the range and the achievements of Progressivism.
The loyalty of immigrant voters to the bosses was one of
the signal reasons why the local reform victories were so
short-lived. It would be hard to imagine types of political
culture more alien to each other than those of the Yankee
reformer and the peasant immigrant. The Yankee's idea
of political action assumed a popular democracy with widespread participation and eager civic interest. To him politics was the business, the responsibility, the duty of all
men. It was an arena for the realization of moral principles of broad application—and even, as in the case of
temperance and vice crusades—for the correction of private habits. The immigrant, by contrast, coming as a rule
from a peasant environment and from autocratic societies
with strong feudal survivals, was totally unaccustomed
to the active citizen's role.[1] He expected to be acted on by
government, but not to be a political agent himself. To
him government meant restrictions on personal movement,
the arbitrary regulation of life, the inaccessibility of the
law, and the conscription of the able-bodied. To him government was the instrument of the ruling classes, characteristically acting in their interests, which were indifferent

The immigrant reaction became most outspoken during the war, when
the Americanizers, startled by the sudden realization of the strength of
alien loyalties, accelerated their efforts. "The immigrant is by no
means stupid," declared an immigrant newspaper in 1919. "He feels
the patronizing attitude the American adopts towards him, and therefore never opens his soul." Hartmann, op. cit., p. 258.
[1] I have drawn here upon the perceptive discussion of the immigrant
in politics by Oscar Handlin: The Uprooted (Boston, 1951), chapter
viii.

or opposed to his own. Nor was government in his eyes an affair of abstract principles and rules of law: it was the actions of particular men with particular powers. Political relations were not governed by abstract principles; they were profoundly personal.[2]

Not being reared on the idea of mass participation, the immigrant was not especially eager to exercise his vote immediately upon naturalization. Nor was he interested in such reforms as the initiative, referendum, and recall, which were intelligible only from the standpoint of the Anglo-American ethos of popular political action. When he finally did assume his civic role, it was either in response to Old World loyalties (which became a problem only during and after the first World War) or to immediate needs arising out of his struggle for life in the American city—to his need for a job or charity or protection from the law or for a street vendor's license. The necessities of American cities—their need for construction workers, street-cleaners, police and firemen, service workers of all kinds—often provided him with his livelihood, as it provided the boss with the necessary patronage. The immigrant, in short, looked to politics not for the realization of high principles but for concrete and personal gains, and he sought these gains through personal relationships. And here the boss, particularly the Irish boss, who could

---

[2] Cf. Henry Cabot Lodge's complaint that the idea of patriotism—devotion to one's country—was Roman, while the idea of devotion to the emperor as the head of state was Byzantine. It was the Byzantine inheritance, he said, that the Eastern immigrants were bringing in. Henry Cabot Lodge: "Immigration—a Review," in Philip David, ed.: *Immigration and Americanization* (Boston, 1920), p. 55.

The boss's code of personal loyalty and the reformer's code of loyalty to civic ideals could not easily be accommodated, with the consequence that when the two had dealings with each other there were irreparable misunderstandings. Thus Woodrow Wilson in New Jersey and Joseph Folk in Missouri were made, respectively, Governor and Attorney General through agreements with bosses, and both turned on their benefactors, Wilson in matters of program and patronage, Folk to the extent of a prosecution for corruption. To bosses Jim Smith and Ed Butler, Wilson and Folk were ingrates and scoundrels. But in their own minds the reformers were justified in placing civic ideals and public commitments over and above mere personal obligations.

see things from the immigrant's angle but could also
manipulate the American environment, became a specialist
in personal relations and personal loyalties.[3] The boss
himself encouraged the immigrant to think of politics as
a field in which one could legitimately pursue one's interests. This was, indeed, his own occupational view of
it: politics was a trade at which a man worked and for
which he should be properly paid. As George Washington
Plunkitt, the sage of Tammany Hall, once said, all the
machines were agreed "on the main proposition that when
a man works in politics, he should get something out of
it." [4] The boss, moreover, was astute enough to see that
the personal interests that were pursued in politics must be
construed broadly enough to include self-respect. Where
the reformers and Americanizers tried to prod the immigrant toward the study of American ways, the boss contented himself with studying the immigrant's ways, attending his weddings and christenings (with appropriate
gifts) and his funerals, and making himself a sympathetic
observer of immigrant life and in a measure a participant
in it. Reformers might try on occasion to compete with
this, but they lacked the means. The boss, rich with graft,
could afford to be more generous; and having doled out
many a favor to businessmen, he could draw upon the
world of private business as well as the public payroll to
provide jobs for his constituents. Where reformers identi-

---

[3] Ross reported the words of a New England reformer: "The Germans
want to know which candidate is better qualified for the office. Among
the Irish I have never heard such a consideration mentioned. They
ask, 'Who wants this candidate?' 'Who is behind him?' I have lined
up a good many Irish in support of Good Government men, but never
by setting forth the merits of a matter or a candidate. I approach my
Irish friends with the personal appeal, 'Do this for me!'" *The Old
World in the New*, p. 262.

　　Later, as new immigrant groups became more Americanized, they
egan to resent the Irish tendency to monopolize political leadership,
and formed factions of their own, with which the Irish bosses learned
to do business.

[4] William L. Riordan: *Plunkitt of Tammany Hall*, ed. by Roy V. Peel
(New York, 1948), p. 52. This work, which consists of a record of
Plunkitt's utterances, was originally published in 1905. It is instruc-
tive to set its basic assumptions alongside those of the reformers.

fied patriotism with knowledgeable civic action and self-denial, the bosses were satisfied to confine it to party regularity, and they were not embarrassed by a body of literature purporting to show that to trade one's vote for personal services was a form of civic iniquity.

While the boss, with his pragmatic talents and his immediate favors, quickly appealed to the immigrant, the reformer was a mystery. Often he stood for things that to the immigrant were altogether bizarre, like women's rights and Sunday laws, or downright insulting, like temperance. His abstractions had no appeal within the immigrant's experience—citizenship, responsibility, efficiency, good government, economy, businesslike management. The immigrant wanted humanity, not efficiency, and economies threatened to lop needed jobs off the payroll. The reformer's attacks upon the boss only caused the immigrant to draw closer to his benefactor. Progressives, in return, reproached the immigrant for having no interest in broad principles, in the rule of law or the public good. Between the two, for the most part, the channels of effective communication were closed. Progressive reform drew its greatest support from the more discontented of the native Americans, and on some issues from the rural and small-town constituencies that surrounded the great cities. The insulation of the Progressive from the support of the most exploited sector of the population was one of the factors that, for all his humanitarianism, courage, and vision, reduced the social range and the radical drive of his program and kept him genteel, proper, and safe.

On some issues, to be sure, especially those, like workmen's compensation, that bore directly on the welfare of the working population, the bosses themselves saw areas of agreement with the reformers. The reformer could preach and agitate over such questions and the machines would help him legislate. Indeed, it was one of the classic urban machine politicians, Al Smith, who made the first effectual bridge between the humanity of the reformers and the humanity of the bosses. But this tendency, which

Smith brought to consummation only during his postwar
governorship of New York, was of slow development in
the Progressive era itself. The uneasy and partial but occasionally effective union between the idealistic reformer
and the boss foreshadowed only vaguely a development
that was to reach its peak under Franklin D. Roosevelt.[5]

II · *Muckraking: the Revolution in Journalism*

To an extraordinary degree the work of the Progressive
movement rested upon its journalism. The fundamental
critical achievement of American Progressivism was the
business of exposure, and journalism was the chief occupational source of its creative writers. It is hardly an
exaggeration to say that the Progressive mind was characteristically a journalistic mind, and that its characteristic
contribution was that of the socially responsible reporter-
reformer. The muckraker was a central figure. Before there
could be action, there must be information and exhorta-

---

[5] Nothing I have said in the text should be taken to imply that the
urban machines based upon immigrant support were the first or only
ones to develop a spirit of political participation based upon the
economics of self-interest. Of course the whole nineteenth-century
sectional-interest scramble, with its tariff trading and its pork-barrel
procedures, would belie any such notion, and it is worth adding that
this political tradition was represented by Anglo-Saxon politicians, many
of them with rural backgrounds. The notion that politics should be
an area for high-minded and disinterested service was revived (it was
by no means new in America among them) by the Mugwump idealists
of the late nineteenth century. After them it became a creed with a
much broader following during the Progressive era. I have singled out,
as a phenomenon of the Progressive era, the antipathy between the
ethos of the boss-machine-immigrant complex and that of the reformer-
individualist-Anglo-Saxon complex not because I hold it to be the only
struggle going on at the time but because it serves as an archetypical
illustration of undercurrents of political feeling that were then beginning to be of especial importance. (For later developments in this
line see chapter vii, section 2.) We need more studies of the types
of political organizations that have flourished in the United States
and of the codes of loyalties they have developed to sustain them.
Such studies would concern themselves with at least five major variants:
not only the immigrant machines and the reform movements, but the
durable reform machines, the native interest-politics machines of the
mid-nineteenth century, and the modes of government developed by
the interlocking local elites of the middle and late eighteenth century.

tion. Grievances had to be given specific objects, and these the muckraker supplied. It was muckraking that brought the diffuse malaise of the public into focus.

The practice of exposure itself was not an invention of the muckraking era, nor did muckraking succeed because it had a new idea to offer. The pervasiveness of graft, the presence of a continuous corrupt connection between business and government, the link between government and vice—there was nothing new in the awareness of these things. Since the 1870's, exposure had been a recurrent theme in American political life. There had been frequent local newspaper crusades. Henry Adams and his brother Charles Francis had muckraked the Erie ring and the "Gold Conspiracy"; the *New York Times*, *Harper's Weekly*, and Thomas Nast had gone after Tammany in the seventies. There had been a great deal of exposure in the nineties, when Parkhurst and the Lexow Committee were active in New York, and W. T. Stead's *If Christ Came to Chicago* had caused a sensation in that city. Henry Demarest Lloyd's *Wealth against Commonwealth*, published in 1894, was a brilliant piece of muckraking. Hamlin Garland's Populist novel, *A Spoil of Office*, showed how general was the familiarity with state corruption. Indeed, during the last three decades of the nineteenth century, literally dozens upon dozens of novels were published which have been designated, because of their concentration upon corruption, "premuckraking" novels.[6]

What was new in muckraking in the Progressive era was neither its ideas nor its existence, but its reach—its nationwide character and its capacity to draw nationwide attention, the presence of mass muckraking media with national circulations, and huge resources for the research that went into exposure. The muckraking magazines had circulations running into the hundreds of thousands. They were able to pour funds into the investigations of their

[6] John Lydenberg: *Premuckraking*, unpublished Ph.D. thesis, Harvard University, 1946.

reporters—S. S. McClure estimated that the famous articles of Ida Tarbell cost $4,000 each and those of Lincoln Steffens $2,000 [7]—and they were able, as very few of the practitioners of exposure had been able before, not merely to name the malpractices in American business and politics, but to name the *malpractitioners* and their specific misdeeds, and to proclaim the facts to the entire country. It now became possible for any literate citizen to know what barkeeps, district attorneys, ward heelers, prostitutes, police-court magistrates, reporters, and corporation lawyers had always come to know in the course of their business.

Behind muckraking there was a long history of change in journalism, the story of a transformation in the newspaper and magazine world. The immensely rapid urbanization of the country had greatly enlarged daily newspaper circulation. In 1870 there were 574 daily newspapers in the country; by 1899 there were 1,610; by 1909, 2,600.[8] The circulation of daily newspapers increased over the same span of time from 2,800,000 to 24,200,000.[9] This expansion had opened up to publishers remarkable promotional opportunities, which brought in their train a number of changes in journalistic practice.

The newspaper owners and editors soon began to assume a new role. Experienced in the traditional function of reporting the news, they found themselves undertaking the more ambitious task of creating a mental world for the uprooted farmers and villagers who were coming to live in the city. The rural migrants found themselves in a new urban world, strange, anonymous, impersonal, cruel, often corrupt and vicious, but also full of variety and fascination. They were accustomed to a life based on primary human contacts—the family, the church, the neighborhood—and they had been torn away from these and thrust

[7] S. S. McClure: *My Autobiography* (New York, 1914), p. 245.
[8] Alfred McClung Lee: *The Daily Newspaper in America* (New York, 1937), pp. 716–17.
[9] Ibid., pp. 725–6.

into a more impersonal environment, in which they experienced a much larger number of more superficial human relationships. The newspaper became not only the interpreter of this environment but a means of surmounting in some measure its vast human distances, of supplying a sense of intimacy all too rare in the ordinary course of its life. Through newspaper gossip it provided a substitute for village gossip. It began to make increased use of the variety and excitement of the city to capture personal interest and offer its readers indirect human contacts.[1] The rural mind, confronted with the city, often responded with shock, and this too the newspaper did not hesitate to exploit. So one finds during the seventies, eighties, and nineties an increasing disposition on the part of editors to use the human-interest story, the crusade, the interview, and the stunt or promotional device to boom circulation. The large newspaper with a growing circulation became less dependent upon the political party. There were more politically independent or quasi-independent papers, and publishers felt more inclined to challenge the political parties and other institutions. In business terms the benefits to booming circulation of crusades and exposés far outstripped the dangers from possible retaliation. In an age when news was at a premium and when more and more copy was needed to surround the growing columns of advertisement, there was a tendency for publishers and editors to be dissatisfied with reporting the news and to attempt to make it. The papers made news in a double sense; they *created* reportable events, whether by sending Nelly Bly around the world or by helping to stir up a war with Spain. They also *elevated* events, hitherto considered beneath reportorial attention, to the level of news occurrences by clever, emotionally colored reporting. They exploited human interest, in short. This was something that had existed almost from the beginning of the popular penny press—one remembers, for instance, the elder James

[1] See Helen MacGill Hughes: *News and the Human Interest Story* (Chicago, 1940).

Gordon Bennett's capacity to exploit his own flamboyant personality. But the new exploitation of human interest was different. There was more of it, of course, and it was more skillfully done, but, most symptomatic, there was a change in its character. Where the old human interest had played up the curious concern of the common citizen with the affairs and antics of the rich, the new human interest exploited far more intensely the concern of comfortable people with the affairs of the poor. The slum sketch, the story of the poor and disinherited of the cities, became commonplace.[2] And it was just this interest of the secure world in the nether world that served as the prototype of muckraking.

All this concern with news, interviews, exposure, and human interest set a premium on the good reporter and reduced the importance of editorial writing and the editorial page. As early as 1871 a writer on journalism observed: "For the majority of readers it is the reporter, not the editor, who is the ruling genius of the newspaper."[3] The old editors of the pre-Civil War era had put a great deal of stock in themselves as makers of opinion through their editorial columns. Now their successors began to realize that their influence on the public mind, such as it was, came from their treatment of the news, not from editorial writing. But getting the news, especially when it came to exposes and human-interest stories, was the reporter's business. Bold reportorial initiative, good reportorial writing, were now very much in demand. In the

---

[2] The modern newspaper reader often shrinks from the vulgarity and sentimentality of sob-sister journalism. While the manifest function of such writing, however, may be to exploit sentiment for the sake of sales, its latent function is to help create an urban ethos of solidarity and to put some limits on the barbarization of urban life. No American newspaper-reader can fail to notice the widespread generous response that is given almost every day to some widely publicized personal disaster. Even a dignified newspaper like the New York Times taps this generosity each year by raising funds for charity on the basis of poignantly written accounts of the city's "Hundred Neediest Cases." A civilization that needs sob-sister journalism is a sad one, but the same civilization incapable of producing it would be worse.

[3] Frank Luther Mott: American Journalism (New York, 1947), p. 385.

period from 1870 to about 1890 the salaries of reporters doubled. Better-educated men were more attracted to the profession and were more acceptable in it.[4] Editors who had scorned college graduates began to look for them. The Spanish-American War, a triumph of the new journalism, was nowhere fought more brilliantly than in the columns of the newspapers, and it was covered by a battery of reporters numerous enough and well enough equipped to be used in emergency as military reinforcements. As the reporter's job rose in status, even in glamour, more and more young men with serious literary aspirations were attracted to it as a provisional way of earning a living. These men brought to the journalistic life some of the ideals, the larger interests, and the sense of public responsibility of men of culture.

Finally, the occupational situation of the reporter was uniquely illuminating. It was not merely that reporters saw and heard things, got the inside story; they sat at the crossroads between the coarse realities of their reportorial beats and the high abstractions and elevated moral tone of the editorial page. Reporters saw what fine things the newspapers said about public responsibility, and they also saw the gross things newspaper managers did to get news or advertising. As Theodore Dreiser, then a young reporter, recalled, they became alert to hypocrisy, perhaps a little cynical themselves, but fundamentally enlightened about the immense gaps between the lofty ideals and public professions of the editorial page and the dirty realities of the business office and the newsroom.[5] And it was

---

[4] Ibid., pp. 488–90.

[5] "While the editorial office might be preparing the most flowery moralistic or religionistic editorials regarding the worth of man, the value of progress, character, religion, morality, the sanctity of the home, charity, and the like, the business office and news room were concerned with no such fine theories. The business office was all business, with little or no thought of anything save success, and in the city news room the mask was off and life was handled in a rough-and-ready manner, without gloves. . . . Pretense did not go here. Innate honesty on the part of any one was not probable. Charity was a business with something in it for somebody. Morality was in the main for public consumption only." Theodore Dreiser: *A Book about My-*

into this gap that the muckraking mind rushed with all its fact-finding zeal.

It was, of course, the popular magazine, not the daily newspaper, that stood in the forefront of muckraking, but the muckraking periodicals were profoundly affected by newspaper journalism. The old, respectable magazines, the *Atlantic*, *Harper's*, the *Century*, and *Scribner's*, had been genteel, sedate enterprises selling at thirty-five cents a copy and reaching limited audiences of about 130,000. These periodicals were run by literary men; implicit in their contents was the notion that the magazine is a book in periodical form; they were managed by the conservative publishing houses. The new magazines that emerged at the turn of the century sold at ten or twelve or fifteen cents a copy and reached audiences of from 400,000 to 1,000,000. Their publishers were not literary men but business promoters; their editors were usually former newspaper editors, and they ran a good deal of news copy written by reporters. These magazines, by contrast, were newspapers in periodical form; they took many of their ideas from daily journalism or the Sunday supplements. They contained not only literature but features that resembled news. And like the daily press they soon began to make news and to become a political force in their own right.

As businessmen, the publishers of these magazines, Frank Munsey, S. S. McClure, John Brisben Walker, and others, resembled their promotion-minded forerunners in daily journalism like E. W. Scripps, Joseph Pulitzer, and William Randolph Hearst. Muckraking for them was the most successful of the circulation-building devices they used. Neither the muckraking publishers and editors nor the muckraking reporters set out to expose evils or to reform society. Although the experience of the *Ladies' Home Journal*, *Munsey's*, and the *Saturday Evening Post* showed that immense circulations could be achieved with-

self (New York, 1922), pp. 151-2. Thus the newspaper itself provided a model for the Progressive dissociation of morals and "reality."

out ever entering in any serious sense upon it, muckraking
was a by-product, perhaps an inevitable one, of the development of mass magazines. Even *McClure's*, the magazine that touched off the movement, had already built a
large circulation upon an enterprising use of popular
fiction and upon Ida Tarbell's series on the lives of Napoleon and Lincoln. The so-called "muckraking" magazines
themselves devoted only a small proportion of their total
space to muckraking articles. Only after exposure had
proved its popularity did other magazines, notably *Hampton's*, boom their circulations by focusing on muckraking.

A significant illustration of the accidental sources of
muckraking was Miss Tarbell's famous series on Standard
Oil. S. S. McClure was running, during the late 1890's,
a series of articles which he describes in his autobiography
as dedicated to "the greatest American business achievements." He had observed that the "feeling of the common
people [about the trusts] had a sort of menace in it; they
took a threatening attitude toward the Trusts, and without much knowledge." [6] He and his editors decided that a
study of Standard Oil, the greatest of the trusts, would
have some educational value, and they called in Ida
Tarbell, who "had lived for years in the heart of the oil
region of Pennsylvania, and had seen the marvelous development of the Standard Oil Trust at first hand." [7] It
happened also that Miss Tarbell, whose family had suffered
the common disastrous fate of the independent oil-pro-
ducers, had a great feeling for them.[8] The methods that
had been used by Standard Oil were altogether too vulnerable to be played down, and although she hoped her
inquiry "might be received as a legitimate historical
study . . . to my chagrin I found myself included in a
new school, that of the muckrakers." She decided that she
would have done with the whole business and seems to
have resented the demand of some of her following that

[6] S. S. McClure, op. cit., pp. 237–8.
[7] Ibid., p. 238.
[8] Ida Tarbell: *All in the Day's Work* (New York, 1939), pp. 202 ff.

she go on with the work of exposure—"I soon found that
most of them wanted attacks. They had little interest in
balanced findings." [9] Later she did some further work in
exposing tariff politics, but she afterwards recalled: "My
conscience began to trouble me. Was it not as much my
business as a reporter to present this [the favorable] side
of the picture as to present the other?" "The public was
coming to believe," she felt, as a result of all the work
of exposure, "that the inevitable result of corporate industrial management was exploitation, neglect, bullying,
crushing of labor, that the only hope was in destroying
the system." So she began to write about achievements
and improvements in business—under the considerable
handicap, to be sure, of her muckraking reputation—became a eulogist of business, and eventually wrote an
apologetic biography of the industrialist Judge Gary.[1]
In her case the impulse that had been expressed by Mc-
Clure when he first set out to publicize business achievements came full circle.

Most of the other outstanding figures of the muckrake
era were simply writers or reporters working on commission and eager to do well what was asked of them. A
few, among them Upton Sinclair and Gustavus Myers, were
animated by a deep-going dislike of the capitalist order,
but most of them were hired into muckraking or directed
toward it on the initiative of sales-conscious editors or publishers. Probably the most socially minded and inquisitive
of the muckrakers, except for the Socialists, was Lincoln
Steffens; but even his muckraking of American cities began
more or less accidentally when McClure refused to allow
him to take over an editorship without getting out and
familiarizing himself with the country.[2] Others were reluctant dragons. Ray Stannard Baker, whose chief desire
was to be a novelist, came to *McClure's* as a writer of

---

[9] Ibid., p. 242.
[1] Ibid., chapter xiv, pp. 364 ff.
[2] Lincoln Steffens: Autobiography, p. 364.

secret-service stories and of a book celebrating America's prosperity. Before he began muckraking he was writing faintly eulogistic articles on big business and the trusts! It is perhaps a significant token of the way in which memory rearranges facts in the light of myth that many years later, when Louis Filler was writing his study of the muckrakers, Baker could—no doubt sincerely—refer him to these pieces as examples of early muckraking articles. In fact Baker's first muckraking work tended in a far different direction—it showed up abuses in labor-unionism. Thomas Lawson, the author of the popular *Frenzied Finance,* was a bruised speculator with a bitter contempt for popular democracy.[3] David Graham Phillips, who wrote *The Treason of the Senate,* was making large sums writing novels for the *Saturday Evening Post* when Bailey Millard, the editor of the *Cosmopolitan,* talked him into writing the attack on the Senate. Phillips was extremely reluctant at first, insisting that someone else be engaged to "gather the facts," and agreed to undertake the work only when Gustavus Myers, the Socialist writer, was hired to do the research. Once engaged upon the task, however, he developed a real interest in it.

If, from the standpoint of the editors and journalists themselves, the beginning of muckraking seemed to be more or less "accidental," its ending did not. The large magazine built on muckraking was vulnerable as a business organization. The publishing firm was so large an enterprise and sold its product for so little that it became intensely dependent upon advertising and credit, and hence vulnerable to pressure from the business community. Advertisers did not hesitate to withdraw orders for space when their own interests or related interests were touched upon. Bankers adopted a discriminatory credit policy, so that modest loans could not be secured even for the maintenance of a business of great value and proved stability. In one case, that of *Hampton's,* even espionage

[3] C. C. Fegier: *The Era of the Muckrakers* (Chapel Hill, 1932), p. 130.

was employed to destroy the magazine.[4] One magazine,
Pearson's, continued to muckrake after 1912, when all the
others had fallen into new hands or changed their policies,
and its vitality, sustained down to the time of the first
World War, has been cited as evidence that muckraking
sentiment did not die a spontaneous death, but was
choked off at its sources by those who were most affected
by its exposures.[5] This is a suggestive, but to my mind
not a conclusive, point. It is conceivable that there may
have been enough muckraking sentiment left to support
one well-run periodical with a large circulation, but not
a half-dozen plus a large number of smaller imitators. Certainly business was hostile and made its hostility felt, but
it also seems that the muckraking mood was tapering off.
By 1912 it had been raging at a high pitch for nine years.
To imagine that it could have gone on indefinitely is to
mistake its character.

Consider who the muckrakers were, what their intentions were, and what it was they were doing. Their criticisms of American society were, in their utmost reaches,
very searching and radical, but they were themselves moderate men who intended to propose no radical remedies.
From the beginning, then, they were limited by the disparity between the boldness of their means and the tame-
ness of their ends. They were working at a time of widespread prosperity, and their chief appeal was not to desperate social needs but to mass sentiments of responsibility,
indignation, and guilt. Hardly anyone intended that these
sentiments should result in action drastic enough to trans-

---

[4] For accounts of the decline of muckraking, see Louis Filler: *Crusaders
for American Liberalism* (New York, 1939), chapter xxviii, and C. C.
Regier, op. cit., chapter xii.
[5] Filler, op. cit., pp. 370–3. The whole subject of the decline of muckraking deserves a full-length study of its own, centering not simply on
the resistance of the business community but on such factors as popular
mood and the internal business and promotional methods of the
magazines themselves. In the latter connection see Walter A. Gaw:
*Some Important Trends in the Development of Magazines in the
United States as an Advertising Medium*, unpublished doctoral dissertation, New York University, 1942.

form American society. In truth, that society was getting along reasonably well, and the muckrakers themselves were quite aware of it. The group of leading muckrakers that left *McClure's* in 1906 to form the *American Magazine*,[6] as Ray Stannard Baker recalled, was "far more eager to understand and make sure than to dream of utopias. . . . We 'muckraked' not because we hated our world but because we loved it. We were not hopeless, we were not cynical, we were not bitter." [7] Their first announcement promised "the most stirring and delightful monthly book of fiction, humor, sentiment, and joyous reading that is anywhere published. It will reflect a happy, struggling, fighting world, in which, as we believe, good people are coming out on top. . . . Our magazine will be wholesome, hopeful, stimulating, uplifting. . . ." [8]

Finally, it is perhaps necessary to point out that within the limited framework of the reforms that were possible without structural alterations in the American social and economic system, the muckrakers did accomplish something in the form of legislative changes and social face-washing. They enjoyed, after all, some sense of real achievement. Presumably the temper of the early writers for *McClure's* was far more akin to that of the majority of their middle-class audience than was the attitude of

---

[6] Most of the principals have left this incident obscure in their memoirs. The most informative account is that of Ida Tarbell, op. cit., pp. 256–7; cf. Steffens: *Autobiography*, pp. 535–6.

[7] Ray Stannard Baker: *American Chronicle* (New York, 1945), p. 226.

[8] Ibid., pp. 226–7. Cf. Miss Tarbell's recollection that the *American Magazine* "had little genuine muckraking spirit. . . . The idea that there was something fundamentally sound and good in industrial relations, that in many spots had gone far beyond what either labor or reformers were demanding, came to the office as a new attack on the old problem." Op. cit., p. 281. "It seems to me," wrote William Allen White, another member of the group, to editor John S. Phillips in 1906, "the great danger before you is that of being too purposeful. People will expect the pale drawn face; the set lips and a general line of emotional insanity. You should fool 'em. Give 'em something like 'Pigs is Pigs.' From the prospectus they will judge that you are going to produce a 'Thin red line of heroes,' and instead of which you should have the sharp claque of the slap stick. . . ." Walter Johnson: *William Allen White's America* (New York, 1947), p. 159.

the Socialist muckrakers like Gustavus Myers, Upton Sinclair, and Charles Edward Russell, who wanted to push the implications of muckraking discoveries to their utmost practical conclusions.

III · Reality and Responsibility

The muckrakers had a more decisive impact on the thinking of the country than they did on its laws or morals. They confirmed, if they did not create, a fresh mode of criticism that grew out of journalistic observation. The dominant note in the best thought of the Progressive era is summed up in the term "realism." It was realism that the current literature and journalism fostered, just as it was realism that the most fertile thinkers of the age brought into philosophy, law, and economics. Although Western sectional consciousness, which was curiously united to a sort of folkish nationalism, made its own contribution to realistic writing, the chief source of realism lay in the city and city journalism. With few exceptions the makers of American realism, even from the days of Mark Twain and William Dean Howells, were men who had training in journalistic observation—Stephen Crane, Theodore Dreiser, Harold Frederic, David Graham Phillips—or men like Edward Kirkland, Edward Eggleston, Hamlin Garland, and Jack London who in some other capacity had also seen the rough side of life to which the reporters and human-interest writers were exposed. What they all had in common—the realistic novelists, the muckrakers, and the more critical social scientists of the period —was a passion for getting the "inside story."

Robert Cantwell once suggested that the primary reason for the success of the muckrakers was not political at all, but literary, and that their work was in a sense the journalistic equivalent of the literary realism that also flourished at the time. It had never been customary in America to write about America, but especially not about the life of industry and labor and business and poverty and vice. Now, while novelists were replacing a literature bred out of other literature with a genre drawn from street scenes and abattoirs or the fly-specked rural kitchens of Hamlin Garland's stories, the muckrakers were replacing the genteel travel stories and romances of the older magazines with a running account of how America worked. "It was not," says Cantwell, "because the muckrakers exposed the corruption of Minneapolis, for example, that they were widely read, but because they wrote about Minneapolis at a time when it had not been written about, without patronizing or boosting it, and with an attempt to explore its life realistically and intelligently. They wrote, in short, an intimate, anecdotal, behind-the-scenes history of their own times. . . . They traced the intricate relationship of the police, the underworld, the local political bosses, the secret connections between the new corporations . . . and the legislatures and the courts. In doing this they drew a new cast of characters for the drama of American society: bosses, professional politicians, reformers, racketeers, captains of industry. Everybody recognized these native types; everybody knew about them; but they had not been characterized before; their social functions had not been analyzed. At the same time, the muckrakers pictured stage settings that everybody recognized but that nobody had written about—oil refineries, slums, the red-light districts, the hotel rooms where political deals were made—the familiar, unadorned, homely stages where the teeming day-to-day dramas of American life were enacted. How could the aloof literary magazines of the East, with their essays and their contributions from distinguished English novelists, tap this rich material?" [9]

What the muckrakers and the realistic writers were doing in their fields the speculative thinkers and social scientists were also doing in theirs. As scholars reached

---

[9] Robert Cantwell: "Journalism—the Magazines," in Harold E. Stearns, ed.: *America Now* (New York, 1938), p. 347.

out for their own "realistic" categories, the formalistic
thought of an earlier and more conservative generation
fell under close and often damaging scrutiny. Economists
were pondering Veblen's effort to replace the economic
man of the classical school with his wasteful consumer
and his predatory captain of industry. Legal realists were
supplanting the "pure" jurisprudential agent of earlier legal
theorists with the flesh-and-blood image of the corporation lawyer dressed in judicial robes and stuffed with
corporation prejudices. Political scientists were losing their
old veneration for the state as an abstract repository of
something called sovereignty and accepting the views of
men like Charles A. Beard and Arthur F. Bentley, who
conceived of the state as a concrete instrument that regis-
tered the social pressures brought to bear upon it by various
interest groups. Historians were beginning to apply the
economic interpretation of history. The new discipline of
sociology, intimately linked with social-settlement work
and Christian social reform, was criticizing the older
notions of individuality and morality and developing a
new, "realistic" social psychology. John Dewey was attacking formalistic categories in philosophy and trying to develop a more descriptive and operational account of the
uses of ideas.[1] The supreme achievement of this pervasive iconoclasm came in 1913 with Charles A. Beard's
*An Economic Interpretation of the Constitution of the
United States,* a book that scandalized the conservative
world. This consummatory attack on the traditional symbols had now carried the Progressive mind to the inner
citadel of the established order: a nation of Constitution-
worshippers and ancestor-worshippers was confronted with
a scholarly muckraking of the Founding Fathers and the
Constitution itself. V. L. Parrington, himself a representative of Populist and Progressive thinking, once suggested
that the "chief contribution of the Progressive movement
to American political thought was its discovery of the es-

---

[1] On the intellectual achievement of this generation see Morton G.
White: *Social Thought in America* (New York, 1949), esp. chapter ii.

sentially undemocratic nature of the federal constitution." [2]

But Beard's treatment of the Founding Fathers also shows some of the limitations of the Progressive conception of reality. When he wrote about the economic interests and activities of the Founding Fathers, especially those activities related to politics in a way not always above question from the highest standards of disinterested morality, he wrote fully and with illumination. When he dealt with their ideas about democracy, he was relatively casual; his mind did not become fully engaged with his object, and he was content with a spare and rather literal-minded compound of scattered quotations from the debates in the Constitutional Convention. [3] The muckraking model of thought had brought with it a certain limiting and narrowing definition of reality and a flattening of the imagination. William Dean Howells, in one of his less fortunate remarks, had accepted the earlier tendency of American literature to deal with "the smiling aspects of life" that were more characteristically American. This complacency the realists reversed with a vengeance. Reality now was rough and sordid. It was hidden, neglected, and off-stage. It was conceived essentially as that stream of external and material events which was most likely to be unpleasant. [4] Reality was the bribe, the rebate, the bought franchise, the sale of adulterated food. It was what one found in *The Jungle, The Octopus, Wealth against Commonwealth,* or *The Shame of the Cities.* It was just as completely and hopelessly dissociated from the world of morals and ideals as, say, a newspaper editorial on Motherhood might be from the facts about infant mortality in the slums.

To the average American of the Progressive era this

---

[2] In his Introduction to J. Allen Smith: *Growth and Decadence of Constitutional Government* (New York, 1930), p. xi.
[3] I have dealt with this problem at greater length in "Beard and the Constitution," *American Quarterly,* Vol. II (Fall 1950), pp. 195–213; the same essay is in Howard K. Beale, ed.: *Charles A. Beard* (Lexington, Ky., 1954), pp. 75–92.
[4] Cf. the discussion of "Reality in America" by Lionel Trilling, in *The Liberal Imagination* (New York, 1950), pp. 3–21.

ugly thing that presented itself as reality was not a final
term. Reality was a series of unspeakable plots, personal
iniquities, moral failures, which, in their totality, had come
to govern American society only because the citizen had
relaxed his moral vigilance. The failures of American society were thus no token of the ultimate nature of man,
of the human condition, much less the American condition; they were not to be accepted or merely modified, but
fought with the utmost strenuosity at every point. First
reality must in its fullness be exposed, and then it must
be made the subject of moral exhortation; and then, when
individual citizens in sufficient numbers had stiffened in
their determination to effect reform, something could be
done. As Josiah Strong put it: "If public opinion is educated concerning a given reform—political, social, industrial, or moral—and if the popular conscience is sufficiently
awake to enforce an enlightened public opinion, the reform is accomplished straightway. This then is the generic
reform—the education of public opinion and of the popular
conscience." [5] First the citizen must reclaim the power that
he himself had abdicated, refashioning where necessary
the instruments of government. Then—since the Yankee
found the solution to everything in laws—he must see that
the proper remediable laws be passed and that existing
laws be enforced. He must choose men of the highest moral
qualities for his political leaders. It was assumed that such
moral qualities were indestructible and that decent men,
once found and installed in office, would remain decent.
When they had regained control of affairs, moral rigor
would not flag again.

An excellent illustration of the spirit of Progressivism as
it manifested itself in the new popular literature is provided by a famous editorial by S. S. McClure in the January 1903 issue of *McClure's*.[6] In this editorial McClure

---

[5] Josiah Strong, op. cit., p. 159.
[6] I have chosen not only this editorial from *McClure's*, but that
periodical's contents during this whole era as being completely representative of the average magazine-reader's fare, and of the thought and
sensibility of the muckraking movement.

stood back and took a fresh look at his publication and suddenly realized what it was that he and his writers were doing. He observed that his current issue, which was running an article muckraking Minneapolis by Lincoln Steffens, another on Standard Oil by Ida Tarbell, and still another by Ray Stannard Baker on labor, showed a striking and completely unplanned convergence upon a central fact in American life: a general disrespect for law on the part of capitalists, workingmen, politicians, and citizens. Who, he asked, was left in the community to uphold the law? The lawyers? Some of the best of them made a living from advising business firms how to evade it. The judges? Among too many of them the respect for law took the form of respect for quibbles by which they restored to liberty men who on the evidence of common sense would be convicted of malfeasances. The churches? "We know of one, an ancient and wealthy establishment, which had to be compelled by a Tammany hold-over health officer to put its tenements in sanitary condition." "The colleges? They do not understand." "There is no one left," concluded McClure, "none but all of us. . . . We all are doing our worst and making the public pay. The public is the people. We forget that we all are the people. . . . We have to pay in the end, every one of us."

The chief themes of the muckraking magazines are stated here. First is the progressive view of reality—evildoing among the most respectable people is seen as the "real" character of American life; corruption is found on every side. Second is the idea that the mischief can be interpreted simply as a widespread breaking of the law. I have remarked that Anglo-Saxon thinking emphasized governance by legal rules, as opposed to the widespread tendency among immigrants to interpret political reality in the light of personal relations. If the laws are the right laws, and if they can be enforced by the right men, the Progressive believed, everything would be better.[7] He had

---

[7] "In brief, so long as the trust question is a question of law, the people may feel as the President does, that it is safe in clean, steady hands

a great and abiding faith in the appeal to such abstractions
as the law and patriotism, and the efficacy of continued
exhortation. Third, there was the appeal to universal personal responsibility and the imputation of personal guilt.

To understand the reform mentality, we must consider
the vigor with which the Progressives attacked not only
such social questions as the powers of trusts and bosses,
but also such objects of reform as the liquor traffic and
prostitution. The Progressive mind, I have said, was pre-
eminently a Protestant mind; and even though much of its
strength was in the cities, it inherited the moral traditions
of rural evangelical Protestantism. The Progressives were
still freshly horrified by phenomena that we now resignedly
consider indigenous to urban existence. However prosperous they were, they lived in the midst of all the iniquities that the agrarian myth had taught them to expect of
urban life, and they refused to accept them calmly. Here it
was that a most important aspect of the Protestant per-

---

and a loyal, legal mind." L. A. Coolidge: "Attorney-General Knox,
Lawyer," McClure's, Vol. XIX (September 1902), p. 473.
   ". . . the dull indifference of the people. They do not insist that
the laws be enforced." S. S. McClure: "The Increase of Lawlessness
in the United States," ibid., Vol. XXIV (December 1904), p. 163.
   "The only remedy is a strict enforcement of all the laws, all along
the line, all the time . . ." Ray Stannard Baker: "What Is a Lynch-
ing?" ibid. (February 1905), p. 430.
   ". . . a failure to observe the elementary principles of law . . ."
Burton J. Hendrick: "Governor Hughes," ibid., Vol. XXX (April
1908), p. 681.
   "I would like to see all saloons legislated out of existence . . ."
"The Story of an Alcohol Slave," ibid., Vol. XXXIII (August 1909),
p. 430.
   ". . . my chief constructive work was devoted to securing a system
by which I could compel the body of men under me—against its old
custom and obvious self-interest—really to enforce the law." General
Theodore A. Bingham: "The Organized Criminals of New York,"
ibid., Vol. XXXIV (November 1909), p. 62.
   This was one of the points at which the more sophisticated thinking
of the era deviated most sharply from common discourse; for while
the Progressive moralists and popular exhorters were demanding a return to the "law," conceived as a glittering abstraction, writers like
Charles A. Beard, Arthur F. Bentley, and Frank G. Goodnow were
trying to show that law too is responsive to political pressures and
that it reflects class interests.

sonality came into play: its ethos of personal responsibility.
American life and American mythology had been keyed to
the conditions of rural simplicity and village neighborliness
under which personal responsibility for the problems—and
the morals—of others could in fact often be assumed.[8]
Moreover it was the whole effect of the Protestant ethic
to heighten the sense of personal responsibility as much as
possible. The more the muckrakers acquainted the Protestant Yankee with what was going on around him, the more
guilty and troubled he felt. The religious institutions of
Protestantism provided no mechanism to process, drain off,
and externalize the sense of guilt.[9] American political
traditions provided no strong native tradition of conservatism to reconcile men to evils that could not easily be
disposed of. The native ethos of mass participation in
politics and citizenlike civic consciousness—so strange, as
we have remarked, to the immigrants—confirmed the idea
that everyone was in some very serious sense responsible
for everything.

---

[8] E. A. Ross wrote a very popular book, *Sin and Society* (Boston, 1907),
whose entire purpose was to show how the new conditions of life
demanded a new code of morality. Sinning—the commission of evil
acts harmful to others—had become corporate and impersonal. The
characteristic wrong arose not out of aggression but from betrayal.
Usually it was committed by men who were entirely virtuous in
private and personal relationships, for the chief problem now was not
the evil impulse itself but moral insensibility. The modern sinners
could not see the results of their own acts because these would be
remote in time and space. Therefore it was necessary to become ever
so much more imaginative than formerly in appraising one's own sins
and those of others. Among other things, directors of companies
should be held personally accountable for every preventable abuse
committed by their corporations.

[9] In evangelical Protestantism the individual is expected to bear almost
the full burden of the conversion and the salvation of his soul. What
his church provides him with, so far as this goal is concerned, is an
instrument of exhortation. In Catholicism, by contrast, as in some
other churches, the mediating role of the Church itself is of far
greater importance and the responsibility of the individual is not
keyed up to quite the same pitch. A working mechanism for the disposal and psychic mastery of guilt is available to Roman Catholics
in the form of confession and penance. If this difference is translated
into political terms, the moral animus of Progressivism can be better
understood.

Frederic C. Howe's candid and highly illuminating auto-biography, *The Confessions of a Reformer,* shows with fine self-awareness how the preachings of evangelical Protestantism and the civic teachings of Mugwumpery laid the foundations for the Progressive sense of responsibility. Howe had been raised in Meadville, Pennsylvania, as the child of moderately well-to-do and sincerely pious Methodist parents. Attending a small sectarian college in the great age of secularization that came in with Darwinism, Howe found himself unable to respond any longer to evangelical revivalism; but, as he reports, the "morality of duty, of careful respectability," that was inculcated in him from his earliest years was not so easily dislodged as the theology that went with it. "Early assumptions as to virtue and vice, goodness and evil remained in my mind long after I had tried to discard them. This is, I think, the most characteristic influence of my generation. It explains the nature of our reforms, the regulatory legislation in morals and economics, our belief in men rather than in institutions and our messages to other peoples. Missionaries and battleships, anti-saloon leagues and Ku Klux Klans, Wilson and Santo Domingo are all a part of that evangelistic psychology that makes America what she is." [1] When Howe went to Johns Hopkins University for graduate study, he was well prepared to respond to the passionate preachings of an academic Mugwump like Woodrow Wilson, who spoke out against the indifference and loss of responsibility among the public, and to the high-minded addresses of Lord Bryce, who lamented the spoils system, corruption, the failure of democracy, and the "decay of a sense of responsibility among the kind of people whom I knew. That was what impressed me most: the kind of people I knew had neglected their duties." [2] As so often happens in the development of ideas and public moods, the remarkable group of teachers and students that gathered at Johns Hopkins in the late 1880's and the 1890's was simply

---

[1] Howe: *The Confessions of a Reformer,* p. 17.
[2] Ibid., p. 3.

anticipating by a few years the civic consciousness that
soon swept over a vastly larger public. What Howe observes of the Johns Hopkins men of the nineties—"We felt
that the world had been wished onto our shoulders"[3]—
became true of a large part of the nation not long after-
ward. After the turn of the century the men who were in
best rapport with public sentiment were preaching to the
whole nation the necessity of taking up, personally and individually, those civic burdens which the previous generation had forsaken. "No hard-and-fast rule can be laid
down," said Theodore Roosevelt, "as to the way in which
such work [reform] must be done; but most certainly every
man, whatever his position, should strive to do it in some
way and to some degree."[4]

One is impressed, in a review of the literature, with the
enormous amount of self-accusation among Progressives.
William Allen White saw it when he attributed much of
the movement to the fact that "in the soul of the people
there is a conviction of their past unrighteousness."[5] The
moral indignation of the age was by no means directed
entirely against others; it was in a great and critical measure directed inward. Contemporaries who spoke of the
movement as an affair of the conscience were not mistaken.

---

[3] Ibid., p. 8.
[4] Theodore Roosevelt: "Reform through Social Work," *McClure's*,
Vol. XVI (March 1901), p. 454.

". . . in the final analysis it was the voters who decided whether
New York should be 'open' or 'shut.'" Josiah Flynt: "In the World
of Graft," ibid. (April 1901), p. 576.

"In short, if we want self-government . . . we have got to work at
it ourselves. President Roosevelt is right when he preaches broad
morality; the necessity of each man getting down and doing something
himself." Ray Stannard Baker: "The Trust's New Tool—the Labor
Boss," ibid., Vol. XXII (November 1903), p. 43. Cf. the same
author's conclusion that everyone was guilty "who has not, himself
obedient to the law, demanded the election of men who will enforce
the law." "The Reign of Lawlessness," ibid., Vol. XXIII (May 1904),
p. 56.

"They [the Christian citizens] could accomplish it by each individual
resolving to vote for God at the polls—that is to say, vote for the
candidate whom God would approve." Anonymous: "Christian Citizenship," ibid., Vol. XXVI (November 1905), p. 110.
[5] William Allen White: *The Old Order Changeth*, p. 30.

Lincoln Steffens had the key to this sense of personal involvement when he entitled his famous muckraking volume
The Shame of the Cities.

Nothing, indeed, illustrates better than the Introduction
to Steffens's volume the fashion in which the Yankee ethos
of responsibility had become transmuted into a sense of
guilt. Again and again Steffens laid the responsibility for
the ugly state of affairs portrayed in his book at the door-
steps of his own readers. "The misgovernment of the American people," he declared, "is misgovernment by the American people. . . . Are the people honest? Are the people
better than Tammany? . . . Isn't our corrupt government,
after all, representative? . . . There is no essential difference between the pull that gets your wife into society or for
your book a favorable review, and that which gets a heeler
into office, a thief out of jail, and a rich man's son on the
board of directors of a corporation. . . . The boss is not
a political, he is an American institution, the product of a
freed people that have not the spirit to be free. . . . We
are responsible, not our leaders, since we follow them. . . .
The spirit of graft and of lawlessness is the American spirit.
. . . The people are not innocent. That is the only 'news'
in all the journalism of these articles. . . . My purpose
was . . . to see if the shameful facts, spread out in all
their shame, would not burn through our civic shamelessness and set fire to American pride." Steffens closed his
introduction by dedicating his book "to the accused—to all
the citizens of all the cities in the United States." [6]

It may seem that there was remarkable boldness in this
accusatory procedure, but such appearances are often
deceptive. Steffens had good reason to know that the substantial American citizen accepted such accusation as valid.
The people of Minneapolis and St. Louis had written not
in resentment but in encouragement after his exposure of
those cities had been published in *McClure's*, and—still

* Lincoln Steffens: *The Shame of the Cities* (New York, 1904); the
quotations are drawn, *passim*, from the introduction, pp. 4–26.

more significant—hundreds of invitations poured in from citizens, as individuals or in organized groups, of many other cities inviting exposure on their own premises: "come and show us up; we're worse than they are." [7]

Steffens's argument that it was the people, and particularly the "best" people, who were responsible for corruption cannot be taken, however, as an ultimate comment on human nature or the human condition. He was not preaching universal sinfulness as a token of the fact that most men would be damned, but because he hoped and expected that all could be saved—saved through this ardent appeal to their pride. This is the real function of the pervasively ugly character of reality that the Progressives so frequently harped on: pervasive as it was, it was neither impenetrable nor irremovable: it was an instrument of exhortation, not a clue to life but a fulcrum for reform. Steffens hoped, at bottom, "that our shamelessness is superficial, that beneath it lies a pride which, being real, may save us yet." [8] For when the chips were down he could not but believe, as he said of the situation in St. Louis, that "the people are sound." [9]

Among some reformers this ethos of responsibility to which Steffens appealed simply took the form of an effort to participate in what the rhetoric of the time called "the race life"—which meant, by and large, to get nearer to those who suffered in a more profound and poignant way from the burdens of "reality." As early as 1892 Jane Addams had delivered a fine, penetrating lecture on "The Subjective Necessity for Social Settlements," in which she explained how the sheltered and well-brought-up young Americans of her generation, reared on the ideal of social justice and on Protestant moral imperatives, had grown uncomfortable about their own sincerity, troubled about their uselessness, and restless about being "shut off from the

[7] Ibid., p. 25.
[8] Ibid., p. 24.
[9] Ibid., p. 140.

common labor by which they live and which is a great
source of moral and physical health." [1] Similarly a character in one of the social novels of H. H. Boyesen, the son of
a rich contractor, professed "a sneaking sense of guilt when
I am too comfortable," and left high society to plunge into
what he called "the great discordant tumultuous life, with
its passions and cries of distress." [2] Characters with the
same motivation were constantly to be found in the pages
of McClure's—now, however, no longer only as the
protagonists of fiction, but as the authors of articles.[3]

[1] Jane Addams et al.: *Philanthropy and Social Progress* (New York,
1893), pp. 1–26.

[2] H. H. Boyesen: *Social Strugglers* (New York, 1893), pp. 78, 83–4,
273. The ethos of guilt and indignation, work and service, and the
idea of an implacable opposition between material gratification and
spiritual development are outstanding themes in the work of the most
popular Progressive novelist, Winston Churchill, who portrayed the
whole movement as "the springing of a generation of ideals from a
generation of commerce." See Richard and Beatrice Hofstadter:
"Winston Churchill: a Study in the Popular Novel," *passim*.

[3] "Blair Carrhart goes as a laborer into the steel works, that he may
better know the men whom he wants to help. . . . With him we live
a life full of dangers and struggles and suffering." A review of I. K.
Friedman's *By Bread Alone*, *McClure's*, Vol. XVII (September 1901),
pp. 502–3.

"She was a woman of superior education and wide social experience,
and, like many other American women of similar qualifications, had
that tireless energy that could not be satisfied with remaining a passive
spectator to the progressive life about her." Lewis E. MacBrayne: "The
Promised Land," *ibid.*, Vol. XX (November 1902), p. 66.

"If we were not reading about matters calculated to fill us with
unutterable shame, we should be captivated by a style so frank, strong,
and fervent. Here is something better than entertainment." *Everybody's*,
reviewing the work of Lincoln Steffens, as quoted in *McClure's*, Vol.
XXIII (November 1904), p. 111. The significance of that last sentence
should not be passed over.

"We were as blind to real civil morals as the Spaniards of the In-
quisition must have been to the morality of Christ." William Allen
White: "Roosevelt: a Force for Righteousness," *ibid.*, Vol. XXVIII
(January 1907), p. 388. ". . . the whole infernal system of money-
bought government, money-bought churches and schools, was as surely
made from the commercial malice in our own hearts as the golden
calf set up in the wilderness was the god of the Israelites." *Ibid.*, p.
394.

See also the article by Rudolph Cronau: "A Continent Despoiled,"
ibid., Vol. XXXII (April 1909), with its "incontrovertible and con-
victing evidence of grave sins of which our nation has been guilty"
(p. 639).

Where this impulse was translated into action it sent a host of earnest reformers into the field to engage themselves in various useful philanthropies. But on the purely verbal level, where of necessity it had to remain for most people, it resulted on occasion in a rather strenuous moral purgation, not unlike the pathetic proletarianism that swept over many American intellectuals in the 1930's. One Florence Wilkinson contributed to *McClure's* a poem entitled "The Tortured Millions":[4]

. . . *They are dying that I may live, the tortured millions.*
By the Ohio River, the Euphrates, the Rhone.
They wring from the rocks my gold, the tortured millions;
Sleepless all night they mix my daily bread;
With heavy feet they are trampling out my vintage;
They go to a hungry grave that I may be fed. . . .
I warm my hands at the fires of ruining houses;
On a dying mother's breast I sink my head;
Last night my feet were faint from idleness,
I bathed my feet in blood her children shed.
O thou eternal Law, I wish this not to be.
Nay, raise them from the dust and punish me.

So the middle-class citizen received quite earnestly the exhortations that charged him with personal responsibility for all kinds of social ills. It was his business to do something about them. Indeed, he must do something if he was ever to feel better. But what should he do? He was too substantial a fellow to want to make any basic changes in a society in which he was so typically a prosperous and

---

[4] *McClure's*, Vol. XXIII (June 1904), pp. 167–8. The same author published (December 1906) another expression of her feelings, "A Salutation to Russia," written in a Whitmanesque manner and beginning: "You, millions of muzhiks, huddled in the smoky doorways of your huts . . ." This should be compared with her "Hands," ibid. (June 1910), p. 229:

> Oh, wonderful hands of toilers,
> Graved with the signs of your crafts, . . .
> I honor you, hands of toilers,
> I kneel and kiss your hands.

respectable figure. What he needed, therefore, was a *feel-ing* that action was taking place, a sense that the moral tone of things was being improved and that he had a part in this improvement. Corruption thus became a particularly fine issue for the moral energies of the Progressive. He was ready to be convinced that the country was thoroughly wicked, and the muckrakers supplied him with a wealth of plausible evidence.

In time the muckraking and reform writers seem to have become half conscious of the important psychic function their work was performing for themselves and their public, quite apart from any legislative consequences or material gains. They began to say, in effect, that even when they were unable to do very much to change the exercise of political power, they liked the sense of effort and the feel-ing that the moral tone of political life had changed. "It is not the material aspect of this," they began to say, "but the moral aspect that interests us." William Allen White dated the beginnings of this shift from "materialism" to "moral values" from the war with Spain when "the spirit of sacrifice overcame the spirit of commercialism," and the people saw "that if we could learn to sacrifice our own interest for those of a weaker people, we would learn the lesson needed to solve the great problem of democracy— to check our national greed and to make business honest." [5] McClure himself gave characteristic expression to this high valuation of the intangibles when he praised Charles Evans Hughes's exposure of the New York life-insurance com-panies for the enormous "tonic effect of the inquiry," which, he felt, had very likely saved thousands of young men from making compromises with honor. They saw that "public disgrace" awaited evildoers, and "there is no punishment so terrible as public disclosure of evil doing." [6] Related to

---

[5] *The Old Order Changeth*, p. 29.
[6] *McClure's*, Vol. XXVI (December 1905), p. 223. Cf. Burton J. Hendrick, who remarked concerning Hughes's governorship that it was too early to judge the permanent effects of his changes but it was clear "that he has permanently increased the influence of his office, established new ideals for his successors, impressed upon legislators new

this emphasis on moral as opposed to material values was a fresh assertion of disdain for money and monetary success, very reminiscent of the disdain of the Mugwump type for the materialists.[7] With this came a disparagement of material achievement. San Francisco, remarked George Kennan, was a successful and prosperous city, but it had put stress "upon material achievement and business prosperity rather than upon civic virtue and moral integrity. But what shall it profit a city if it gain the whole world and lose its own soul?"[8] Probably no statesman of the time had a better intuitive understanding of the interest of the reform mind in moral intangibles than Theodore Roosevelt, whose preachments exploited it to the full. And no observer had a better insight into T. R.'s relation to his time than the Sage of Emporia, who declared quite properly that "Roosevelt's power in this land is a spiritual power. His is not a kingdom of this earth. . . . It is immaterial whether or not the Supreme Court sustains him in his position on the rate bill, the income tax, the license for corporations, or the inheritance tax; not for the establishment of a system of statutes was he born into this world; but rather like all great

conceptions of their responsibilities and greatly improved the tone and efficiency of public life." "Governor Hughes," ibid., Vol. XXX (April 1908), p. 681 (italics added).

[7] Cf. Miss Tarbell's "John D. Rockefeller: a Character Study," ibid., Vol. XXV (July-August 1905).

[8] George Kennan: "Criminal Government and the Private Citizen," ibid., Vol. XXX (November 1907), p. 71. (This George Kennan, 1845–1924, the explorer and journalist, should not be confused with George F. Kennan the diplomat, who is his nephew.) Cf. the opinion of Judge Ben B. Lindsey that the most appalling price of lawlessness and corruption was not the material but the moral cost. "The bottom of the whole trouble is a kind of selfishness that in this country is exalting money above manhood, and no business is ever going to be permanently successful so long as it is based upon an iniquitous doctrine like that." Ibid. (January 1908), p. 386. Compare with this the extraordinary idealization of both business and the professions expressed in Brandeis's famous essay "Business—a Profession," in which it is argued that "success in business must mean something very different from mere money-making" and that the joys of business must not be "the mere vulgar satisfaction which is experienced in the acquisition of money, in the exercise of power or in the frivolous pleasure of mere winning." *Business—a Profession* (Boston, 1944), pp. 3, 5; this essay was originally written in 1912.

teachers, that by his life and his works he should bear wit-
ness unto the truth." [9] This was a penetrating comment
upon the meaning of the reform literature as a kind of symbolic action. For, besides such material accomplishment as
they had to show for themselves, the Progressive writers
could claim that they had provided a large part of the
American people with a necessary and (as they would have
said) wholesome catharsis.

---

[9] William Allen White: "Roosevelt, a Force for Righteousness," ibid.,
Vol. XXVIII (January 1907), p. 393.

CHAPTER VI

THE STRUGGLE
OVER ORGANIZATION

❖

1 · *Organization and the Individual*

Progressivism, at its heart, was an effort to realize familiar
and traditional ideals under novel circumstances. As I have
emphasized, the ordinary American's ideas of what political
and economic life ought to be like had long since taken
form under the conditions of a preponderantly rural society with a broad diffusion of property and power. In that
society large aggregates had played a minor role. Corporate businesses were then just emerging, and they had
not yet achieved the enormous size and national scope
which they acquired during the closing decades of the
nineteenth century, when the Progressive generation was
still growing up. Political machines, though an important
feature of American life since the days of Aaron Burr, had
not played the massive managerial role that they now assumed in American cities and states, and in any case had
appeared less formidable threats to civic virtue and democratic politics than they now seemed to be in the corrupting presence of the great corporations. The American
tradition had been one of unusually widespread participation of the citizen in the management of affairs, both
political and economic.[1] Now the growth of the large cor-

---

[1] On the historic roots of this participation, see the illuminating essay
by Stanley Elkins and Eric McKitrick: "A Meaning for Turner's
Frontier, Part I: Democracy in the Old Northwest," *Political Science
Quarterly*, Vol. LXIX (September 1954), pp. 321–53.

poration, the labor union, and the big impenetrable political machine was clotting society into large aggregates and presenting to the unorganized citizen the prospect that all these aggregates and interests would be able to act in concert and shut out those men for whom organization was difficult or impossible. As early as 1894 William Dean Howells, who had grown up in a small Midwestern community, remarked that the character of American life had undergone a drastic change. "The struggle for life," he said, "has changed from a free fight to an encounter of disciplined forces, and the free fighters that are left get ground to pieces between organized labor and organized capital." [2] Ray Stannard Baker, writing in *McClure's* almost a decade later, pointed out that a number of well-knit local combinations of capital and labor had recently been organized, and gave voice to the fears of the potential victims: "The unorganized public, where will it come in? The professional man, the lecturer, the writer, the artist, the farmer, the salaried government employee, and all the host of men who are not engaged in the actual production or delivery of necessary material things, how will they fare? . . . Is there any doubt that the income of organized labor and the profits of organized capital have gone up enormously, while the man-on-a-salary and most of the great middle class, paying much more for the necessaries of life, have had no adequate increase in earnings?" [3] The central theme in Progressivism was this revolt against the industrial discipline: the Progressive movement was the complaint of the unorganized against the consequences of organization.

Of course there was a problem underlying this effort that did not escape the most astute contemporaries, including many who sympathized deeply with the Progressives. The processes of modern technology and machine industry

---

[2] Howells: *A Traveler from Altruria* (Edinburgh, 1894), p. 164.
[3] Ray Stannard Baker: "Capital and Labor Hunt Together," *McClure's*, Vol. XXI (September 1903), p. 463; cf. the remarks of Mr. Dooley [Finley Peter Dunne]: *Dissertations by Mr. Dooley* (New York, 1906), p. 64.

—not to speak of the complex tasks of civic life—make organization, specialism, hierarchy, and discipline utterly necessary. The Progressives, object though they might to the many sacrifices of traditional values that the new society demanded, did not seriously propose to dismantle this society, forsake its material advantages, and return to a more primitive technology. Nor did they always make the mistake of thinking that the revolt against organization could go on without itself developing new forms of organization. They were trying, in short, to keep the benefits of the emerging organization of life and yet to retain the scheme of individualistic values that this organization was destroying. In order to understand them sympathetically, then, it is important to think of them not as stupid or incapable men who fumbled a simple task, but as men of reasonable and often indeed of penetrating intelligence whose fate it was to attempt, with great zeal and resourcefulness, a task of immense complexity and almost hopeless difficulties.

Long before the Progressives arose, some Americans had seen that organization had its disadvantages and dangers, but it was in the Progressive era that the social types expropriated and alienated by the new organization reached a new peak in numbers and a pitch of restiveness such as they have not shown since. Many historians have pointed out that Progressivism appealed powerfully to small businessmen who were being overwhelmed or outdistanced by great competitors. It also appealed—as all the rhetoric about the trusts and the consumer made evident—to the new middle class of technicians and salaried professionals, clerical workers, salespeople, and public-service personnel that multiplied along with the great corporations and the specialized skills of corporate society. This was by far the most rapidly growing stratum in the population. From 1870 to 1910, when the whole population of the United States increased two and one-third times, the old middle class—business entrepreneurs and independent professional men—grew somewhat more than two times; the

working class, including farm labor, grew a little more
than three times; the number of farmers and farm tenants
doubled. But the new middle class grew almost eight times,
rising from 756,000 to 5,609,000 people. When we compare the latter figure with the 3,261,000 independent
enterprisers and self-employed professionals, we have some
notion of the relative strength of these two strata of the
population from which Progressivism drew so much of its
urban following.[4]

A large and significant political public had emerged that
was for the most part fairly well educated, genteel in its
outlook, full of aspiration, and almost completely devoid of
economic organization. It had no labor unions, no trade
associations; its professional societies were without bargaining power. It had only political means through which
to express its discontents. While it could not strike or fix
prices or support expensive lobbies, it could read the
muckraking magazines, listen to the Progressive orators,
and vote. I suspect that this class was recruited in very
large measure from people who had either risen upwards
or moved sideways in the social scale—of Yankee farmers'
sons who had come to the city, of native workmen's children aspiring to white-collar respectability—of people, in
short, who had been bred upon the Horatio Alger legend
and the American dream of success and who had not given
up hope of realizing it. Today the white-collar class is
more apathetic and more self-indulgent; it hopes chiefly for
security, leisure, and comfort and for the enjoyment of the
pleasures of mass entertainment. But in the Progressive
era this class still lived within the framework of the old
ambitions.[5] While it resented the swollen wealth of the

---

[4] The new middle class had risen from 33 per cent of the entire middle
class in 1870 to 63 per cent in 1910. I have followed the computa-
tions of Lewis Corey: "The Middle Class," Antioch Review (Spring
1945), based upon Population: Comparative Occupational Statistics for
the United States, 1870 to 1940, published by the United States
Bureau of the Census. For a critical view of the new middle class today, see C. Wright Mills: White Collar (New York, 1951).
[5] The decline of career aspiration and the growing tendency to seek
comfort and interpret life from the standpoint of the consumer is the

tycoons and the crass impersonal conditions of economic life under the corporate economy, it none the less maintained a half-suppressed feeling of admiration and envy for the captains of industry who had after all done no more than fulfill the old dream of heroic personal ascendancy. This may explain why the very journals that ran the devastating muckrakers' exposures of the predations and excesses of the corporations also published hero tales about the outstanding figures of American industry. It may also explain why the same Progressive periodicals, and even the Socialist periodicals,[6] that pilloried the evils of American society, tore into its established ideas, and offered blueprints for progress and reform were full of little individualistic advertisements intended to tell clerks how they could improve themselves and "get ahead"—so that simply by moving one's eye from left to right, from one column to the next, one could pass from the world in which the Beef Trust or Standard Oil was being exposed and denounced, to the world in which "You Too Can Be a Certified Public Accountant."

The discontent over the trusts expressed familiar ideals of entrepreneurship and opportunity which great numbers of Americans were quite unwilling to abandon. In the old society upon which American ideas of the right and the good had been founded, the fluid capital of the middle classes had commonly found an outlet in investments over which the investors exercised a large measure of control.

---

theme of Leo Lowenthal's suggestive study: "Biographies in Popular Magazines," in Paul F. Lazarsfeld and Frank Stanton, eds.: *Radio Research 1942–1943* (New York, 1944), pp. 507–48.

[6] Daniel Bell points out how common in the columns of the *International Socialist Review*, the chief magazine of American Socialism, were the advertisements instructing readers in the art of "DOUBLING OR TRIPLING YOUR MONEY THROUGH CLEAN HONEST INVESTMENT," or earning $300 a month selling cream separators. Socialists seem to have been very fond of real-estate promotions and gold-mine stocks. Daniel Bell: "Marxian Socialism in the United States," in Donald Drew Egbert and Stow Persons, eds.: *Socialism and American Life* (Princeton, 1952), Vol. I, pp. 298–9. On the middle-class character of American Socialism, see David A. Shannon: "The Socialist Party before the First World War," *Mississippi Valley Historical Review*, Vol. XXXVIII (September 1951), pp. 279–88.

The typical business unit of the early and middle nineteenth century was owned by an individual or a small
group, was limited in size by the personal wealth of the
individuals who controlled it, and was managed either
directly by them or by their agents. As the corporate form
of organization grew and a large market in corporate
securities was developed, the savings and investments and
insurance of the substantial middle class, and with these
more and more of the power to make the vital economic
decisions of society, passed into the hands of the masters
of corporations and the investment bankers. The restlessness of the Progressive era owed much of its force to a
class of substantial property-owning citizens whose powers
of economic decision had been expropriated by the system
of corporate organization.

It would be misleading to imply that the development of
the corporation eliminated profitable direct small-scale
investments. Quite the contrary, for the urbanization of the
country brought a growing need for the work of service
industries that are usually organized in small units, and
such lines of enterprise continued to offer much opportunity for small investors who were satisfied to operate profit-
ably on a small scale in marginal lines of business. But
such enterprises could not absorb more than a part of
middle-class savings; and after 1870 the decisive and
strategic lines of enterprise that called the tune for the
economy as a whole, that afforded the richest profits and
aroused the highest excitement in the entrepreneurial imagination, passed increasingly under the corporate form of
organization. Confined in the pre-Civil War period to a
few types of industries, the business corporation had taken
a new lease on life as a consequence of the Civil War. The
necessities of war finance and the success of Jay Cooke in
reaching the domestic investor with government securities
had awakened men to the possibilities of a domestic investment market. In the period after the war this market had
grown swiftly, spreading from the railroad and banking
fields into public utilities, mining and quarrying, manufac-

turing, and eventually merchandising. By 1900 there were estimated to be 4,400,000 stockholders in American corporations; by 1917, 8,600,000.[7]

One area in which middle-class savings became a focus of poignant conflict was that of life insurance. As a major pivot of finance, life insurance was a product of the post-Civil War era. Life-insurance protection in the United States, which amounted to $5.47 per capita in 1860, rose to $40.69 in 1885, and to $179.14 in 1910.[8] The aggregate of insurance in force rose by 577 per cent between 1870 and 1896, while the total admitted assets of the insurance companies rose by 958 per cent.[9] With these changes in the size of the business came internal changes in company policy. The adoption of the so-called deferred-dividend contract made available to the insurance managers large undistributed surpluses that did not have the legal status of liabilities in the companies' accounts. These surpluses, supposedly to be distributed at the end of stated periods to policy-holders, were drawn upon by the managers of some of the large companies and used for speculative purposes through subsidiary companies. The exposure of these life-insurance practices in the work of the New York State legislature's Armstrong Committee and in such books as Burton J. Hendricks's *The Story of Life Insurance* made it painfully clear to the policy-holding public that even in the citadels of security they were being shamelessly and ruthlessly gulled.[1]

A thought most galling to middle-class investors was that the shrinkage of their own power and the growth in the power of the "plutocracy" were based upon their own sav-

---

[7] A. A. Berle and G. Means: *The Modern Corporation and Private Property* (ed. New York, 1947), p. 56.

[8] Shepard B. Clough: *A Century of Life Insurance* (New York, 1946), pp. 3, 6.

[9] Ibid., pp. 128–30.

[1] Ibid., chapter xii; Marquis James: *The Metropolitan Life* (New York, 1947), chapters viii and ix; Merlo J. Pusey: *Charles Evans Hughes* (New York, 1951), Vol. I, chapter xv; and Douglass North: "Capital Accumulation in Life Insurance between the Civil War and the Investigation of 1905," in William Miller, ed.: *Men in Business* (Cambridge, 1952), pp. 238–53.

ings—that, as Louis D. Brandeis put it, "the fetters which
bind the people are forged from the people's own gold." [2]
The American had been brought up to accept as "natural"
a type of economy in which enterprise was diffused among
a multitude of firms and in which the process of economic
decision, being located everywhere, could not be located
anywhere in particular. Now it was shocking to learn that
this economy had been self-destructive, that it was giving
way to small bodies of men directing great corporations
whose decisions, as Woodrow Wilson protested, were
"autocratic," who could concentrate in themselves "the resources, the choices, the opportunities, in brief, the power
of thousands." The poor stockholder, Wilson continued,
"does not seem to enjoy any of the substantial rights of
property in connection with [corporate stocks]. He is
merely contributing money for the conduct of a business
which other men run as they please. If he does not approve
of what they do, there seems nothing for it but to sell
the stock (though their acts may have depreciated its
value immensely). He cannot even inquire or protest without being told to mind his own business—the very thing
he was innocently trying to do!" [3] The Pujo Committee
investigators underlined this argument when they revealed
that none of the witnesses that appeared before them was
able to mention a single instance in the country's history
in which stockholders had either successfully overthrown
the management of any large corporation or secured an
investigation of its conduct.[4]

People readily acknowledged that in spite of all this they
were prosperous. But many of them could not help feeling
that this prosperity was being obtained on false pretenses,
that it was theirs in disregard of sound and ancient principles, and that for this disregard they would in good time
come to grief. It had been their tradition to believe that

[2] Louis D. Brandeis: *Other People's Money* (1914; ed., National Home
Library Foundation, 1932), pp. 12–13.
[3] Woodrow Wilson: "The Lawyer and the Community," *North American Review*, Vol. CXCII (November 1910), pp. 612, 617–18.
[4] Brandeis, op. cit., p. 41.

prosperity and economic progress came not through big or monopolistic businesses—that is, through the gains and economies of organization—but rather through competition and hard work and individual enterprise and initiative. They had been brought up to think of the well-being of society not merely in structural terms—not as something resting upon the sum of its technique and efficiency—but in moral terms, as a reward for the sum total of individual qualities and personal merits. This tradition, rooted in the Protestant ethic itself, was being wantonly defied by the system of corporate organization.

In 1905 Judge Peter S. Grosscup of the United States Circuit Court of Appeals published in *McClure's* an article that reveals, coming as it did from a man of impeccable conservatism,[5] how widespread this concern was. Although Grosscup acknowledged that the nation was enjoying a prosperity and power such as it had never seen before, he expressed his fear that it was losing its soul. It was the intangibles that worried him. Neither the prosperity nor the power was in danger, but "the soul of republican America . . . is individual opportunity. . . . The loss that republican America now confronts is the loss of individual hope and prospect—the suppression of the instinct that . . . has made us a nation of individually independent and prosperous people." The country was in the midst of a trend that, if not deflected, would eventually reach a point at which "the acquisition of property, by the individuals who constitute the bulk of the people, will cease to be one of the opening and controlling purposes of their lives. This means that, as a republican political institution, America will have lost the spirit which alone promises its life. It means social and, eventually, political revolution." The

---

[5] A McKinley Republican and a distinguished jurist, Grosscup had been one of two judges issuing the injunction against Debs and other American Railway Union officials in 1894, and he had been among those calling on President Cleveland to use troops in the Pullman strike. He also was presiding judge of the Circuit Court of Appeals that reversed District Judge Kenesaw Mountain Landis's imposition of a $29,240,000 fine on Standard Oil for accepting rebates.

widespread apprehension about corporations was not merely a consequence of anxiety over high prices. It was rather the result of an "intuitive perception that, somewhere, something is wrong—that in the face of the future there is a disturbing, even sinister look." What was wrong was that the corporation was putting an unbearable strain on the institution of private property, upon which the civilization of the world rested; for it was the desire and the hope of acquiring private property upon which the entire moral discipline of an individualist society must rely. The nation was at a crossroad leading on one side to corporate paternalism and on the other to state socialism—both fatal to individual liberties. Fortunately there was another path that could still be taken: "Individual Opportunity—the opportunity, actual as well as in theory, to each individual to participate in the proprietorship of the country."

Grosscup proposed, in short, to reverse the entire process by which the individual had been expropriated. This he thought could be done if the matter was taken out of the hands of the states and vested in the federal government, if "stock-jobbing" and stock-watering were prevented (that is, if the corporation was "regenerated"), and if the "road to proprietorship" was opened to the wage-earners of the country.[6] How such proprietorship could be made possible he did not say.

Grosscup was expressing an attitude toward economic life that was to appear with increasing frequency down to the end of the Progressive era. While the great theoretician and technician of this protest was Louis D. Brandeis, its master spokesman in politics was Woodrow Wilson, whose campaign speeches in 1912 provide us with a magnificently articulate expression of the whole impulse. Like Grosscup's article, Wilson's evocative speeches express the tendency of the middle-class public to think of the economic order not quite so much as a system organized for the production and distribution of goods as a system intended to stimulate

---

[6] Peter S. Grosscup: "How to Save the Corporation," *McClure's*, Vol. XXIV (February 1905), pp. 443–8.

and reward certain traits of personal character. The public to which Wilson appealed had been brought up on the nineteenth-century ideal of opportunity and the notion that success was a reward for energy, efficiency, frugality, perseverance, ambition, and insight. In their thinking, people competed—or ought to compete—in the exercise of these qualities, and success ought properly to go to those who had the most of them. The metaphor they most often and most significantly used in describing their economic ideal was that of a race—"the race of life," as it was commonly called. What Wilson was pointing to—and what he refused to accept as a governing principle for American industry—was the fact that this race was no longer being run. It had once been true that a man could "choose his own calling and pursue it just as far as his abilities enable him to pursue it." America had been committed to "ideals of absolutely free opportunity, where no man is supposed to be under any limitations except the limitations of his character and of his mind . . . where men win or lose on their merits." By various means the new system of organization had destroyed this body of ideals. But: "America will insist upon recovering in practice those ideals which she has always professed." [7]

Wilson saw that Americans were living under "a new organization of society," in which the individual had been "submerged" and human relations were pervasively impersonal. Wilson's hero, the rising individual entrepreneur of classical economics and of earlier days of diffused property management, had been done in by just such impersonal organization. This entrepreneurial hero—referred to by Wilson as the "beginner," the "man with only a little capital," the "new entry" in the race, "the man on the make" —was the figure for whom he was particularly solicitous. For Wilson was profoundly interested, he said, in "the constant renewal of society from the bottom," upon which the genius and enterprise of America had always depended. And while it was true that the country was still prosperous,

[7] Wilson: *The New Freedom* (New York, 1913), pp. 14–15, 30.

the "middle class is being more and more squeezed out by the processes which we have been taught to call processes of prosperity. Its members are sharing prosperity, no doubt; but what alarms me is that they are not *originating* prosperity." The real treasury of America lay in the ambitions and energies that were not restricted to a special favored class but depended upon the inventions and originations of "unknown men." "Anything that depresses, anything that makes the organization greater than the man, anything that blocks, discourages, dismays the humble man, is against all the principles of progress." [8] According to the ideals of individualism, then, the acknowledged power and prosperity of the country had been achieved by means that must in the long run be considered retrogressive. For was it not true that the big fellows had narrowed and stiffened the lines of endeavor, cut the little man off from credit, and shut the markets against him? [9] This process had gone so far that men were about to forget "the ancient time when America lay in every hamlet, when America was to be seen in every fair valley, when America displayed her great forces on the broad prairies, ran her fine fires of enterprise up over the mountainsides and down into the bowels of the earth, and eager men were everywhere captains of industry, not employees; not looking to a distant city to find out what they might do, but looking about among their neighbors, finding credit according to their character, not according to their connections, finding credit in proportion to what was known to be in them and behind them, not in proportion to the securities they held that were approved where they were not known." [1]

While the worst forebodings of the Progressives were not to be realized, one must see with sympathy the view of affairs taken by the men of their generation whose historical consciousness had been formed on the American experience with individual enterprise. The drama of American history

---

[8] Ibid., pp. 3, 5, 6, 15–18, 82, 85, 86–7.
[9] Ibid., pp. 14–19.
[1] Ibid., pp. 18–19.

had been played out on a continent three thousand miles wide and almost half as long. Great political issues had been fought out over this terrain, great economic risks taken on it, fantastic profits exacted from it. The generation that had not yet passed from the scene had produced and admired, even as it resented and feared, a Carnegie, a Rockefeller, a Hill, a Harriman, a Morgan. America had engendered a national imagination keyed to epic dimensions, a soul unhappy without novelty and daring, raised on the conquest of a continent, the settlement of an immense domain, the creation within the life span of one man of a gigantic system of industry and transportation. Its people had pioneered, improvised, and gambled their way across the continent. And now were its young men to become a nation of employees, at best of administrators, were they to accept a dispensation under which there was nothing but safe investment, to adapt themselves passively to a life without personal enterprise even on a moderate scale? How, then, was the precious spiritual bravura of the whole American enterprise to be sustained? And if it could not be sustained, what would become of America? The Progressives were not fatalists; they did not intend quietly to resign themselves to the decline of this great tradition without at least one brave attempt to recapture that bright past in which there had been a future.

II · *The State and the Trusts*

The Progressive case against business organization was not confined to economic considerations, nor even to the more intangible sphere of economic morals. Still more widely felt was a fear founded in political realities—the fear that the great business combinations, being the only centers of wealth and power, would be able to lord it over all other interests and thus to put an end to traditional American democracy. Here Wilson eloquently expressed a fear that troubled a great many men who did not fully share his burning interest in creating economic opportuni-

ties for small entrepreneurs and for men out of unknown
homes. While the entrepreneurial resentment of the trusts
had its greatest meaning for small businessmen, the lower
middle class, and those who had inherited Populistic traditions, the fear of the trusts as a threat to democratic government, which of course disturbed the same groups, also
affected other types—urban lawyers, professionals and
intellectuals, practical politicians recruited from the old
elites, who often looked with disdain upon the purely economic jealousies of would-be competitors of big business.
Only in limited numbers did men aspire to go into business,
but men in any segment of society might become concerned as to whether the enormous combinations of capital
were at all compatible with a free society.

By the close of his 1912 campaign there was no doubt
left in Wilson's mind that a great part of the public considered an attack on business monopoly necessary to political freedom, for he had seen campaign crowds respond
with marked enthusiasm to his denunciation of restraints
and his effort to link political and economic liberties. He
was engaged, he said, in "a crusade against powers that
have governed us—that have limited our development—
that have determined our lives—that have set us in a
straitjacket to do as they please." Drawing himself up to
assert the full import of his own ideas, he continued: "This
is a second struggle for emancipation. . . . If America is
not to have free enterprise, then she can have freedom of
no sort whatever." [2]

The fear that Americans might be completely divested of
control over their own affairs confirmed a well-established

---

[2] Arthur S. Link: *Wilson: the Road to the White House* (Princeton,
1947), p. 514. When one reflects that this idea, that "free enterprise"
is the cornerstone upon which all other freedoms rest, has become the
rallying cry of the conservatives in America and the supreme shibboleth
of the National Association of Manufacturers, one realizes why so
many men who were ardent Progressives before the first World War
could have become equally ardent conservatives during the past twenty
years without any sense that they were being inconsistent. Indeed, they
had held to the same ideas with great constancy; it was history itself
that was inconsistent, and the world at large that had changed.

trait in the national character: the distrust of authority. While it has been a familiar observation at least since the time of Tocqueville that the American yields all too readily to the tyranny of public opinion, it is important to understand that in this context public opinion is hard to locate rigorously: it is diffuse and decentralized, and it belongs, after all, to the people themselves—or so it seems. But authority that can be clearly located in persons, or in small bodies of persons, is characteristically suspect in America. Historically, individual enterprise has been at a premium. For the many tasks that cannot be handled by individuals Americans have preferred to found voluntary group associations. For the remaining tasks that cannot be handled without the sanction of government and law they have preferred where possible to act through local government, which seems close to them, and then through state government; and only when these resources have failed have they called upon the federal government for action. This distrust of authority has often been turned against government, particularly when government was felt to be strong or growing in strength. It was called upon during the agitations that led to the American Revolution, and it gave tenacity to the most ardent supporters of the Revolutionary War. It helped impede the adoption of the Federal Constitution, it was invoked to justify secession, it caused Americans to postpone into the twentieth century governmental responsibilities that were assumed decades earlier among other Western societies, and in recent years it has sustained a large part of the population in its resistance to the innovations of the New Deal.

But this distrust of authority has on other occasions been turned primarily against business, or at least against some portions of the business community. In the Jackson era the United States Bank paid dearly for its growing power over the country's credit. In the Progressive era the entire structure of business similarly became the object of a widespread hostility which stemmed from the feeling that business was becoming a closed system of authoritative action.

Suppose, it was argued, that the process of business combination goes on in the future as it has in the past, with
ever larger combinations emerging. Then suppose that,
perhaps under the auspices of the investment bankers, there
should covertly come to be a "combination of the combinations . . . 'a community of interest' more formidable
than any conceivable single combination that dare appear
in the open." [3] What then would be the situation of American democracy? Already the power of economic decision
had been expropriated from the owners of property in the
great lines of corporate enterprise. The next step would
be the expropriation of political decision, for it would not
be too difficult for such a great combination to buy up the
political process, as it were, to bend the corrupt political
machines and the venal politicians to its purposes—as,
indeed, on a local and limited scale some of the existing
combinations had already done. Then the voice of the ordinary voter would be as effectually eliminated from political
influence as the voice of the ordinary stockholder had been
from the conduct of the giant corporation. Even if the intentions of the masters of industry should prove benevolent,
it would not suit a free people to submit to paternalism,
to guardianship, to restraints imposed from without. In a
more moderate and more justified form Progressive thinking thus displays some of that same fear of a secret conspiratorial plutocracy which had had such a melodramatic
formulation among the Populists. It was less common
among the Progressives to impute sinister intent or all-
embracing design to the plutocrats, but they were still
restive under the awareness that vital decisions were being
made with which they had nothing to do. "Somewhere, by
somebody," said Wilson, "the development of industry is
being controlled." It was imperative for "the law to step
in" and create new and more tolerable conditions of life
under which there would be no more secrecy of decision.
"There ought to be no place where anything can be done
that everybody does not know about." All legislation, all

---

[3] The phrase is Wilson's: *The New Freedom*, p. 187.

economic operations, should take place in the open. If the people knew what decisions were being made, knew how they were being governed, and had in their hands the instruments of action, they would have a fair opportunity to elect men who would devise the necessary remedies.[4] (Here, as in so many instances, one can see the domestic analogue of Wilson's foreign policy: in business, as in world affairs, there was to be no more secret diplomacy, nothing but open covenants of business, openly arrived at.)

In the past the state and federal governments had been limited in their functions, in the size of their operations, in their power to regulate. In the earlier nineteenth century these governments, considered as units of organization, had been small entities in a world of small entities. Into the midst of this system of diffused power and unorganized strength the great corporations and investment houses had now thrust themselves, gigantic units commanding vast resources and quite capable of buying up political support on a wholesale basis, just as they bought their other supplies. The Progressives were thus haunted by the specter of a private power far greater than the public power of the state. As early as 1888 Charles William Eliot, in a well-known essay on "The Working of the American Democracy," had pointed out that the great corporations, as units of organization, had far outstripped the governments of the states. He remarked that a certain railroad with offices in Boston employed 18,000 persons, had gross receipts of about $40,000,000 a year, and paid its highest-salaried officer $35,000. At the same time the Commonwealth of Massachusetts employed only 6,000 persons, had gross receipts of about $7,000,000 and paid no salary higher than $6,500. And a really great railroad like the Pennsylvania would overshadow the Commonwealth far more imposingly than the Boston organization.[5] As units

---

[4] Ibid., pp. 20, 22, 62, 114, 125–6, and chapter vi *passim*.
[5] Charles William Eliot: *American Contributions to Civilization* (New York, 1907), pp. 85–6. Eliot was not so much in fear of corporate

of organization the state governments were now relatively
small enough to become the fiefs of the corporations.

Eliot wrote at a time when the movement toward combination was still far from its peak. The organization of the
giant corporations after 1898 and the system of interlocking
directorates revealed during the Progressive era suggested
that all government, federal as well as state, was overshadowed. The capital, for instance, raised to organize the
billion-dollar steel trust in 1901 was enough to pay the
costs of all functions of the federal government for almost
two years. In March 1908 Senator La Follette made a
memorable speech in the Senate on the control of American industry, transportation, and finance, in which he attempted to prove with careful documentation from the interlocking directorates of American corporations that fewer
than one hundred men, acting in concert, controlled the
great business interests of the country. "Does anyone
doubt," he asked, "the community of interest that binds
these men together?" [6]

Four years later the investigations of the Pujo Committee spelled out in alarming detail what La Follette had
pointed to: the Morgan interests at the peak of the financial system held 341 directorships in 112 corporations
(insurance companies, transportation systems, manufacturing and trading corporations, and public utilities) with aggregate resources or capitalization of $22,245,000,000.
This inventory—an incomplete one—thus showed a single
network of interests commanding more than three times the
assessed value of all the real and personal property in New
England; or more than twice the assessed value of all the
property in the thirteen Southern states; or more than all
the property in the twenty-two states west of the Missis-

power as some of the Progressives came to be, but he was concerned
to make the observation that "the activity of corporations, great and
small, penetrates every part of the industrial and social body, and their
daily maintenance brings into play more mental and moral force than
the maintenance of all the governments on the [American] Continent
combined." Cf. the remarks of Wilson: The New Freedom, pp. 187–8.
[6] Congressional Record, 60th Cong., 1st Sess., March 17, 1908, p.
3450.

sippi.[7] The mind reeled in horror at the thought of such a vast power, unchecked by any comparable or equal power responsible to the public, moving quietly and relentlessly toward the achievement of its political goals. Ignatius Donnelly's nightmare about a society ruled by an inner council of plutocrats now seemed, even to much soberer minds than his, not altogether fantastic. "If monopoly persists," declared Wilson, "monopoly will always sit at the helm of the government. I do not expect to see monopoly restrain itself. If there are men in this country big enough to own the government of the United States, they are going to own it." [8]

Now, reluctantly rather than enthusiastically, the average American tended more and more to rely on government regulation, to seek in governmental action a counterpoise to the power of private business. In his resentment against the incursions of business organization upon his moral sensibilities and his individualistic values, he began to support governmental organization and to accept more readily than he had been willing to do before the idea that the reach of government must be extended. Since the state governments, so long the central agencies of political action, had been clearly outdistanced by business interests (which were in any case constitutionally beyond the reach of state control), he looked to the federal government as his last resource for the control of business, thus ironically lending support to another step in the destruction of that system of local and decentralized values in which he also believed. The long-range trend toward federal regulation, which found its beginnings in the Interstate Commerce Act of 1887 and the Sherman Act of 1890, which was quickened by a large number of measures in the Progressive era, and which has found its consummation in our time, was thus at first the response of a predominantly individualistic public to the uncontrolled and starkly original collectivism of big business. In America the growth of

[7] Brandeis: *Other People's Money*, pp. 22-3.
[8] Wilson: *The New Freedom*, p. 286.

the national state and its regulative power has never been
accepted with complacency by any large part of the middle-class public, which has not relaxed its suspicion of
authority, and which even now gives repeated evidence of
its intense dislike of statism. In our time this growth has
been possible only under the stress of great national
emergencies, domestic or military, and even then only in
the face of continuous resistance from a substantial part of
the public. In the Progressive era it was possible only
because of a widespread and urgent fear of business
consolidation and private business authority. Since it has
become common in recent years for ideologists of the
extreme right to portray the growth of statism as the result
of a sinister conspiracy of collectivists inspired by foreign
ideologies, it is perhaps worth emphasizing that the first
important steps toward the modern organization of society
were taken by arch-individualists—the tycoons of the
Gilded Age—and that the primitive beginning of modern
statism was largely the work of men who were trying to
save what they could of the eminently native Yankee values
of individualism and enterprise.

But if the power of the state had to be built up, it would
be more important than it had ever been that the state be
a neutral state which would realize as fully as possible the
preference of the middle-class public for moderation, impar-
tiality, and "law." If big business sought favoritism and
privilege, then the state must be powerful enough to be
more than a match for business. But the state must not be
anti-business, nor even anti-big-business: it must be severely
neutral among all the special interests in society, subordi-
nating each to the common interest and dealing out evenhanded justice to all. It would be for neither the rich man
nor the poor man, for labor nor capital, but for the just and
honest and law-abiding man of whatever class. It would
stand, in fact, where the middle class felt itself to be
standing—in the middle, on neutral ground among self-
seeking interests of all kinds. The government's heightened
power was to represent not its more intimate linkage with

any of these interests, but rather its ability with greater effectuality to stand above them, and where necessary against them.

The first major political leader to understand this need of the public for faith in the complete neutrality of the powerful state was Theodore Roosevelt, whose intuitive sense of the importance of this motive, as well as his genuine personal sympathy with it, explains much of his popularity.[9] In this respect the most important year of his presidency was 1902, when he brought the great anthracite strike to a successful arbitration and launched the prosecution of the Northern Securities Company. These moves, by suggesting that the country at last had a President capable of taking a strong and independent stand in such matters, gave people confidence. They were symbolic acts of the highest importance.[1] While previous Presidents had intervened in labor disputes—Hayes, for instance, in the rail-

---

[9] No one familiar with T. R.'s writings will fail to recognize the assertion of this impulse in his vigorously equivocal rhetoric. "This sums up my whole attitude in the matter. . . . [it] is, after all, simply the question of treating each man, rich or poor, on his merits, and making him feel that at the White House, which is the Nation's property, all reputable citizens of the Nation are sure of like treatment." *The Letters of Theodore Roosevelt*, ed. by Elting R. Morison, Vol. IV (Cambridge, 1951), p. 880. ". . . the success of such suits as that against the Northern Securities Company which gave a guaranty in this country that rich man and poor man alike were held equal before the law, and my action in the so-called Miller case which gave to trades-unions a lesson that had been taught corporations—that I favored them while they did right and was not in the least afraid of them when they did wrong." Ibid., p. 993. "At the same time I wished the labor people absolutely to understand that I set my face like flint against violence and lawlessness of any kind on their part, just as much as against arrogant greed by the rich, and that I would be as quick to move against one as the other." Ibid., Vol. III, p. 482. There are scores of similar utterances in T. R.'s public and private writings. For a penetrating analysis of T. R.'s presidential role see John Morton Blum: *The Republican Roosevelt* (Cambridge, 1954).

[1] The character of such action was also recognized by Roosevelt's friend Senator Henry Cabot Lodge. "You have no power or authority, of course," he wrote to the President as the coal crisis grew acute. ". . . Is there anything we can appear to do?" Henry Cabot Lodge, ed.: *Selections from the Correspondence of Theodore Roosevelt and Henry Cabot Lodge, 1884–1918* (New York, 1925), Vol. I, pp. 528–32; italics added.

road strikes of 1877, Cleveland in the Pullman strike—it
had been as partisans of the captains of industry, not as an
independent force representing a neutral view and the
"public" interest. Now T. R. seemed in the public eye to
stand not only apart from but above the opposing sides.
During the course of the negotiations that led up to the
final compromise, he loomed larger than either the mine
workers or the operators. At first he saw his independence
as the source of a considerable disadvantage: "Unfortu-
nately the strength of my public position before the country
is also its weakness," he wrote to Lodge. "I am genuinely
independent of the big monied men in all matters where I
think the interests of the public are concerned, and probably I am the first President of recent times of whom this
could be truthfully said. I think it right and desirable that
this should be true of the President. But where I do not
grant any favors to these big monied men which I do not
think the country requires that they should have, it is out
of the question for me to expect them to grant favors to me
in return. . . . The sum of this is that I can make no private or special appeal to them, and I am at my wits' end
how to proceed." [2]

In fact T. R.'s wits were much more with him than he
had imagined—and so were the sympathies of a few of the
big moneyed men. Ironically, it was Mark Hanna and
J. Pierpont Morgan, both of them paramount symbols of
the public of the bloated plutocracy, whose help and influence made the ultimate settlement possible,[3] for without
them the obstinate mine operators might never have been
prevailed upon to agree to arbitration. Nor did Hanna or
Morgan expect in return any direct and immediate "favors"
of the sort Roosevelt felt he could not grant. His own conduct in the affair, after all, was intended to fend off widespread suffering, mass discontent, possible mob violence,
a potential sympathetic general strike, and perhaps even

<hr />

[2] *The Letters of Theodore Roosevelt*, Vol. III, p. 332.
[3] See T. R.'s cordial letters of thanks to both men, ibid., pp. 353, 354.
The whole episode, which is enormously instructive, can be followed in
T. R.'s letters, ibid., pp. 323–66.

"socialistic action," [4] and he appealed to these men primarily in their capacity as responsible conservatives who might be able to head off a social disaster. In the public mind the incident redounded much to Roosevelt's credit, and properly so. The historian, however, cannot refrain from adding that it ill accorded with the stereotypes of Progressive thinking that "Dollar Mark" Hanna and J. P. Morgan should have attended as midwives at the birth of the neutral state.

The psychological impact of the Northern Securities prosecution was comparable to that of the strike settlement, though the economic content was relatively meaningless. This great railroad merger, which had been consummated only after a spectacular war for control between financial forces directed by E. H. Harriman and others directed by James J. Hill and Morgan, had brought about a frightful financial panic in which a great many personal fortunes were made and unmade. Of necessity the new combination had attracted a great deal of public attention, and it was everywhere known as a Morgan interest. To move for its dissolution, though hardly a blow at any vital concern either of Morgan or of the business community, was to appear to challenge the dragon in his den. (And indeed Morgan, offended because he had not been informed in advance, came bustling down to Washington to find out if T. R. intended "to attack my other interests.") The government's suit encouraged everyone to feel at last that the President of the United States was really bigger and more powerful than Morgan and the Morgan interests, that the country was governed from Washington and not from Wall Street. Roosevelt was immensely gratified when the dissolution was finally upheld by the Supreme Court in 1904, and he had every right to be—not because he had struck a blow at business consolidation, for the decree was ineffective and consolidation went on apace, but because for the first time in the history of the presidency he had done something to ease the public mind on this vital issue. It

[4] Ibid., p. 337; cf. pp. 329–30, 336, 338, 340–1, 349, 357, 360, 362–3.

was, he said, "one of the great achievements" of his first
administration, "for through it we emphasized in signal
fashion, as in no other way could be emphasized, the fact
that the most powerful men in this country were held to
accountability before the law." [5] Henceforth, whatever he
might do or say, a large part of the public persisted in
thinking of him as a "trust-buster."

Representing as they did the spirit and the desires of the
middle class, the Progressives stood for a dual program of
economic remedies designed to minimize the dangers from
the extreme left and right. On one side they feared the
power of the plutocracy, on the other the poverty and
restlessness of the masses. But if political leadership could
be firmly restored to the responsible middle classes who
were neither ultra-reactionary nor, in T. R.'s phrase, "wild
radicals," both of these problems could be met. The first
line of action was to reform the business order, to restore
or maintain competition—or, as the case might be, to limit
and regulate monopoly—and expand credit in the interests
of the consumer, the farmer, and the small businessman.
The second was to minimize the most outrageous and in-
defensible exploitation of the working population, to cope
with what was commonly called "the social question." The
relations of capital and labor, the condition of the masses
in the slums, the exploitation of the labor of women and
children, the necessity of establishing certain minimal
standards of social decency—these problems filled them
with concern both because they felt a sincere interest in
the welfare of the victims of industrialism and because they
feared that to neglect them would invite social disintegration and ultimate catastrophe. They were filled with a passion for social justice, but they also hoped that social

---

[5] Ibid., Vol. IV, p. 886. Some years later he admitted, in effect, that
the intangible, ceremonial consequences of the prosecution—i.e., establishing "the principle that the government was supreme over the great
corporations"—were the only consequences. Works, Memorial Edition
(New York, 1923–6), Vol. XIX, p. 448; cf. Outlook, Vol. CII
(September 21, 1912), p. 105.

justice could be brought about, as it were, conspicuously. Men like Roosevelt were often furious at the plutocrats because their luxury, their arrogance, and the open, naked exercise of their power constituted a continual provocation to the people and always increased the likelihood that social resentments would find expression in radical or even "socialistic" programs.

Writing to Taft in 1906 about the tasks of American political leadership as he envisaged them for the next quarter century, Roosevelt declared: "I do not at all like the social conditions at present. The dull, purblind folly of the very rich men; their greed and arrogance, and the way in which they have unduly prospered by the help of the ablest lawyers, and too often through the weakness or shortsightedness of the judges or by their unfortunate possession of meticulous minds; these facts, and the corruption in business and politics, have tended to produce a very unhealthy condition of excitement and irritation in the popular mind, which shows itself in part in the enormous increase in the socialistic propaganda. Nothing effective, because nothing at once honest and intelligent, is being done to combat the great amount of evil which, mixed with a little good, a little truth, is contained in the outpourings of the *Cosmopolitan,* of *McClure's,* of *Collier's,* of Tom Lawson, of David Graham Phillips, of Upton Sinclair. Some of these are socialists; some of them merely lurid sensationalists; but they are all building up a revolutionary feeling which will most probably take the form of a political campaign. Then we may have to do, too late or almost too late, what had to be done in the silver campaign when in one summer we had to convince a great many good people that what they had been laboriously taught for several years previous was untrue." [6]

---

[6] *The Letters of Theodore Roosevelt,* Vol. V, pp. 183–4. It hardly needs to be said that Roosevelt was unduly concerned. The writers he mentioned were doing far more to build up support for him among the public than they were to create "revolutionary feeling." Six years later Roosevelt himself was building up a "revolutionary feeling" about as menacing as that created by the *Cosmopolitan* et al.

Roosevelt represented, of course, the type of Progressive
leader whose real impulses were deeply conservative, and
who might not perhaps have been a Progressive at all if it
were not for the necessity of fending off more radical
threats to established ways of doing things. The characteristic Progressive thinker carried on a tolerant and mutually
profitable dialogue with the Socialists of the period, perhaps glancing over his shoulder with some anxiety from
time to time, to be sure that Marxian or Fabian ideas were
not gaining too much ground in the United States, but
chiefly because in this age of broad social speculation he
was interested to learn what he could from Socialist criticism. Fundamentally, however, the influence of such
criticism was negative: if the Socialist said that the growing combinations of capital were natural products of social
evolution and that the challenge they represented to democracy must be met by expropriating their owners, the
typical Progressive was only spurred all the more to find
ways of limiting or regulating monopoly within a capitalist
framework; when the Socialist said that the grievances of
the people could be relieved only under Socialism, the
typical Progressive became the more determined to find
ways of showing that these grievances were remediable
under capitalism. In these ways the alleged "threat" of
Socialism, much talked about in the Progressive period,
actually gave added impetus to middle-class programs.[7]

[7] The growth of Socialist sentiment had greater leverage than it is
usually credited with on the more conservative politicians of the Progressive era. It enabled a man like T. R. to argue more plausibly that
the sort of moderate and gradual reform he stood for was urgently
needed, over the long run, to stave off more drastic forms of protest.
Of course, few of the more ardently Progressive men of the age were
much worried by the advancing interest in Socialism. Many of them
saw in it simply another variant of the general protest rather than a
genuine interest in creating a Socialist society. Cf. Wilson: *The New
Freedom*, pp. 26-7. The general interest in Socialist speculation is
attested by the attention paid to Socialist muckrakers and publicists
such as W. J. Ghent, Robert Hunter, Jack London, Gustavus Myers,
Algie M. Simmons, Upton Sinclair, John Spargo, and William English
Walling. Eugene Debs's vote in the presidential elections rose from
94,000 in 1900 to 402,000 and 420,000 in the succeeding campaigns
and finally to 897,000 in 1912, which represented the highest figure

At bottom, the central fear was fear of power, and the greater the strength of an organized interest, the greater the anxiety it aroused. Hence it was the trusts, the investment banking houses, the interlocking directorates, the swollen private fortunes, that were most criticized, and after them the well-knit, highly disciplined political machines. The labor unions, being far weaker than the big businesses and the machines, held an ambiguous place in Progressive thinking. The Progressive sympathized with the problems of labor, but was troubled about the lengths to which union power might go if labor-unionism became the sole counterpoise to the power of business. The danger of combinations of capital and labor that would squeeze the consuming public and the small businessman was never entirely out of sight. The rise in the price of coal after the anthracite strike aroused much public concern. And wherever labor was genuinely powerful in politics—as it was, for instance, in San Francisco, a closed-shop town where labor for a time dominated the local government—Progressivism took on a somewhat anti-labor tinge.[8]

Where the labor movement was of no more than moderate strength and where it clearly represented the middle-class aspirations of native workers and of business unionism, it was readily accepted, if only as a minor third partner in the alliance between agrarians and the urban middle

---

and the largest percentage (almost 6 per cent) ever received by a Socialist Party candidate. While voters rarely sent Socialists to Congress or the state legislatures, they frequently put them into municipal offices, largely in connection with protest against local corruption. By May 1912, 1,039 Socialists had been elected to office, including 56 mayors, 160 councilmen, and 145 aldermen. The Socialist press had grown to the point at which there were eight foreign-language and five English dailies, and 262 English and 36 foreign-language weeklies. J. A. Wayland's Socialist weekly, *Appeal to Reason*, which was published in Kansas, reached a circulation of 500,000. On Socialist political successes see R. F. Hoxie: "The Rising Tide of Socialism," *Journal of Political Economy*, Vol. XIX (October 1911), pp. 609–31, and Daniel Bell: "Marxian Socialism in the United States," pp. 259, 283–4, and passim.
[8] For the situation in San Francisco see the excellent account by Walton Bean: *Boss Ruef's San Francisco* (Berkeley, 1952); George Mowry: *The California Progressives*, p. 295, points to a similar development in Los Angeles during a period of labor militancy.

class that constituted the Progressive movement. Those Progressives who lived in the midst of industrial squalor and strife seem to have felt that the best way of meeting the "social question" was through means more benevolently disinterested than those of direct labor action. Here again the ideal of the neutral state came into play, for it was expected that the state, dealing out evenhanded justice, would meet the gravest complaints. Industrial society was to be humanized through law, a task that was largely undertaken in the state legislatures. In the years following 1900 an impressive body of legislation was passed dealing with workmen's compensation, the labor of women and children, hours of work, minimum wages for women, and old-age pensions.[9] Even when much allowance is made for spottiness in administration and enforcement, and for the toll that judicial decisions took of them, the net effect of these laws in remedying the crassest abuses of industrialism was very considerable. Today it is perhaps necessary to make a strong effort of the imagination to recall the industrial barbarism that was being tamed—to realize how much, for instance, workmen's compensation meant at a time when every year some 16,000 or 17,000 trainmen (about one out of every ten or twelve workers so classified) were injured. The insistence that the power of law be brought to bear against such gratuitous suffering is among our finest inheritances from the Progressive movement.

Progressivism was effective, moreover, not only for the laws it actually passed but for the pressure it put on business to match public reform with private improvements. American business itself had entered a new phase. Before the 1890's it had been too much absorbed in the problems of plant construction, expanding markets, and falling prices to pay much attention to either the efficiency or the morale of its working force. American plant management had been backward. But in the early twentieth century thoughtful American businessmen, pressed by the threat of

---

[9] This legislation is summarized in John R. Commons, ed.: *History of Labor in the United States*, Vol. III (New York, 1935).

union organization, condemned by muckrakers, and smarting under comparisons with the most efficient managers in Europe, began to address themselves to poor working conditions and employee morale and to the reformation of their haphazard shop methods.[1] Between 1900 and 1910, 240 volumes on business management were published. Frederick Winslow Taylor's interest in efficiency was popularized among businessmen. The emerging business schools, nonexistent in the country before 1898, provided numerous new agencies for discussion, education, and research in the field of management. Employers began to study personnel problems, consider devices for cutting fatigue and improving work conditions, and launched in some cases upon their own welfare and pension programs and profit-sharing schemes.[2] Much of this was resisted by labor unions as an attempt to set up a system of paternalistic control, and much was indeed associated with the fostering of company unions. Few employers went as far as Edward A. Filene in encouraging labor participation in managerial decisions. But the whole Progressive atmosphere did help to give rise to a system of private welfare capitalism alongside the statutory system of business regulation that was growing up. During and after the first World War this private system developed with notable rapidity.

So far as those important intangibles of political tone were concerned in which so many Progressives were deeply interested, they won a significant victory, for they heightened the level of human sympathy in the American political and economic system. One of the primary tests of the mood of a society at any given time is whether its comfortable people tend to identify, psychologically, with the power and achievements of the very successful or with the needs and sufferings of the underprivileged. In a large and striking measure the Progressive agitations turned the

[1] On this movement see Cochran and Miller: *The Age of Enterprise*, pp. 243–8, and Commons, op. cit., Vol. III, section III.
[2] See the comments on this movement in W. J. Ghent: *Our Benevolent Feudalism*, pp. 59–66.

human sympathies of the people downward rather than upward in the social scale. The Progressives, by creating a climate of opinion in which, over the long run, the comfortable public was disposed to be humane, did in the end succeed in fending off that battle of social extremes of which they were so afraid. Thanks in part to their efforts, the United States took its place alongside England and the Scandinavian countries among those nations in which the upper and middle classes accepted the fundamental legitimacy of labor aspiration and labor-unionism, and took a different path from those countries of the Continent where the violence of class antagonism and class struggle was heightened by the moral rejection of Labor. To realize the importance of the change in the United States itself, one need only think of the climate of opinion in which the Pullman strike and the Homestead strike were fought out and compare it with the atmosphere in which labor organization has taken place since the Progressive era. There has of course been violence and bloodshed, but in the twentieth century a massive labor movement has been built with far less cost in these respects than it cost the American working class merely to man the machines of American industry in the period from 1865 to 1900.

Although the Progressives were thus capable, except in special instances, of coming to terms with the organization of labor, the objective problem as well as the confusing mixture of feelings involved in their approach to business organization gave them far greater trouble. While the Progressive citizen was alarmed at the threat to economic competition and political democracy, he was also respectful of order, aware of prosperity, and cautious about launching any drastic attack upon propertied institutions. While he was hostile to private business power, he also admired bigness, efficiency, and success. While he was devoted to the moral virtues and believed in the material benefits of price competition, he was also willing to reckon with social change, and he worshipped that god of progress which the consolidation of business was said by many men to represent.

The Progressive discussion of the so-called trust or monopoly question is therefore filled with all that uneasiness and inconsistency which we may expect to see when men find themselves enmeshed in institutions and practices that seem to be working to considerable effect but that violate their inherited precepts and their moral preferences. When a social problem is, in its largest aspects, insoluble, as this one was, and when the feelings aroused over it are as urgent as the feelings of the Progressive generation, what usually happens is that men are driven to find a purely ceremonial solution. Among later generations, which do not approach the problem in the same way or have feelings of the same urgency about it, such ceremonial solutions are a temptation to the satirical intelligence. But we must be wary of falling too readily into that easy condescension which one may feel when speaking with hindsight about the problems of an earlier age. Since we no longer experience with anything like the same intensity some of the Progressives' anxieties or their sense of loss, we have outgrown the problem of business organization that they faced; and in so far as we recognize it as a real problem—as we do, for instance, in relation to the preservation of democracy—we have by no means solved it.

From the very beginning, at any rate, when the Sherman Anti-Trust Act was passed in 1890, it was recognized by most of the astute politicians of that hour as a gesture, a ceremonial concession to an overwhelming public demand for some kind of reassuring action against the trusts. Senator Orville Platt was candid enough to say at the time that it was just the result of a desire "to get some bill headed: 'A Bill to Punish Trusts' with which to go to the country." [3] Before the time of Theodore Roosevelt's presidency very little attempt had been made, and negligible results had been achieved, in employing the act to check business

---

[3] L. A. Coolidge: *An Old-fashioned Senator: Orville H. Platt* (New York, 1910), p. 444.

consolidations, and the Supreme Court had already made it clear that enforcement would be no simple matter. T. R., as we have seen, dramatized the issue in his Northern Securities prosecution, which was followed in time by a few other selected prosecutions of comparable public-relations value. The readiness with which his reputation as a "trust-buster"—a reputation that despite all the efforts of the historians still clings to his name—grew up around these prosecutions is itself striking testimony to the public's need to believe in the effectiveness of action in this sphere;[4] for not only did T. R. fail to prosecute many trusts, and fail to check the accelerating business consolidation that occurred during his administrations, but he did not even believe in the trust-busting philosophy and he was utterly and constantly candid in saying so in his presidential messages and other public statements. He inveighed regularly and with asperity against attempting "the impossible task of restoring the flintlock conditions of business sixty years ago by trusting only to a succession of lawsuits under the antitrust law. . . ."[5] "The man who advocates destroying the trusts," he said early in his presidency, "by measures which would paralyze the industries of the country is at least a quack and at worst an enemy to the Republic."[6] Lacking faith in the viability or workability of all efforts to restore the old competitive order, he urged, as did those Progressive intellectuals who followed the lead of Herbert Croly, that the whole system of organization be accepted as a product of modern life, and that such efforts as must be made to control and check overgrown organization be carried out along the lines of counter-organization: "A simple and poor society can exist as a democracy on a basis of sheer individualism. But a rich

---

[4] It was characteristic of the age that Taft, who started twice as many anti-trust actions as T. R., but had not half his gift for dramatization, was not thought of as a trust-buster.

[5] *Works*, Memorial Edition (New York, 1923–6), Vol. XIX, p. 401; this was his speech before the Progressive National Convention of 1912.

[6] *Presidential Addresses and State Papers* (New York, 1910), Vol. I, p. 139; from a speech at Fitchburg, Massachusetts, September 2, 1902.

and complex industrial society cannot so exist; for some individuals, and especially those artificial individuals called corporations, become so very big that the ordinary individual . . . cannot deal with them on terms of equality. It therefore becomes necessary for these ordinary individuals to combine in their turn, first in order to act in their collective capacity through that biggest of all combinations called the government, and second, to act also in their own self-defense, through private combinations, such as farmers' associations and trade unions." [7]

These remarks come as close as a brief statement could do to foreshadowing the important developments in this sphere since Roosevelt's time. It was his belief that while business combinations should be accepted and recognized, their affairs, their acts and earnings, should be exposed to publicity; and that they should be subject to regulation and be punished when they were "bad." The Bureau of Corporations, which was created at his instance in 1903, did in fact carry out useful studies of the conduct of a number of major industries, including lumber, meat-packing, oil, steel, and tobacco. Roosevelt seems to have thought of the Bureau of Corporations as the tentative beginning of a somewhat more effective system of regulation, whose ultimate form was, not surprisingly, rather vague in his mind.[8] As time passed, however, he put more and more emphasis on the distinction between good and bad trusts. Monopoly power itself was not to be the object of concern, but only such monopoly or near-monopoly as was achieved or maintained by unfair methods. This distinction might be difficult to realize satisfactorily in positive law— but such a consideration seems not to have concerned him. The facilities of the Antitrust Division of the Department of Justice were limited to five attorneys working with a budget of about $100,000 a year. By definition, since only

[7] John Morton Blum: *The Republican Roosevelt*, p. 110; for a more elaborate statement of this argument, see Herbert Croly: *The Promise of American Life* (New York, 1909), esp. chapter xii.
[8] *The Letters of Theodore Roosevelt*, Vol. III, pp. 591–2, 680.

a handful of suits could be undertaken each year, there could hardly be very many "bad" businesses. Such was the situation as T. R. left it during his presidency.

Despite the efforts of President Taft to put some force into the anti-trust movement, public dissatisfaction continued to grow, as the appetite for the regulation of business consolidation seemed to enlarge with such small evidences of success as the politicians were able to produce. There was a growing awareness of the danger of what Wilson called "a combination of the combinations"—the union of all the great business interests under the leadership of the chief investment banking houses. More and more Americans were coming to the conclusion that what had been done thus far did not go nearly deep enough. The view expressed by Herbert Croly, T. R., Charles H. Van Hise, and some others that monopoly must be accepted and regulated may have had widespread appeal among many lawyers, intellectuals, and the more sophisticated businessmen, but it was probably not the predominant sentiment among those who had strong feelings about the matter. The idea of Brandeis, Wilson, La Follette, and Bryan that a real effort should be made to restore, maintain, and regulate competition rather than regulate monopoly seems to have been more congenial to the country at large, to most of the reformers, and especially to rural people and small businessmen in the West and South, where Populist anti-monopoly traditions had some strength.[9] No doubt it was this large public that Vice-President Thomas R. Marshall had in mind when he declared in 1913: "The people were told in the last campaign that trusts were a natural evolution, and that the only way to deal with them was to regulate them. The people are tired of being told such things. What

---

[9] George Mowry points out that Roosevelt's paternalistic philosophy, with it's acceptance of regulated consolidation, its labor reforms, and its protective tariff had more urban than rural appeal, and that in the eighteen largest cities he ran 10 per cent ahead of his vote in the country at large. *Theodore Roosevelt and the Progressive Movement,* p. 280.

they want is the kind of opportunity that formerly existed in this country." [1]

This remark summarizes the issue of business consolidation as it had been dramatized in the election campaign of 1912. Both Wilson and Roosevelt ran on platforms so generally Progressive that only their difference on the trust issue clearly marked them off from each other. The issue, as Brandeis put it, was regulated competition versus regulated monopoly, and although it was vigorously debated in these terms, giving strong expression to the feelings of the two schools of thought, it is doubtful that the difference was in fact as sharp as the debate made it seem. To be sure, men like Wilson and La Follette at times seemed really to believe that the tide of business consolidation could be swept back by Sherman Act methods. La Follette declared in 1912 that "the executive could have saved the people from the appalling conditions which confront us today, if all the power of this government had been put forth to enforce the [Sherman] Anti-Trust law." [2] Wilson asserted in the same year that the community of business interests by which the United States was in danger of being governed was "something for the law to pull apart, and gently, but firmly and persistently dissect" [3]—a threat that raises the image of a surgical president, perhaps with Brandeis and La Follette in attendance, exercising his scalpel over the palpitating body of the American business community.

In fact Wilson's approach was not so straightforward or unequivocal as this menacing surgical metaphor suggests—for he too recognized that "the elaboration of business upon a great co-operative scale is characteristic of our time and has come about by the natural operation of modern civilization," and admitted that "we shall never return to the old order of individual competition, and that the organization of business upon a grand scale of co-operation is, up to a

---

[1] Quoted in William English Walling: *Progressivism and After* (New York, 1914), p. 104.
[2] *Autobiography*, pp. 704–5.
[3] *The New Freedom*, p. 188.

certain point, itself normal and inevitable." [4] While he believed deeply in the little entrepreneur and in competition, he rested his hope in what he called "free competition," not in "illicit competition." Free competition was anything that promoted the victory of superior efficiency, while illicit competition was the use of unfair means to surpass competitors by firms that were not actually more efficient. Wilson had to admit that free competition, too, would kill competitors, and that these competitors would be just as dead as those killed by illicit competition. But in such cases the net result would be good, because it would add to the total efficiency of the nation's production. Thus a big business that grew big through superior efficiency was good; only one that grew big by circumventing honest competition was bad. [5] "I am for big business," said Wilson in one of his more inscrutable sentences, "and I am against the trusts." [6] But no one, not even Brandeis, knew how to define or measure superior efficiency, or to draw a line in the progress toward bigness beyond which a business would lose rather than gain in efficiency. While it was possible to draw up a list of business practices that most honest men would agree to condemn, no one knew a constructive or responsible way of dissolving great businesses that had already grown up by employing just such practices. No one knew how to make empirical sense out of Wilson's distinction between the big business he favored and the trusts he disliked. And no one could be sure that there was any real working difference between the distinction T. R. made between good and bad trusts and the distinction Wilson made between free and illicit competition.

A Progessive voter who felt impelled to take a rational view of the trust question might well have been confused, and may have wondered whether the warm debate expressed a really profound difference between the candi-

---

[4] Ibid., p. 163; William Diamond: *The Economic Thought of Woodrow Wilson* (Baltimore, 1943), p. 108.

[5] See the discussion of "Monopoly or Opportunity," *The New Freedom*, chapter viii.

[6] Ibid., p. 180.

dates. In fact, by the time of the 1912 campaign the decisions of the Supreme Court had already whittled the Sherman Act down to the point at which it was no longer possible to imagine that the law could be—without a juridical revolution—an instrument for a broad frontal attack on business consolidation.[7] What remained was the possibility that particular businesses guilty of flagrantly unfair competition could occasionally be singled out for action—a procedure not signally different from the Rooseveltian distinction between good and bad trusts. What is perhaps most worthy of comment is that the further antitrust legislation of the Wilson administration, the Clayton Act and the creation of the Federal Trade Commission, did not include any provisions aimed at circumventing the Supreme Court's extremely damaging approach to antitrust suits. Nor was any serious effort made by Wilson to launch a vigorous policy. Under him the Antitrust Division was expanded, but only to eighteen men—and even this was done only after wartime conditions had sent prices skyhigh. (The most elementary policing of the economy, more recent experience has shown, calls for a staff of well over ten times as many attorneys.[8]) Wilson also disappointed those who hoped that the Federal Trade Commission

---

[7] This was completely clear after the American Tobacco Company and the Standard Oil cases, both decided in 1911, as a consequence of the application of the "rule of reason" to anti-trust suits. In his dissenting opinion in the latter case Mr. Justice Harlan declared that the Court had "by mere interpretation, modified the act of Congress, and deprived it of practical value as a defensive measure against the evils to be remedied." This was the view generally taken of these decisions by the anti-trust reformers.

[8] When the Antitrust Division was revived under Franklin D. Roosevelt after 1938, with the intention not of launching a frontal attack on consolidation but of policing price policies and competitive practices, it acquired a force of about 250 lawyers and economists. The Securities and Exchange Commission needs a personnel of over 1,200 to carry out its work today. Walton Hamilton and Irene Till: *Antitrust in Action*, T.N.E.C. Monograph No. 16 (Washington, 1941), pp. 23–6 gives a good brief account of the historic non-enforcement of the Sherman Act; cf. Walton Hamilton: *The Pattern of Competition* (New York, 1940), pp. 58–82, on difficulties and limitations of enforcement; and Thurman Arnold: *The Bottlenecks of Business* (New York, 1940), esp. chapter viii.

would become an effective agency of regulation by choosing commissioners who were either ineffectual or primarily interested in making the agency useful to business.[9] Brandeis, who had helped to draft the act creating the Federal Trade Commission, later dismissed its management under Wilson as "a stupid administration."[1]

No one who follows the trust question at the level of both public discussion and legislative action can fail to be impressed by the disparity between the two: the discussions were so momentous in their character and so profound —for nothing less was at stake than the entire organization of American business and American politics, the very question of who was to control the country—and the material results were by comparison so marginal, so incomplete, so thoroughly blocked at all the major strategic points. It is impossible not to conclude that, despite the widespread public agitation over the matter, the men who took a conservative view of the needs of the hour never lost control. It was not merely that, on the main issues to be adjudicated, the Supreme Court stood with them, but that the executive leaders who occupied the White House and the sober gentry of the Senate were in the final analysis quite reliable. It proved impossible for me like Byran and La Follette, who did not enjoy the confidence of at least large segments of the business community, to find their way to the White House; and the considerable influence that these men had throughout the country was carefully filtered through the hands of more conservative politicians before it was embodied in legislative or administrative action. A leader like Theodore Roosevelt, and with him several prominent Republicans, who understood the urgency of Progressive sentiments, knew also how to act as a balance wheel between what he considered to be the most irresponsible forces of left and right. (In 1912 George Roosevelt re-

[9] Arthur S. Link: *Woodrow Wilson and the Progressive Era* (New York, 1954), pp. 70–5.
[1] Ibid. p. 74

marked to him that whereas earlier he had been the progressive leader of the conservatives, he was now the conservative leader of the progressives. " 'Yes, yes,' T. R. muttered, as he rocked back and forth in his favorite rocking chair, 'that's it. I have to hold them in check all the time. I have to restrain them.' " [2])

Historians have long been aware how T. R., while enjoying the support and indeed even on occasion whipping up the sentiments of the insurgent forces in American life, turned for advice in the solution of his problems to the great conservative leaders in the Senate and to the great spokesmen of Eastern industry and finance capital; and how much support he accepted for his campaigns from the financial interests whose custodians these men always were. Woodrow Wilson had a different temperament, and in his administration the same forces worked in a somewhat roundabout way. To preserve his own sense of integrity, Wilson had fewer direct dealings with the captains of industry and finance; but his closest adviser, Colonel House, became a personal agent through whom the needs and views of capital could be expressed to the White House, and House's diary records frequent conferences with J. P. Morgan, Felix M. Warburg, Henry Clay Frick, Francis L. Higginson, Otto H. Kahn, and Frank Vanderlip.[3] Moreover, when a depression developed late in 1913 which grew more serious in the following year, Wilson himself began openly and assiduously to cultivate the support of business, began to welcome bankers and business leaders back to the White House, and issued unequivocal reassurances to the effect that the wave of reform legislation was nearing its end.[4] Progressive intellectuals, who were familiar with the praise Herbert Croly had lavished upon the circumspect Roosevelt, must have been bemused to

---

[2] Nicholas Roosevelt: *A Front Row Seat* (Norman, Oklahoma, 1953), p. 53.
[3] Matthew Josephson: *The President Makers* (New York, 1940), is most penetrating on this aspect of Progressive politics.
[4] Arthur S. Link: *Woodrow Wilson and the Progressive Era*, pp. 75–9.

see this editor scold Woodrow Wilson in 1914 for his failure to go very far with the program of Progressive reform.[5]

But to say all this about the ceremonial function of the agitation over big business should not divert us from our search for its other uses. The relations of the reform movement to business were not limited to the effort to restore competition or check monopoly. There were other, more pragmatic reforms under consideration; and it was the effect of all the monitory writing and speaking, and all the heated agitation over the trusts and their threat to democracy and enterprise and liberty, to throw big business and the vested interests on the defensive and to create a climate of public opinion in which some reform legislation was possible. The Progressives may not have been able to do much about business consolidation, but they did manage, in the Hepburn Act, to take the first step toward genuine regulation of the railroads, a thing long overdue; they did manage, in the creation of the Federal Reserve System, to establish a more satisfactory system of credit subject to public control; they did bring about, in the Underwood tariff, a long-sought downward revision of duties; and on a number of fronts, both state and national, they won other legislative reforms of real value to farmers and workers and the consuming public that would have been far more difficult to achieve in a social atmosphere unaffected by the widespread demand to challenge the power of big business.

In a number of ways the problem of business consolidation now presents itself, even to liberals and reformers, in different forms from those in which it appeared to the men of the Progressive generation. Fewer men by far experience the passing of independent entrepreneurship with the same anguish. The process of capital formation has changed in such a way as to reduce the importance of the investment banking houses and thus to lay the specter of the money trust. Product competition has in some respects replaced

[5] Ibid., pp. 79–80.

the old price competition. The great distributive agencies, themselves giant concerns, have given consumers some protection from the exactions of monopoly. Big business has shown itself to be what the Progressives of the Brandeis school resolutely denied it would be—technologically more progressive than the smaller units it has replaced. The political power of capital has been more satisfactorily matched by an enormous growth in labor organization. The very dissociation of ownership from control, so alarming to the Progressives, has created a class of salaried managers who have a stake in their own respectability and civic comfort that is as large as or greater than their stake in profits-at-any-cost. It is conceivable that such men may continue to show more industrial flexibility than the hard-pressed entrepreneurs of old-fashioned enterprise could afford.

None the less, subsequent generations of Americans still owe a great debt to the anti-trust inheritance they hold from the Progressive era. The rise of big business may have been inevitable, but if so it was salutary that it should have taken place in a climate of opinion that threw it intermittently on the defensive. Even Thurman Arnold, whose name is conspicuously identified with the argument that the chief effect of the anti-trust rhetoric "was to promote the growth of great industrial organizations by deflecting the attack on them into purely moral and ceremonial channels," [6] had to concede, when he elaborated this thesis in *The Folklore of Capitalism*, that the same anti-trust rhetoric, by encouraging the notion that great corporations could be disciplined and made respectable, had something to do with the fact that they finally did become respectable; and that without the presence of hostile laws the pricing policies of big business might have been a good deal more unfavorable to the public interest.[7] His own subsequent career as Assistant Attorney General in charge of the Anti-

---

[6] Thurman Arnold: *The Folklore of Capitalism* (New Haven, 1937), p. 212; the thesis seems to have been foreshadowed by C. H. Van Hise: *Concentration and Control*, p. 233.

[7] Arnold, op. cit., pp. 221, 228.

trust Division of the Department of Justice was, in a broad
historical sense, built upon intangibles of sentiment inherited from the Progressives and their anti-monopoly
predecessors. For even though he and the other planners
of the latter-day New Deal movement against monopoly
planned no such general assault on bigness as was foreshadowed in the more exalted campaign talk of the Bran-
deis-Wilson school, they did rely upon political sentiments
that the Progressives had nourished and strengthened.
Franz Neumann, examining the conditions that led to the
collapse of the Weimar Republic and the rise of the Nazis
in Germany, pointed out that in Germany there had never
been anything like a popular anti-monopoly movement
such as the United States experienced under Theodore
Roosevelt and Woodrow Wilson, that the middle classes
had not been articulate against the cartels and the trusts,
and that labor, looking at concentration through Marxist
eyes, had consistently favored it. This, he suggests, weakened the opposition, within the business order, to authoritarian controls. This comparison suggests another respect in
which the anti-trust tradition has justified itself.[8] Paradoxi-
cally, while hostility to big business and finance has on
occasion led to local authoritarianism and to unhealthy
modes of rebellion,[9] it has also been one of the resources
upon which American democracy has drawn. So, after all,
even the overblown rhetoric of the anti-trust movement
finds its place, and even the Progressive charade of anti-
monopoly takes on a function that goes beyond mere entertainment. No doubt the immediate material achievement
was quite small in proportion to all the noise; but there are
many episodes in history in which intense struggle has to
be waged to win modest gains, and this too must be remembered before we pass too severe a judgment on the
great Progressive crusade against the trusts.

---

[8] Franz Neumann: Behemoth (New York, 1942), pp. 15–16.
[9] Lipset and Bendix: "Social Status and Social Structure," passim.

iii · *The Citizen and the Machine*

If big business was the ultimate enemy of the Progressive, his proximate enemy was the political machine. The problem of political organization gave him somewhat the same sort of perplexity as that of economic organization; it similarly divided the Progressive community between those who proposed an aggressive and uncompromising struggle against organization as such and those who proposed to meet it by counterorganization, by increasing specialism and leadership, and by the assumption of new responsibilities. Unless the machine and its leader, the boss, could be broken, unless the corrupt alliance between special interests and the machine could be smashed, it seemed that no lasting reform could be accomplished. Hence this particular form of the struggle over organization was prominent in political discussions from the beginning to the end of the Progressive era. What the majority of the Progressives hoped to do in the political field was to restore popular government as they imagined it to have existed in an earlier and purer age. This could be done, it was widely believed, only by revivifying the morale of the citizen, and using his newly aroused zeal to push through a series of changes in the mechanics of political life—direct primaries, popular election of Senators, initiative, referendum, recall, the short ballot, commission government, and the like. Such measures, it was expected, would deprive machine government of the advantages it had in checkmating popular control, and make government accessible to the superior disinterestedness and honesty of the average citizen. Then, with the power of the bosses broken or crippled, it would be possible to check the incursions of the interests upon the welfare of the people and realize a cleaner, more efficient government.

The Progressives set about the task of political reform with great energy and resourcefulness. By 1910 they had had a considerable measure of success in getting their reforms incorporated into the electoral and governmental machinery, and this success engendered in some quarters a high optimism about the future of the movement for popular government. William Allen White's book *The Old Order Changeth*, published in that year, deserves analysis as a hearty expression of this optimism and as a statement of what was probably the dominant popular philosophy of politics. America, White believed, was in the midst of an inexorable "drift" toward democracy, which had produced gain after gain in the sphere of popular government—victories for the secret ballot and the direct primary, the widespread adoption of the recall of officials, the impending triumph of the popular referendum. Such changes would not have been dreamed of ten years before, "and to have told the campaign managers of '84 or '88 that within a quarter of a century the whole nation would be voting a secret ballot, the candidates nominated in two-thirds of the American states by a direct vote of the people, without the intervention of conventions or caucuses, and that . . . every dollar spent by a candidate or by a party committee would have to be publicly accounted for," would have aroused only a cackle of derision. Now in twenty-six states of the Union, Senators had to go directly to the people for their nomination, not to the railroads and utilities as before. "Capital is not eliminated from politics, but it is hampered and circumscribed, and is not the dominant force it was ten years ago." "It is safe to say that the decree of divorce between business and politics will be absolute within a few years." "Now the political machine is in a fair way to be reduced to mere political scrap iron by the rise of the people. . . . Under the primary system any clean, quick-witted man in these states can defeat the corporation senatorial candidate at the primary if the people desire to defeat him." [1]

White fully shared the dominant Progressive philosophy concerning organization. The business of reform in politics, he said, had to be done by taking the power to nominate

[1] White: *The Old Order Changeth*, pp. 34, 36, 39, 47–53.

and elect candidates and to set policies out of the hands of the old ruling caste of the machines. Such a thing "could always be done by breaking the machine of the moment or of any locality and establishing another machine." But such a remedy was no good—and here was the crux of the matter—because it was not "a permanent cure." The only permanent cure was in changing the system.[2] If theory was to be effective in practice, one would have no machines at all. White did not hesitate to emphasize the underlying individualism of the popular revolt: it was a change in "the public's moral average," the aggregate result of the transformation of a multitude of individual wills. Yet for all its need to bring property under control, it was far from socialistic: "the modern movement in American politics is bristling with rampant, militant, unhampered men crowding out of the mass for individual elbow-room." [3]

None of this movement for elbow-room was considered to be excessively self-regarding. White's book was full of references to the intelligence, the self-restraint, the morality, the breadth of view of the average man, the emergent New Citizen. The whole process of revolt was indeed so benign that he could only attribute it to the workings of "a divinely planted instinct." For it was essential that the individual be —as he was proving himself—disinterested. The New Citizen was the guilty and neglectful citizen of the muckraking literature after he had been reformed and aroused by all the exhortatory literature of the age. "The people are controlling themselves. Altruism is gaining strength for some future struggle with the atomic force of egoism in society." [4] It followed from this view of the citizen that his contribution to the public weal grew not out of his pursuit in politics of his own needs but, in the manner of the old Mugwump ideal, out of his disinterested reflection upon the needs of the community. Of course the struggle against the machines could not take place without the benefit of

---

[2] Ibid., p. 39.
[3] Ibid., p. 121.
[4] Ibid., pp. 57, 60–3, 66, 71, 120.

some form of counterorganization; but it was characteristic
of this style of thought to conceive of these counterorganizations as private organizations based upon high principles
rather than group interests—organizations like the National
Civil Service Reform League, the Pure Food Association,
the Child Labor Committee, the Consumers' League, the
National Civic Federation, the Masons, and other fraternal
groups. What all such things rested upon for their success
was the civic virtue—White spoke rather of "righteousness"
and "altruism"—of the individual, his willingness not to
pursue his interests but to transcend them. "Democracy is,
at base, altruism expressed in terms of self-government."
"Practically all the large national organizations which jam
the trains annually going to their conventions are fundamentally altruistic." [5]

We can see now in its broad outlines the persistent individualism of these Progressives. Although it was necessary for them to make some use of organization, they had a
profound inherited distrust of it. At the core of their conception of politics was a figure quite as old-fashioned as
the figure of the little competitive entrepreneur who represented the most commonly accepted economic ideal. This
old-fashioned character was the Man of Good Will, the
same innocent, bewildered, bespectacled, and mustached
figure we see in the cartoons today labeled John Q. Public
—a white collar or small business voter-taxpayer with perhaps a modest home in the suburbs. William Graham Sumner had depicted him a generation earlier as "the forgotten
man," and Woodrow Wilson idealized him as "the man on
the make" whose type, coming "out of the unknown
homes," was the hope of America. In a great deal of
Progressive thinking the Man of Good Will was abstracted
from association with positive interests; his chief interests
were negative. He needed to be protected from unjust taxation, spared the high cost of living, relieved of the exactions of the monopolies and the grafting of the bosses. In
years past he had been careless about his civic responsibil-

---

[5] Ibid., pp. 132, 143; see chapter vi passim.

ities, but now he was rising in righteous wrath and asserting himself. He was at last ready to address himself seriously to the business of government. The problem was to devise such governmental machinery as would empower him to rule. Since he was dissociated from all special interests and biases and had nothing but the common weal at heart, he would rule well. He would act and think as a public-spirited individual, unlike all the groups of vested interests that were ready to prey on him. Bad people had pressure groups; the Man of Good Will had only his civic organizations. Far from joining organizations to advance his own interests, he would dissociate himself from such combinations and address himself directly and high-mindedly to the problems of government. His approach to politics was, in a sense, intellectualistic: he would study the issues and think them through, rather than learn about them through pursuing his needs. Furthermore, it was assumed that somehow he would really be capable of informing himself in ample detail about the many issues that he would have to pass on, and that he could master their intricacies sufficiently to pass intelligent judgment.

Without such assumptions the entire movement for such reforms as the initiative, the referendum, and recall is unintelligible. The movement for direct popular democracy was, in effect, an attempt to realize Yankee-Protestant ideals of personal responsibility; and the Progressive notion of good citizenship was the culmination of the Yankee-Mugwump ethos of political participation without self-interest. But while this ethos undoubtedly has its distinct points of superiority to the boss-machine ethos of hierarchy, discipline, personal loyalty, and personal favors, it was less adapted to the realities of the highly organized society of the late nineteenth and the twentieth century. It is not surprising, then, that so much of the political machinery designed to implement the aims of direct democracy should have been found of very limited use.

Of course, not all his Progressive contemporaries were quite so optimistic as William Allen White. There were a

number of Progressive spokesmen who found fault with his
assumptions, and there were a few outstanding Progressive
leaders who surmounted them in their practical political
dealings. Just as Progressive discussions of the business
order were pervaded by an argument between two schools
with contrasting schemes for dealing with the trusts, so the
discussions of political reform took place between two sides
that were divided by a difference in philosophy. On the
left was a populistic school of thought that seemed to have
hardly any reservations about the extent to which the management of affairs could and should be given into the
hands of the populace. This school, which can be traced as
far back as the time when Jackson argued for rotation in
office on the ground that "the duties of all public offices
are, or at least admit of being made, so plain and simple
that men of intelligence may readily qualify themselves for
their performance," found its contemporary expression in
William Jennings Bryan's contention that the people were
competent "to sit in judgment on every question which has
arisen or which will arise, no matter how long our government will endure," and his argument that the great political questions were in the final analysis moral questions
concerning which the intuitions of the people were as good
as almost any degree of experience. Even a man like
Woodrow Wilson, whose native impulses and earlier philosophy ran quite to the contrary, fell into this populistic
conception of democracy when he asserted that the Democratic Party aimed "to set up a government in the world
where the average man, the plain man, the common man,
the ignorant man, the unaccomplished man, the poor man
had a voice equal to the voice of anybody else in the settlement of the common affairs, an ideal never before realized in the history of the world." [6]

This faith in the lowest common denominator of political action was frequently coupled with an attack on political organization. The political evils that plagued the country, it was often argued, were not the consequences of defi-
_____
[6] Link: *Wilson: the Road to the White House*, p. 518.

cient organization but of over-organization. The answer to these evils was to move as close as possible to a system of "direct government" by the people. It was considered not only that the people were capable of acting effectively as individuals, but that they were at their best when acting in this capacity because only then were they free of the corrupting and self-interested influence of parties and machines. Thus Albert Baird Cummins, when he ran for the governorship of Iowa in 1910, declared that his great object was "to bring the individual voter into more prominence, and to diminish the influence of permanent organization in the ranks of the party." [7]

Those who shared this style of thought tended to deny that the parties should be the property of the party organizations—that is, of the groups of persons who did the work of the party and held offices under its name—and to insist that the parties properly belonged to the voters at large. Indeed, the rhetoric of American party politics had encouraged this notion, and it was easy to conclude that in so far as the party was in fact not the property of the voters, democracy was being flouted. Democracy was considered to require not merely competition between party organizations that would afford the voters a choice, but rank-and-file control or dissolution of the organizations

---

[7] *Dictionary of American Biography*, Vol. IV (New York, 1930), p. 597. This point of view was expressed as late at 1923 by Senator George W. Norris in a defense of the direct primary: "One of the [most important] objections that is always made to the direct primary is that it takes away party responsibility and breaks down party control. . . . Politicians, political bosses, corporations and combinations seeking special privilege and exceptional favor at the hands of legislatures and executive officials, always urge this as the first reason why the direct primary should be abolished. But this objection thus given against the direct primary I frankly offer as one of the best reasons for its retention. The direct primary will lower party responsibility. In its stead it establishes individual responsibility. It does lessen allegiance to party and increase individual independence, both as to the public official and as to the private citizen. It takes away the power of the party leader or boss and places the responsibility for control upon the individual. It lessens party spirit and decreases partisanship." "Why I Believe in the Direct Primary," *Annals* of the American Academy of Political and Social Science, Vol. CVI (March 1923), p. 23.

themselves. The movement for the direct primary was the chief embodiment of this conception of democracy.[8] Its historical inspiration presumably came from the town-meeting model, and from the widespread direct participation of the American citizen in civic affairs in the early and middle years of the nineteenth century.

Counterposed to this philosophy was a more conservative view, expressed by a good many men who recognized the value of the Progressive demands for reform and saw the importance of popular discontent, but who looked to new forms of political organization under responsible leadership as the most desirable and effective remedy for the evils against which the Progressives were working. The historical root of this point of view lay in the long-standing Mugwump concern with good government and in the implicit Mugwump belief in elite leadership. Brandeis, as we have seen, expressed its impulse when he called upon the lawyers to assume "a position of independence between the wealthy and the people, prepared to curb the excesses of either," and so did T. R. when he entitled one of his talks to businessmen "The Radical Movement under Conservative Direction." [9] Henry L. Stimson, writing to Roosevelt in 1910, gave vent to a somewhat partisan statement of this philosophy: "To me it seems vitally important that the Republican party, which contains, generally speaking, the richer and more intelligent citizens of the country, should take the lead in reform and not drift into a reactionary position. If, instead, the leadership should fall into the hands of either an independent party, or a party composed, like the Democrats, largely of foreign elements and the classes which will immediately benefit by the reform, and if the solid business Republicans should drift into new obstruction, I fear the necessary changes could hardly

---

[8] See E. E. Schattschneider: *Party Government* (New York, 1942), pp. 53–61.

[9] Theodore Roosevelt: *Works*, National Edition (New York, 1926), Vol. XVI, pp. 86–99.

be accomplished without much excitement and possible violence." [1]

Somewhat more congenial to Mugwump traditions was the idea that the evils against which the Progressives were fighting could be remedied by a reorganization of government in which responsibility and authority could be clearly located in an executive, whose acts would be open to public view. The power of the boss, they argued, like the overweening power of great corporations, was a consequence of the weakness of the political executive and the more general division of authority and impotence in government. Spokesmen of this view scoffed at the inherited popular suspicion of executive power as an outmoded holdover from the days of the early Republic when executive power was still identified with royal government and the royal governors. "The true remedy for American misgovernment," said Stimson, "would lie, then, in exactly the opposite direction from that indicated by the advocates of direct democracy. The elected officials must have more power, not less. . . ." [2] The purpose of such devices would not be to flout public opinion, but to give expression to its demands in conformity with principles of organization that accepted the realities of a complex society.

The most ardent debate, however, did not take place between the two schools of reformers, but between the direct-government reforms and the ultraconservatives. To attend to the terms in which the various reforms intended to promote direct democracy were debated—and to these one should add the proposal for women's suffrage—one might think that the issue was utopia versus apocalypse. The conservatives moaned and admonished as though each new reform proposal portended the end of the nation, while many Progressives seemed to imagine and often, indeed, said that these reforms, once achieved, would

---

[1] Henry L. Stimson and McGeorge Bundy, op. cit., p. 22.
[2] Ibid., p. 58; see the general argument of chapter iii, "Responsible Government," pp. 56–81.

open the way to a complete and permanent victory over the machines and corruption. Woodrow Wilson, for instance, once said of the short ballot that it was "the key to the whole problem of the restoration of popular government in this country"[3]—which was a heavy burden, sound reform though it was, for the short ballot to bear. There were of course more moderate men on both sides,[4] and in retrospect it is clearly these men who were right; for the popular reforms neither revolutionized nor restored anything; they had, indeed, only a marginal effect on the conduct of American government.

Here the more general Progressive uprising against bossism, corruption, and misgovernment must be distinguished from the attempt to realize mechanical changes that would guarantee permanent popular rule. Where the reform movements succeeded as they did in sufficient measure to bring a distinct improvement in American government, it was largely because they came in on a strong wave of popular enthusiasm or indignation or under the guidance of local leaders of exceptional magnetism. Such leaders and such public sentiments, I believe, would have had somewhat the same results within the framework of the older mechanism of government. In their search for mechanical guarantees of continued popular control the reformers were trying to do something altogether impossible—to institutionalize a mood. When the mood passed, some of the more concrete reforms remained; but the formal gains for popular government, while still on the books, lost

---

[3] Quoted in Austin F. Macdonald: *American City Government and Administration*, 3rd ed. (New York, 1941), p. 279. Cf. Walter Lippmann in 1914: "I have just read a book by a college professor which announces that the short ballot will be as deep a revolution as the abolition of slavery. There are innumerable Americans who believe that a democratic constitution would create a democracy." *Drift and Mastery*, p. 187. Cf. La Follette's hopes for the direct primary, *Autobiography*, pp. 197–8.

[4] An excellent contemporary discussion of the whole problem of the public will and representative institutions was A. Lawrence Lowell's *Public Opinion and Popular Government* (New York, 1913); see also the critical reflections of Herbert Croly in *Progressive Democracy* (New York, 1914).

meaning because the ability of the public to use them effectively lapsed with the political revival that brought them in, and the bosses and the interest promptly filtered back. Herbert Croly, while by no means unsympathetic to the "professional democrats," as he called them, argued cogently that their tendency "to conceive democracy as essentially a matter of popular political machinery" was one of their great weaknesses. Their dominant impulse was to protect the people against knavery, a negative goal, rather than "to give positive momentum and direction to popular rule." They sought, above all, "to prevent the people from being betrayed—from being imposed upon by unpopular policies and unrepresentative officials. But to indoctrinate and organize one's life chiefly for the purpose of avoiding betrayal is to invite sterility and disintegration." He concluded that the impulse toward popular rule was without meaning whenever it was divorced from a specific social program.[5]

The history of Progressive reform justified Croly's argument, for under the impact of the Progressive movement the people in many places won better public services, better parks, better schools, better tax policies, but they did not destroy narrowly partisan government, break up machines, or gain direct control of their affairs. With a few exceptions, the bosses found ways either to deflect or to use the new reforms that were meant to unseat them.[6] The direct primary, for instance, for all its wide adoption throughout the country, did not noticeably change the type of men nominated for office. It was expensive both

---

[5] Croly: *Progressive Democracy*, pp. 213–14; see in general chapters x and xiii.

[6] Where the tone of a community was congenial to bossism it was impossible to find political mechanics that would prevent it. One of the signal illustrations of this comes from New Jersey, where the Walsh Act of 1911 permitted municipalities to change to the commission system of government. This was one of the reforms that worked to good effect in some places, but in New Jersey Frank Hague used his position as commissioner of public safety—i.e., the police and fire departments—as a stepping-stone toward that execrable regime for which he became notorious. Dayton D. McKean: *The Boss: the Hague Machine in Action* (Boston, 1940), pp. 37–45.

to the government and to the candidates—for it introduced
two campaigns in the place of one. It put a new premium
on publicity and promotion in nominating campaigns, and
thus introduced into the political process another entering
wedge for the power of money. Without seriously impair-
ing the machines, it weakened party government and partly
responsibility. The initiative and referendum were also
disappointing as instruments of popular government. As
critics like Herbert Croly pointed out, they were perfectly
designed to facilitate minority rule in so far as the complex
questions set before the voters in referendums could be
passed with a distinct minority of the total registration.[7]
Confronted by an array of technical questions, often
phrased in legal language, the voters shrank from the responsibilities the new system attempted to put upon them.
Small and highly organized groups with plenty of funds
and skillful publicity could make use of these devices, but
such were not the results the proponents of initiative and
referendum sought; nor was the additional derationaliza-
tion of politics that came with the propaganda campaigns
demanded by referendums. Finally, the more ardent reformers who expected that the public will, once expressed
directly, would bring a radical transformation of the old
order were surprised to find the voters exercising their
prerogative in the most conservative way, rejecting, for
instance, proposals for municipal ownership, the single tax,
and pensions for city employees.[8]

[7] Herbert Croly: *Progressive Democracy*, p. 306.
[8] There is an extensive literature on such practices as direct primaries,
the short ballot, initiative, referendum, recall, commission government,
the city-manager plan, and other reforms of the age. For a brief
general critique see William B. Munro: *The Government of American
Cities*, 4th ed. (New York, 1933).
    Some sober party estimates of the direct primary may be found in
Annals of the American Academy of Political and Social Sciences, Vol.
CVI (March 1933). The comments of working politicians on the
direct primary in Ralph S. Boots: *The Direct Primary in New Jersey*
(New York, 1917), pp. 262–76, are of unusual interest.
    One of the more successful changes, useful chiefly in smaller munici-
palities, was the city-manager plan, which paid more deference to the
need for concentration of power and expertise than the devices aimed

The reformers were, of course, entirely right in feeling that effective action against the old political machines and their bosses was both possible and desirable. Reform has been the balance wheel of the governmental system. The existing machines did their work at unnecessary cost and with gross inequities, and their humane care of their own constituents was matched by the outright brutality and the crass disregard of civil liberties with which they frequently dealt with opposition. Unopposed by the reform principle, the machine principle tended to deteriorate to the point at which good government and liberal politics both were threatened. But the characteristic mistake of the more dogmatic enthusiasts for direct government was their unwillingness to consider the possibility of a synthesis between the two principles, their faith in contrivances that would somehow do away with the machine process and even with party responsibility. Too many of these enthusiasts failed to see that the machine organizations they were trying to destroy did have a number of real functions, however badly they often performed them, and that any attempt to replace the existing machines had to provide not William Allen White's "permanent cure" for the whole machine system, but rather alternative machines. There are machines and machines. The real choice that lay before the reformers was not whether to have direct popular government or party organizations and machines, but whether, in destroying the existing organizations, they could create organizations of their own, with discipline enough to survive, that would be cleaner and more efficient than those they were trying to break up. It must be admitted at once that in this respect the practice of some skilled Progressive leaders was often superior to their theories and their rhetoric. La Follette was an excellent case in point. Although he expressed great faith in the

---

to bring about direct popular government. The value even of this plan, however, has been impaired by the unwillingness of American voters to see their city managers (or their other administrators or political leaders) paid adequate salaries. On this see Thomas H. Reed: *Municipal Governments in the United States* (New York, 1934), chapter xiv.

efficacy of the direct-government reforms, he remained in
power for a long time and exerted a strong and salutary
influence on Wisconsin life because he was an extremely
astute machine-master, who knew the techniques of the
bosses and used some of them to build a militant and
well-disciplined state organization.[9]

It is in our own times that the most notable decline in
the strength and importance of the old-fashioned machines
has taken place. This has occurred not because the machines have yielded to frontal assault but because some
of their former functions have ceased to be necessary and
others have been taken over by new agencies. There is no
longer the great mass of immigrants to be patronized and
introduced to American life. Federal centralization, especially since the New Deal, has nibbled away at the role
of the local organizations, particularly in the sphere of
social welfare. The growth of the mass trade unions has
displaced the machines in some respects, while the development of stronger executives in state and local government has deprived them of some of their former patronage
and power. Much of the work of political indoctrination
and education that once belonged to them has been assumed by the mass media—radio, television, and the mass
periodicals, while the work of sounding public sentiment
has been taken over in some part by professional pollsters.
These latter developments suggest that we are in a certain
sense moving closer to the plebiscitarian ideals, the mass

---

[9] The whole subject of the types of political machines and the character
of what might be called reform machines needs study by historians and
political scientists. See, however, the suggestive article by Robert S.
Maxwell: "La Follette and the Progressive Machine in Wisconsin,"
Indiana Magazine of History, Vol. XLVIII (March 1952), pp. 55–70,
in which the author briefly analyzes the La Follette machine as a
particular instance of the general proposition: "On those rare occasions
when successful reform organizations have been welded together they
have developed techniques of political astuteness, leadership, and discipline not unlike the traditional machines." Cf. George Mowry's remarks on Hiram Johnson's California machine: *The California Progressives*, pp. 138–9, 292. The administration of Fiorello La Guardia in
New York affords a municipal example of a reform movement that
used machine methods.

democracy, that the advocates of direct government had in mind. But they would not have been pleased with the prospect of having their goals approached in this way, for the means of influencing mass sentiment on a grand scale require the big money and the crass manipulative techniques that the Progressives were trying to eliminate from politics. This brings us back again to a central problem of the modern democrat: whether it is possible in modern society to find satisfactory ways of realizing the ideal of popular government without becoming dependent to an unhealthy degree upon those who have the means to influence the popular mind. Without taking an excessively indulgent view of the old machines or imagining that their failings were any less serious than they actually were, it is still possible to wonder whether the devices that are replacing them are superior as instruments of government.

CHAPTER VII

FROM PROGRESSIVISM
TO THE NEW DEAL

❀

1 · *Progressivism and War*

War has always been the Nemesis of the liberal tradition
in America. From our earliest history as a nation there has
been a curiously persistent association between democratic
politics and nationalism, jingoism, or war. Periodically war
has written the last scene to some drama begun by the
popular side of the party struggle. In the age of Jefferson
and Madison it was the Jeffersonian Republican Party, and
particularly that faction of the Republican Party associated
with the democratic hinterland and the frontier, that did
most to bring on the War of 1812, and it was the war that
finally liquidated the Jeffersonian policies and caused their
reversal. Jacksonian democracy, the next popular upsurge,
was at first built upon nationalist hero-worship and the
military reputation of a leader whose ideas about domestic
policies were unknown. Although it fell short of actual war
with a European power, the diplomacy of Jacksonian
democracy was pugnacious. After their primary domestic
reforms were accomplished, Jacksonian leaders prodded
the nation toward bellicose expansionism, risked war with
England, and finally did go to war with Mexico. In the
subsequent "young America" movement of the 1850's,
democracy and nationalism were again marching hand in
hand. After the long period of continental settlement that
followed the Civil War, a period of predominantly peaceful
relations with foreign countries, it fell for the first time in

1898 to the more conservative forces to be at the helm in a time of war—but, as I pointed out in dealing with the Populists, it was the more radical and popular and dissenting forces in American life that felt the strongest impulse toward the Cuban crusade, and it was the Mark Hanna, Wall Street kind of Republican that showed the strongest initial opposition to the war. Again, as after Jeffersonian and Jacksonian democracy, the war, soon followed by prosperity, was a strong if only temporary solvent of the reform impulse.

By the turn of the century, it is possible to distinguish two chief strains of feeling in the Populist-Progressive tradition. The first, more Populist than Progressive, more rural and sectional than nationwide in its appeal, represents, in a sense, the roots of modern American isolationism. But this Populist impulse was less pacifistic and isolationist than it was nationalist, anti-European, and anti-English. Although it was by no means devoid of belligerent potential, it was opposed to imperialism or colonialism or militarism. To the good Populist, imperialism was doubly accursed—appeal though it might to his national pride—because it was held to benefit the capitalist and the Wall Streeter rather than the nation at large, and because it was too strongly imitative of the British example. To the Populist who was also a Southerner, imperialism was further questionable because it brought new alien races into the national fold. Hence a great many Americans who had responded with enthusiasm to the war against Spain as a crusade to liberate underdogs in Cuba and to strike at a decadent European aristocratic and Catholic power became as ardently anti-imperialist as they had been prowar, just as soon as they saw some capitalists express an interest in the Philippines as an imperial outpost.

When all this has been said, it must be added that alongside this nationalist belligerence and crusading credulity of the native American, there was a genuine streak of Christian pacifism, too inconsistently held to be an overruling force and yet far from a negligible influence in the

conduct of national affairs. It was this pacifism that Bryan
at times appealed to and that Wilson in good part relied
on during the period when he was "too proud to fight."
Both men drew on the same strain of moral idealism in
their conduct of what Arthur S. Link has called "missionary
diplomacy," in relation to China, Mexico, and the Caribbean countries.[1]

The second source of patriotic and imperialist sentiment
was neither among the Populists nor the ultraconservatives
of the country, but among the fervently patriotic and nationalistic middle-class Americans in all parts of the country who were deeply attracted to Republican insurgency.
It is true that there were among the Republican Progressives a few ardent pacifists like Jane Addams as well as a
small group of isolationists who followed men like the
elder La Follette and George W. Norris in their courageous
last-ditch resistance to American participation in the first
World War. But the main stream of feeling in the ranks
of insurgency was neither anti-war nor anti-imperialist.
Its real spiritual leader, in this as in other respects, was
T. R., with his militarist preachments and his hearty appeals to unselfish patriotism and manliness against self-
seeking and materialistic motives. As William Leuchtenburg has shown, the Progressives, with few exceptions on
scattered issues, either supported the imperialist policies
of the era or quietly acquiesced in them. The majority of
them voted for increased naval expenditures, leaving to
conservatives the task of leading the opposition to big-navy
measures. They took no issue with "Dollar Diplomacy,"
or with Taft's policy when he landed marines in Nicaragua.
Most of them supported T. R. in his adventures in Panama
and the Far East, and his naval expansion. They fought

[1] For an excellent assessment of the merits and defects of missionary
diplomacy, see Arthur S. Link: *Woodrow Wilson and the Progressive
Era* (New York, 1954), chapters iv, v. In the following account I have
benefited from the detailed analysis of the rhetoric of our foreign policy
in Robert Endicott Osgood: *Ideals and Self-Interest in America's Foreign Relations* (Chicago, 1953). See also George F. Kennan: *American
Diplomacy, 1900–1950* (Chicago, 1951), chapter iv.

and voted for policies underwriting American hegemony in
the Caribbean, followed Roosevelt in his contemptuous
(and not altogether unjustified) criticisms of Taft's arbitration treaties, opposed Wilson's magnanimous bill to repeal
the Panama Canal tolls. By 1914 the Progressive Party,
which owed its origins in no small degree to insurgency
over the tariff issue, came out for a higher protective tariff,
and by 1916 it was entirely committed to the defense of
"national honor," excoriation of Wilson, preparedness, and
Americanism. By 1916 "imperialism and militarism had replaced the old liberal formulas of protest, and within a
year the party was dead." [2]

Participation in the war put an end to the Progressive
movement. And yet the wartime frenzy of idealism and
self-sacrifice marked the apotheosis as well as the liquidation of the Progressive spirit. It would be misleading to
imply that American entrance into the war was in any special sense the work of the Progressives, for the final movement toward war was a nationwide movement, shared by
the majority of Americans in both major parties. What is
significant, however, is that the war was justified before
the American public—perhaps had to be justified—in the
Progressive rhetoric and on Progressive terms; and that
the men who went to work for George Creel (himself a
crusading journalist) in the Committee on Public Information, whose job it was to stimulate public enthusiasm for
the war, were in so many instances the same men who
had learned their trade drumming up enthusiasm for the
Progressive reforms and providing articles for the muckraking magazines. By 1912 the Progressive spirit had become so pervasive that any policy—whether it was entrance into the war as rationalized by Wilson or abstention

---

[2] William E. Leuchtenburg: "Progressivism and Imperialism: the Progressive Movement and American Foreign Policy, 1898–1916," *Mississippi Valley Historical Review*, Vol. XXXIX (December 1952), p.
496. Leuchtenburg points out that the Progressives felt that their
idealism and anti-materialism in domestic policies were not contra-
dicted but in fact complemented by their militancy in foreign policy
and their strong faith in the mission of America.

from the war as rationalized by La Follette—could be strengthened if a way could be found to put it in Progressive language. In the end, when the inevitable reaction came, the Progressive language itself seemed to have been discredited.

In the course of the long struggle over neutrality Wilson is the key figure, not merely because of the central power of leadership he exercised but because he was, on this issue, a representative American and a good Progressive citizen who expressed in every inconsistency, every vacillation, every reluctance, the predominant feelings of the country. He embodied, too, the triumph of the Progressive need to phrase the problems of national policy in moral terms.[3] At first, while sharing the common reluctance to become involved in the struggle, he eschewed the "realistic" formula that the whole struggle was none of America's business and that the essence of the American problem was to stay out at all costs. Even his plea for neutrality was pitched in high moral terms: the nation must stay out in order to be of service, to provide a center of sanity uncorrupted by the strains and hatreds of belligerence. It must —the phrase was so characteristic—maintain "absolute self-mastery" and keep aloof in order that it might in the end bring a "disinterested influence" to the settlement.

[3] Although T. R. prided himself on his "realism," I do not think the case was much different with him. He too was a moralist, except that where Wilson invoked pacifistic moral considerations, T. R. was constantly crying for the hairy-chested Darwinian virtues, attacking "cowardice," "ease and soft living," "the pleasures of material well-being," and the like, and dealing with international relations in terms of the "timidity" of a man whose wife has been slapped and who will not fight, and similar juvenile comparisons. "The just war," he once wrote, "is a war for the integrity of high ideals. The only safe motto for the individual citizen of a democracy fit to play a great part in the world is service—service by work and help in peace, service through the high gallantry of entire indifference to life, if war comes on the land." Osgood, op. cit., p. 140. Osgood concludes (ibid., p. 143) that "for more than two years before the United States entered the war Roosevelt's appeals to the American people were couched in terms of saving civilization and the national honor rather than the United States itself. . . . His influence . . . was not, after 1914, directed toward arousing a realistic appraisal of the imperatives of self-preservation."

Then, as the country drew closer to involvement under the pressure of events, Wilson again chose the language of idealism to formulate the American problem—the problem not only whether the United States should intervene, but what might be the valid reasons for intervening. One view —a view widely shared within the Wilson administration and among thoughtful men in the country at large—rested chiefly upon the national interest and cool calculations of the future advantage of the United States. According to this view, a victory for imperial Germany would represent a threat to the long-term interests of the United States in some sense that a victory for the Allies would not. It was expected that a victorious Germany would be more aggressive, more formidable, more anti-American, and that after the defeat of the Allies and the surrender of the British fleet it would either turn upon the United States at some future time or at least present so forceful and continuous a threat as to compel this country to remain a perpetual armed camp in order to protect its security. Therefore, it was argued, it was the business of the United States, as a matter of self-interest, to see to it that the Allies were not defeated—acting if possible as a nonbelligerent, but if necessary as a belligerent. Another view was that intervention in the war could not properly be expressed in such calculating and self-regarding terms, but must rest upon moral and ideological considerations—the defense of international law and freedom of the seas, the rights of small nations, the fight against autocracy and militarism, the struggle to make the world safe for democracy.[4] To be

---

[4] This is not to say that the conception of a German invasion of the United States played no part in pre-intervention discussions of the subject. Fantasies about such an invasion were common in the press. (Osgood, ibid., pp. 132–3.) In its issues from May 1915 to February 1916, *McClure's* ran two series of articles about an imaginary German invasion of the United States in 1921, under the titles "The Conquest of America," and "Saving the Nation." In the end, after the assassination of the President, Theodore Roosevelt, Herman Ridder the German-American, William Jennings Bryan, and Charles Edward Russell the Socialist, all join hands to lead the American people in a spiritual awakening. Much of the discussion of preparedness in this period was in the Rooseveltian vein. Cf. Porter Emerson Browne, "We'll Dally 'round

sure, the argument from self-preservation and national interest and the argument from morals and ideals were not
mutually contradictory, and both tended to have a place
in the course of public discussion. But Wilson's course,
the characteristically Progressive course, was to minimize
and subordinate the self-regarding considerations, and to
place American intervention upon the loftiest possible
plane. He committed himself to this line of action quite
early in the game when he rested so much of his diplomacy
on the issue of the conduct of German submarine warfare
and the freedom of the seas. This was quixotically formulated because it linked the problem of American intervention or non-intervention to an issue of international law—
though one entirely congenial to the Progressive concern
over lawlessness. To Wilson's critics it seemed hypocritical
because in purely formal terms British violations of mari-
time law were about as serious as German violations.
American concern over them could never be pressed so
vigorously because such a course of action would trip over
the more urgent desire to do nothing to impair the chances
of Allied victory.

Our experience after the second World War suggests
that in the long run there was nothing Wilson could have
done to prevent a reaction against both the war itself and
the Progressive movement that preceded the war. But
this too seems almost certain: that by pinning America's
role in the war so exclusively to high moral considerations
and to altruism and self-sacrifice, by linking the foreign
crusade as intimately as possible to the Progressive values
and the Progressive language, he was unintentionally
insuring that the reaction against Progressivism and moral
idealism would be as intense as it could be. For he was
telling the American people, in effect, not that they were
defending themselves, but that as citizens of the world

the Flag, Boys!" *McClure's*, Vol. XLIX (October 1916), p. 81: "Here
we are, the richest nation in the world, and the most supine and the
fattest, both in body and in head. Wallowing in physical luxury, we have
become spiritually so loose, so lax and so lazy that we have almost
lost the capacity to act."

they were undertaking the same broad responsibilities for world order and world democracy that they had been expected, under the Yankee ethos of responsibility, to assume for their own institutions.[5] The crusade for reform and for democratic institutions, difficult as it was at home, was now to be projected to the world scene.[6]

Wilson turned his back on the realistic considerations that might be offered as reasons for intervention, and continually stressed the more grandiose idealistic reasons. He did more than ignore the self-regarding considerations: on occasion he repudiated them. "There is not a single selfish element, so far as I can see, in the cause we are fighting for," he told the people shortly after American entry. "We are fighting for what we believe and wish to be the rights of mankind and for the future peace and security of the world." [7] Again: "We have gone in with no special grievance of our own, because we have always said that we were the friends and servants of mankind. We look for no profit. We look for no advantage." [8] "America," he said, all too truthfully, during the debate over the treaty, ". . . is the only idealistic Nation in the world." [9]

---

[5] Daniel J. Boorstin has pointed out that while Americans had previously hoped on occasion to encourage the growth of representative institutions abroad, as in the period after the revolutions of 1848, it was not until the time of Wilson that there was in this country any serious expectation that this could be done, much less that Americans could be considered to have any responsibility to see to it. The prevailing notion had been, rather, that American institutions were distinctive and that Europe was incapable of adopting them. It was Wilson who first urged Americans to be "citizens of the world" and insisted that their principles were "not the principles of a province or of a single continent . . . [but] the principles of a liberated mankind." "L'Europe vue par l'Amérique du Nord," in Pierre Renouvin et al., eds.: L'Europe du XIXe et du XXe siècles: problèmes et interprétations historiques (Milan, 1955).

[6] And quite literally too. Cf. Bryan as late as 1923: "Our Nation will be saloonless for evermore and will lead the world in the great crusade which will drive intoxicating liquor from the globe." "Prohibition," Outlook, Vol. CXXXIII (February 7, 1923), p. 265.

[7] The Public Papers of Woodrow Wilson (New York, 1925–7), Vol. V, p. 22.

[8] Ibid., p. 33.

[9] Ibid., Vol. VI, p. 52. It is worth noting, by way of contrast, that F. D. R. suggested that the second World War be designated simply the War for Survival.

What takes the sting of chauvinism out of this extraordinary assertion is that Wilson justified it by going to the peace conference without a single distinctively nationalist demand to make, without a single claim for territory, indemnities, or spoils, with no more self-regarding national object than to restrain his allies, make a durable and just peace, and form a League that would secure such a peace for an incalculable future. It was an amazing episode in the history of diplomacy, an episode that repeated with ironic variations the themes of American domestic Progressivism: for here was Wilson, the innocent in the presence of the interests, the reformer among such case-hardened "bosses" of Europe as Lloyd George and Clemenceau, the spokesman of the small man, the voiceless and unrepresented masses, flinging his well-meaning program for the reform of the world into the teeth of a tradition of calculating diplomacy and an ageless history of division and cynicism and strife. But it was not merely upon Europe that Wilson was making impossible demands: he had pushed the idealism and the resolution of his own people— and even, among his own people, of those who were closest to him—beyond the breaking-point. The vein of idealism he was trying to mine was there; but the demands he made upon it assumed that it would be inexhaustible, and his effort to give to the idealism of America an internationalist form reckoned without the fact that his country was not, even in the remotest sense, a country with an internationalist outlook. The traditional American idea had been not that the United States was to lead, rescue, or redeem Europe, but that it was to take its own people in a totally different direction which Europe was presumably incapable of following. The United States was to be a kind of non-Europe or anti-Europe.[1] Where European institutions were old, static, decadent, and aristocratic, American institutions were to be modern, progressive, moral, and democratic. This undercurrent of feeling was as strong in the native American as the uplifting passions of Progres-

[1] Cf. Boorstin, op. cit., passim.

sivism and far stronger than the ephemeral passions of the war period. For a moment the Western Allies might be thought of as exempt from these charges, but before long they would again be considered, as England for instance so characteristically was in the populistic mind, as the embodiment of them.[2]

It was remarkable that Wilson should have succeeded even for a moment in uniting behind him as large a part of the country as he did in an enterprise founded upon the notion of American responsibility for the world. But it is in no way surprising that he should have been resoundingly repudiated in the election of 1920—more resoundingly than any administration before or since. Not long after they began to pay the price of war, the people began to feel that they had been gulled by its promoters both among the allies and in the United States. In this respect the historical revisionists of the postwar period were merely tardy in catching up with them. The war purged the pent-up guilts, shattered the ethos of responsibility that had permeated the rhetoric of more than a decade. It convinced the people that they had paid the price for such comforts of modern life as they could claim, that they had finally answered to the full the Progressive demand for sacrifice and self-control and altruism. In repudiating Wilson, the treaty, the League, and the war itself, they repudiated the Progressive rhetoric and the Progressive mood—for it was Wilson himself and his propagandists who had done so much to tie all these together. Wilson had foreseen that the waging of war would require turning the management of affairs over to the interests the Progressives had been fighting—but this was hardly the change that he had imagined it to be, for only on limited issues and in superficial respects had the management of

[2] Note La Follette's objection to Wilson's argument that it was impossible for democratic America to remain friendly with Prussian autocracy: "But the President proposes alliance with Great Britain which . . . is a hereditary monarchy . . . with a . . . House of Lords, with a hereditary landed system, with a limited . . . suffrage for one class." *Congressional Record*, 65th Congress, 1st Sess., p. 228.

affairs ever been very far out of those hands. The reaction
went farther than this: it destroyed the popular impulse
that had sustained Progressive politics for well over a
decade before 1914. The pressure for civic participation
was followed by widespread apathy, the sense of responsibility by neglect, the call for sacrifice by hedonism. And
with all this there came, for a time, a sense of self-disgust.
By 1920, publishers were warning authors not to send them
manuscripts about the war—people would not hear of it.[8]
When at last they were willing to think about it at all, they
thought of it as a mistake, and they were ready to read
books about the folly of war.

II · Entr'acte

Progressivism had been founded on a mood, and with
the reaction that followed the war that mood was dissipated. Many months before Wilson and his party were
repudiated in the election of 1920 the reaction had begun
under Wilson's own administration. For it was his Attorney
General who did more than any other man to make the
postwar Red scare official. Wilson himself, in refusing a
pardon to Eugene Debs for opposition to the war (a
pardon that was eventually granted by Harding), merely
expressed the political absolutism of a style of thought
whose exponents intended to wipe out every vestige of
sympathy with Bolshevism, just as their fellows had been
planning to wipe out all political corruption and then to
put a final end to the consumption of alcohol. Moods are
intangible, and yet the change in America hung on mood
as much as anything else. It will not do to say, as it has
often been said, that the returning conservatism of the
1920's can be attributed simply to the return of prosperity,
though it is doubtless true that this age of conservatism
would have been shorter if the prosperity itself had not
lasted until 1929. The reaction, in fact, was at its most

[8] *Literary Digest*, Vol. LXVI (August 21, 1920), p. 35.

intense pitch right after the war and during the brief post-war depression. But still more important, the whole Progressive mood from 1900 to 1914 had been a response, we must remember, not to depression but to prosperity and economic well-being.

Naturally it was impossible that a mood so completely dominant in, say, 1912 should have evaporated without any trace ten years later. Yet what stands out is the extent to which Progressivism had either disappeared or transmuted its form. The independent La Follette campaign of 1924 is commonly cited as evidence that Progressivism was not dead during the twenties. Certainly La Follette's platform of 1924, calling for a number of bold and unmistakably Progressive proposals—public ownership of water power, eventual public ownership of railroads, recognition of collective bargaining, greater governmental aid to farmers, a child-labor law, and several mechanical reforms aimed to expand popular democracy—went somewhat farther than the characteristic pre-war Progressivism; and La Follette, without substantial funds or machine support outside his home state, did well to poll 16.6 per cent of the popular vote. But twelve years earlier, when T. R. snatched the banner of Republican insurgency from La Follette, Progressive sentiment had been so general in the country that Taft, the only avowed conservative in the field, could not, even with the aid of several state machines and ample funds, muster so much as one fourth of the total vote. It is the disappearance of this Progressive consensus of 1912 that seems most significant. Moreover, the La Follette vote, often considered as measuring the minimum of Progressive sentiment in the country, was doubtless much stronger than Progressive sentiment itself: much of his support was an ethnic vote based upon his reputation as an opponent of the war; much of it, also, came from disgruntled farmers who resented their exclusion from the general prosperity but who would not have supported the broad program of social-democratic reform promised in

La Follette's platform.[4] Four years later most of La Follette's supporters seem to have voted for Hoover.

There was, throughout the twenties, a continuous sput-
tering of insurgency in the Senate, set off primarily by the
agricultural depression and the refusal of the Republican
Presidents to support strong measures of farm relief. Now
and then the old Populist rhetoric could be heard on Capi-
tol Hill, but it came chiefly from Western leaders who

An analysis of La Follette's vote suggests two considerations of primary importance: first, its sharp sectional character, and second, the
extent to which it drew upon elements not distinctly or consistently
Progressive.

La Follette carried only his own state, Wisconsin. While he ran
well in a number of industrial counties, he carried only one county
east of the Mississippi River, that in southern Illinois. He ran second
to Coolidge in eleven states, almost all of them in the spring wheat,
ranching, mining, or lumbering country of the North Central states
and the Northwest: Minnesota, Iowa, North Dakota, South Dakota,
Montana, Wyoming, Idaho, Washington, Oregon, and California. Six of
these had been carried by Bryan in 1896.

While in most states where he ran second La Follette seems to have
cut chiefly into Republican support, on the West Coast he got much
support from dissident Democrats who had hoped for a liberal nominee
and were disappointed with Davis. See Kenneth C. MacKay: *The
Progressive Movement of 1924* (New York, 1947), p. 223. Roy Peel
and Thomas Donnelly point out that most of the La Follette counties
went for Hoover in 1928: "Smith carried only 43 of the 409 La Follette counties. The Progressives of 1924 were only Republicans in dis-
guise." *The 1928 Campaign: an Analysis* (New York, 1931), p. 122.
In terms of class, La Follette seems to have appealed chiefly to
farmers suffering from agricultural depression and to the railroad
workers, who had been victimized by an extremely sweeping injunction
obtained by Harding's Attorney General, Harry Daugherty, in a major
strike in 1922. MacKay, op. cit., pp. 27–33.

A very large portion of the La Follette vote appears to have been an
anti-war, anti-British, pro-German vote, chiefly among Germans but in
some part among Irish-Americans. MacKay (op. cit., pp. 216–17) doubts
that this was very significant, but for reasons which seem insubstantial.
Samuel Lubell, in a closer study of voting patterns, points to La
Follette's strength in isolationist German-American counties that had not
been Progressive-Bull Moose in 1912 and in counties that turned strongly
against Franklin D. Roosevelt in 1940, after foreign relations became
an important issue. Lubell concludes: "The 4,800,000 votes which La
Follette got in 1924 were often described loosely as the irreducible
minimum of liberal strength in America. Much of that vote, representing approval of La Follette's opposition to war with Germany, actually had nothing to do with liberalism." *The Future of American
Politics* (New York, 1952), p. 140.

could be relied on not to bolt in the presidential elections, and who indeed, as Hiram Johnson saw when he referred to Senator William E. Borah as "our spearless leader," could usually be expected to do nothing drastic. Congressmen from farm states, expressing the "hard" side of agrarian thinking, formed the Farm Bloc to advance agrarian interests. But the Congressional Progressives of the twenties, except for the activities of a rare soul like George W. Norris and the exposure of the Teapot Dome scandal, were on the whole a fake, and many contemporaries knew it.[5]

Under the cover of public indifference, and even with a large measure of public applause, an old-style conservative leadership, of a sort that the country had almost forgotten in the years since 1900, came back into power, unchecked by any serious opposition. While here and there, notably in New York, where Alfred E. Smith's administrations continued to extend social legislation, the reforms of Progressivism still had some modicum of meaning, in the nation at large it was a simple matter to reverse the Progressive policies. The Republican administrations of the twenties raised the tariff to unheard-of heights, devised tax policies that would benefit the "plutocrats" and the large corporations, applauded and assisted in the continued process of business consolidation, and even used such an agency as Wilson's Federal Trade Commission to further the process of consolidation that it had been created to check. Secure in their domination of national politics, the Republican Presidents of the twenties dared even to spurn the farmers and to veto schemes to uphold domestic prices.

---

[5] See the condemnation by A Washington Correspondent: "The Progressives of the Senate," *American Mercury*, Vol. XVI (April 1929), pp. 385–93, in which the Progressives, excepting George W. Norris and Thomas Walsh, are denounced for their lack of militancy and competence and for their underlying party regularity. Senator Peter Norbeck, who was often in the Progressive camp, wrote confidentially to a friend: "The American Mercury article is making quite a sensation around here because much of it is true." Reinhard Luthin: "Smith Wildman Brookhart of Iowa: Insurgent Agrarian Politician," *Agricultural History*, Vol. XXV (October 1951), p. 194.

With the first of these Presidents, corruption, always more
or less normal in state and municipal politics, moved to
Washington; when it was exposed by insurgents, no one
seemed to care, for the Republicans were returned to power
with overwhelming majorities.[6] Nothing else could have
made quite so clear how little the nation at large responded
to the old Progressive rallying cries.

Among the intellectuals themselves, upon whose activities the political culture of Progressivism had always been
so dependent, there was a marked retreat from politics and
public values toward the private and personal sphere, and
even in those with a strong impulse toward dissent, bohe-
mianism triumphed over radicalism. Among the writers of
the younger generation John Dos Passos was almost alone
in his concern for what had been called "the social question." As for the generation of the muckrakers, it was now
becoming the older generation, by and large; for a man
who had been thirty in the year of Theodore Roosevelt's
sudden accession to the presidency was fifty-three in the
year of La Follette's gallant campaign, and if he was characteristic of his type he was in all probability the "Tired
Radical" of Walter Weyl's essay. On the whole, it must be
said, the Progressive generation had few regrets. In 1926,
when Frederic C. Howe in his autobiography, *Confessions
of a Reformer,* raised the question: Where are the radicals?
a liberal magazine held a symposium on the subject which
sounded out a good sample of Progressive opinion.[7] Almost
none of the old reformers found it necessary to indulge in
self-recrimination or apologetics, and a few expressed the
conviction that the very success of the reformers had made

---

[6] What is in fact most striking is the reaction of the respectable press,
which at first thought that the men who exposed the scandal were
beneath contempt. The *New York Times* called them "assassins of
character," the *New York Tribune* "the Montana scandal-mongers";
others accused them of "pure malice and twittering hysteria." Frederick
Lewis Allen: *Only Yesterday* (New York, 1931), pp. 154–5. But in
the Progressive era men had grown fat and famous exposing iniquities
not one tenth as significant as Teapot Dome.

[7] For the symposium, see "Where Are the Pre-War Radicals?" *The
Survey,* Vol. LV (February 1, 1926), pp. 536–66.

a continuation of their work unnecessary. Several believed that the spirit of reform would revive and attach itself, when it was needed, to new causes, perhaps more radical than the old ones. But the dominant note was the feeling that at least for the moment prosperity had cut the ground from under all movements of reform. All seemed to have forgotten the prosperity of the Progressive era,[8] but underneath this misconception lay one implicit prediction that proved correct: the new indifference would last as long as the new prosperity.

But indifference is too strong, or at least too categorical a word. For if the course of American politics and the control of affairs by the grosser and more obtuse type of businessman was widely accepted, the battle with America went on among the intellectuals on a double front. This was the age of "the revolt against the village," the attack on the country mind, that savage repudiation of the old pieties that one found, for instance, in H. L. Mencken's famous diatribe against the American farmer and in his acidulous sketches of Wilson, Bryan, and Roosevelt. And if American capitalism was almost everywhere accepted as a hard fact, it was not accepted as an ideal. Where the writers of the Progressive era had attacked the businessman for his economic and political role, the intellectuals of the twenties still assailed him for his personal and cultural incapacities. Where once he had been speculator, exploiter, corrupter, and tyrant, he had now become boob and philistine, prude and conformist, to be dismissed with disdain along with

---

[8] This common tendency to forget how much dissent the country had been able to generate during prosperity was, of course, quickened by the depression and New Deal experience. Possibly the reformers felt that the prosperity of the 1920's was better distributed than that of the Progressive era, though the surface evidence seems to contradict this notion. Two differences between the two eras of prosperity do stand out: the prosperity of the twenties was characterized by a high degree of price stability, and hence there was no class in the urban population that found itself engaged in the race against inflation that I noted in chapter iv; second, the prosperity of the twenties was marked by the broad diffusion among the public of new consumers' goods that greatly eased life and made it more entertaining—automobiles, radios, telephones, refrigerators, movies, electrified kitchen gadgetry.

most of the institutions of the country. Aloofness from practical politics was not the same as complacency; but if American intelligence, could be measured by the Scopes trial, American justice by the Sacco-Vanzetti case, American tolerance by the Klan, and American political morals by the Prohibition farce and Teapot Dome, it seemed simpler to catch the first liner to Europe or to retire to the library with the *American Mercury* than to engage oneself seriously with proposals to reform American life.

The widespread revolt among liberals and intellectuals against the village mind and the country mind was altogether symptomatic of the breach in Progressivism, for it had been essential to Progressivism to keep the rural and urban insurgents in harmony. For its achievements in the national arena—whether in the line of railroad regulation, anti-trust laws, or financial reform—the Populist-Progressive tradition had always been dependent upon the support it could muster from the West and the South, from the agrarian flanks of reform. Now it was precisely in the West and the South, in the old Bryan country, that the public mood swung most sharply away from the devotion to necessary reforms that had characterized Progressivism at its best. To be sure, the new prosperity of the twenties was spottiest in the farm belt, and there the old Populist discontents were not altogether forgotten. But the strongest enthusiasms of the rural and small-town Americans who understood and loved Bryan were now precisely what the more sophisticated urban Progressive leadership disdained: the crusade to protect fundamentalist religion from modern science, which had its culmination in the Scopes trial; the defense of the eighteenth amendment from all criticism at all costs; and the rallying of the Ku Klux Klan against the Catholics, the Negroes, and the Jews. The pathetic postwar career of Bryan himself, once the bellwether for so many of the genuine reforms, was a perfect epitome of the collapse of rural idealism and the shabbiness of the evangelical mind. For was it not Bryan who made a fortune lecturing on old-time religion, attacking freedom of thought, and promoting Prohibition, while his erstwhile followers celebrated him, no doubt inaccurately, as "the greatest Klansman of our time"?

When the crusading debauch was over, the country's chief inheritance from the Yankee-Protestant drive for morality and from the tensions of the war period was Prohibition. To the historian who likes to trace the development of the great economic issues and to follow the main trend of class politics, the story of Prohibition will seem like a historical detour, a meaningless nuisance, an extraneous imposition upon the main course of history. The truth is that Prohibition appeared to the men of the twenties as a major issue because it *was* a major issue, and one of the most symptomatic for those who would follow the trend of rural-urban conflicts and the ethnic tensions in American politics. It is also one of the leading clues to the reaction against the Progressive temper. For Prohibition, in the twenties, was the skeleton at the feast, a grim reminder of the moral frenzy that so many wished to forget, a ludicrous caricature of the reforming impulse, of the Yankee-Protestant notion that it is both possible and desirable to moralize private life through public action.

To hold the Progressives responsible for Prohibition would be to do them an injustice. Men of an urbane cast of mind, whether conservatives or Progressives in their politics, had been generally antagonistic, or at the very least suspicious, of the pre-war drive toward Prohibition; and on the other side there were many advocates of Prohibition who had nothing to do with other reforms. We cannot, however, quite ignore the diagnostic significance of prohibitionism. For Prohibition was a pseudo-reform, a pinched, parochial substitute for reform which had a widespread appeal to a certain type of crusading mind.[9] It was linked not merely to an aversion to drunkenness and to the evils that accompanied it, but to the immigrant drinking

---

[9] It is perhaps significant that such an early test of Prohibition as the Webb-Kenyon law of 1913 tended to be supported by the Progressives in the Senate and that most of its opponents were conservatives.

masses, to the pleasures and amenities of city life, and to the well-to-do classes and cultivated men. It was carried about America by the rural-evangelical virus: the country Protestant frequently brought it with him to the city when the contraction of agriculture sent him there to seek his livelihood. Students of the Prohibition movement find it easy to believe that the majority sentiment of the country stood in favor of Prohibition at the time the amendment was passed and for some years before; for even many drinking people were sufficiently persuaded by the note of moral uplift to concede that Prohibition might, after all, be a good thing.[1] And even if the desire for Prohibition was a minority sentiment, it was the sentiment of a large minority, one whose intensity and insistency gave its members a power disproportionate to their numbers. Politicians, at any rate, catered to their demands, and there were among them some—one thinks of Bryan as Secretary of State with his much-ridiculed wineless dinners or of Josephus Daniels with his absurd insistence on depriving the Navy officers of their drink—who unquestionably believed that the conquest of the demon rum was one of the important tasks of political life.

Prohibition had not been a sudden product of the war. The demand for liquor reform, long familiar in American politics, seems to have quickened during the Progressive era, notably after about 1908, and the final victory of the amendment was the culmination of five years of heightened agitation by the Anti-Saloon League. The alcohol issue had been approached with the usual Populist-Progressive arguments: it was one of the means by which the interests, in this case the "whisky ring," fattened on the toil of the people. Drinking was pre-eminently a vice of those classes—the plutocrats and corrupt politicians and ignorant immigrants—which the reformers most detested or feared. The saloon, as an institution pivotal in the life of vice on one side and of American urban politics on the

---

[1] Peter Odegard: *Pressure Politics* (New York, 1928), p. 176; cf. Charles Merz: *The Dry Decade* (Garden City, 1931), chapters i, ii.

other, fell under particular reprobation. Like everything else, drink was subject to muckraking, and the readers of the magazines were entertained by articles on alcohol as "the arch enemy of progress," "The Experiences and Observations of a New York Saloon-Keeper," and "The Story of an Alcohol Slave, as Told by Himself," and were even titillated by such pale efforts as "Confessions of a Moderate Drinker." [2]

George Kibbe Turner, a leading muckraker for S. S. McClure, who specialized in exposing prostitution, probably went to the heart of the Prohibition sentiment when he wrote an article attacking the city saloon in which he pointed out that city people constituted each year a larger and larger portion of the whole population and insisted that the first thing to be done in the movement for city reform was "to remove the terrible and undisciplined commercial forces which, in America, are fighting to saturate the populations of cities with alcoholic liquor." [3] During the war the alleged need to conserve materials and the Germanic names of the leading brewers added some force to the prohibitionist propaganda; but what stood the drys in the best stead was the same strong undercurrent of public self-castigation, the same reaction against personal and physical indulgence and material success, that underlay the Progressive tirades against the plutocracy and instigated those appeals to Lincoln Steffens to "come and show us up." The sense that others were fighting battles and making sacrifices in which one somehow *ought* to share was greatly heightened by the war; and the dry agitation, with its demand for self-denial, struck an increasingly con-

---

[2] See *McClure's*, Vol. XXXII (December 1908), pp. 154–61; ibid. (January 1909), pp. 301–12; Vol. XXXIII (August 1909), pp. 426–30; Vol. XXXIV (February 1910), pp. 448–51.

[3] George Kibbe Turner: "Beer and the City Liquor Problem," *McClure's*, Vol. XXXIII (September 1909), p. 543. For the importance of the saloon, which was a central institution for urban politics, see Peter Odegard, op. cit., chapter ii, which also gives an excellent account of the drys' conception of the saloon. It is unfortunate that no one has written a full-dress history of the old-time saloon as an institution, though there are interesting reminiscences on the subject by George Ade and Brand Whitlock.

genial note.[4] When one of the muckrakers wrote the fantasy I have mentioned about the liberation of the country from German invasion, he did not fail to celebrate the heroism of the women's clubs that drew together in a "Women's National War Economy League," whose members all pledged, among many other pledges, to buy "no jewelry or useless ornaments," to buy fewer clothes and cut their entertaining, and "to abstain from cocktails, highballs and all expensive wines, also from cigarettes, to influence husbands, father, brothers, sons and men friends to do the same, and to contribute the amount thus saved to the Woman's National War Fund."[5] Of course this sort of thing could not last forever, but while it was at its pitch the dry lobbyists struck, and when they were finished the Prohibition mania was fixed in the Constitution; and there it remained for almost fifteen years, a symbol of the moral overstrain of the preceding era, the butt of jokes, a perennial source of irritation, a memento of the strange power of crusades for absolute morality to intensify the evils they mean to destroy.

But Prohibition was more than a symbol—it was a means by which the reforming energies of the country were transmuted into mere peevishness. All through the period before the passage of the Volstead Act—and especially before the emergence of the Anti-Saloon League—when the dry crusade spoke the language of social and humanitarian reform, leading Prohibitionists had often been leading reformers,[6]

---

[4] "In almost every case, I am firmly convinced, the drink problem is fundamentally a problem in moral education; and until parents fully appreciate this, and endeavor, in the upbringing of their children, really to establish self-control and self-denial as guiding principles of conduct, we must expect to be called on to extend helping hands to the unhappy victims of drink." H. Addington Bruce: "Why Do Men Drink?" McClure's, Vol. XLII (April 1914), p. 132; italics added. Here, one may see, is another arena for the exercise of that "absolute self-mastery" to which Woodrow Wilson exhorted the American people.

[5] Cleveland Moffett: "Saving the Nation," McClure's, Vol. XLVI (December 1915), pp. 20 ff.

[6] Like Frances E. Willard, for instance, and Upton Sinclair, who as late as 1931 wrote a book against liquor, The Wet Parade (Pasadena, 1931). A political leader like Bryan linked the defense of Prohibition to the

and the churches that gave the strongest support to the Social Gospel movement in American Protestantism were all by the same token supporters of the dry cause. The victory of Prohibition, the transformation of the drinker from a victim of evil to a lawbreaker, the necessity of defending a law that was widely violated, drew many one-time reformers toward the camp of the conservatives, while the circumstances of American politics led them into Catholic-baiting and city-baiting in 1924 and 1928. Prohibition became a low-grade substitute for the old Social Gospel enthusiasms.[7]

The Ku Klux Klan, another rural Protestant enthusiasm of the twenties, also seemed to mock at the old reforming energies of the pre-war period. I say rural, though the important centers of Klan activity were the small towns of the nation almost everywhere outside the Northeast. It did not pay the often mercenary organizers of the Klan to do the traveling and hard work that is necessary to organize the widely scattered dirt farmers; but in the small towns, where gullible nativists were gathered in sufficient numbers to be worth organizing, the spirit of country Protestantism was still strong, and there it was that the fiery crosses were to be found burning. The Klan appealed to relatively unprosperous[8] and uncultivated native white Protestants who had in them a vein of misty but often quite sincere idealism. Generally they lived in areas where they had little real contact with the Catholics and Jews against whom their voices were raised, though of course in the South the Klan became the chief carrier of white supremacy.

The Klan impulse was not usually a response to direct

---

defense of popular rule. See his "Prohibition," *Outlook*, Vol. CXXXIII (February 7, 1923), p. 263.
[7] This process has been analyzed and documented by Paul Carter: *The Decline and Revival of the Social Gospel . . . 1920–40*, unpublished doctoral dissertation, Columbia University, 1954, chapter iii, "Prohibition, Left and Right."
[8] "You think the influential men belong here?" asked an observer in Indiana City. "Then look at their shoes when they march in parade. The sheet doesn't cover the shoes." Frederick Lewis Allen: *Only Yesterday* (New York, 1931), p. 67.

personal relationship or face-to-face competition, but rather
the result of a growing sense that the code by which rural
and small-town Anglo-Saxon America had lived was being
ignored and even flouted in the wicked cities, and especially by the "aliens," and that the old religion and morality
were being snickered at by the intellectuals. The city had
at last eclipsed the country in population and above all as
the imaginative center of American life. For a century and
more the surplus rural population, coming to the city, had
been able to bring to its life a tincture of rural nostalgia
and rural ideals, but now the city was providing to the
nation at large the archetype of the good life. It was the
city that enjoyed the best of the new prosperity, the countryside that lagged behind. But, above all, the city was the
home of liquor and bootleggers, jazz and Sunday golf, wild
parties and divorce. The magazines and newspapers, the
movies and radio, brought tidings of all this to the countryside, and even lured children of the old American stock
away from the old ways. The blame fell upon the immigrants, the Catholics, the Jews—and not really upon the
harmless ones who lived in the neighborhood, but upon
those who peopled the remoter Babylons like New York
and Chicago. The Anglo-Saxon Americans now felt themselves more than ever to be the representatives of a threatened purity of race and ideals, a threatened Protestantism,
even a threatened integrity of national allegiance—for the
war and its aftermath had awakened them to the realization that the country was full of naturalized citizens still
intensely concerned with the politics of Europe and divided in their loyalties.[9]

The Klan's Imperial Wizard and Emperor, Hiram Wesley
Evans, once wrote a candid and at points eloquent statement of Klan aims which states as clearly as any analyst
could the relation between the movement and the decline
of rural Protestant America:[1] ". . . Nordic Americans for

[9] In understanding the Klan, John M. Mecklin's *The Ku Klux Klan*
(New York, 1924) is helpful.
[1] Hiram Wesley Evans: "The Klan's Fight for Americanism," *North
American Review*, Vol. CCXIII (March–April–May 1926), pp. 33–63.

the last generation have found themselves increasingly uncomfortable and finally deeply distressed. There appeared first confusion in thought and opinion, a groping hesitancy about national affairs and private life alike, in sharp contrast to the clear, straightforward purposes of our earlier years. There was futility in religion, too, which was in many ways even more distressing. . . . Finally came the moral breakdown that has been going on for two decades. One by one all our traditional moral standards went by the boards, or were so disregarded that they ceased to be binding. The sacredness of our Sabbath, of our homes, of chastity, and finally even of our right to teach our own children in our own schools fundamental facts and truths were torn away from us. Those who maintained the old standards did so only in the face of constant ridicule.

"Along with this went economic distress. The assurance for the future of our children dwindled. We found our great cities and the control of much of our industry and commerce taken over by strangers, who stacked the cards of success and prosperity against us. Shortly they came to dominate our government. The *bloc* system by which this is done is now familiar to all. . . .

"So the Nordic American today is a stranger in large parts of the land his fathers gave him. . . . Our falling birth rate, the result of all this, is proof of our distress. We no longer feel that we can be fair to children we bring into the world, unless we can make sure from the start that they shall have capital or education or both, so that they need never compete with those who now fill the lower rungs of the ladder of success. We no longer dare risk letting our youth 'make its own way' in the conditions under which we live. . . .

"We are a movement of the plain people, very weak in the matter of culture, intellectual support, and trained leadership. We are demanding . . . a return of power into the hands of the everyday, not highly cultured, not overly intellectualized, but entirely unspoiled and not de-Americanized, average citizen of the old stock. Our members and leaders are all of this class—the opposition of the intellectuals and liberals who held the leadership, betrayed Americanism . . . is almost automatic.

"This is undoubtedly a weakness. It lays us open to the charge of being 'hicks' and 'rubes' and 'drivers of second hand Fords.' We admit it. . . . Every popular movemen has suffered from just this handicap, yet the popular mov ments have been the mainsprings of progress, and have usually had to win against the 'best people' of their time."

The Klansmen felt themselves to be on the defensive against encroaching evils—but these evils were also temptations. The Klansmen had the characteristic preoccupation of censors with the thing censored. (For this reason it was a particularly terrible blow to them when one of their most exalted hobgoblins, the leader of the powerful Indiana Klan, was convicted for a rape-murder.) In many places they presumed to set themselves up as custodians of the public morals or as informal enforcement agents for Prohibition. If a covert yearning for the license of the city underlay some of their activities, an acknowledged need for romance and the exotic may have heightened their hatred of Catholicism. While the Catholics were the primary objects of their resentment, at least outside the South, among the most striking features of the Klan was its enthusiasm for things suggestive of Catholic practices—its elaborate hierarchy of Cyclopses, Kleagles, Klaliffs, Klokards, Kluds, Kligrapps, Klabees, and Klexters, its pride in its ritual (which, said the Imperial Wizard, the members of other orders admitted to be beautiful and extremely dignified), and its clean white vestments, which every layman could wear.[2]

Some estimates of Klan strength indicate that at its peak the Klan had a membership of a little less than

---

[2] There were, it should be recalled, four "Kloranic Orders," of which the two most dignified were "Knights of the Great Forrest (The Order of American Chivalry)" and "Knights of the Midnight Mystery (Superior Order of Knighthood and Spiritual Philosophies)." Stanley Frost: The Challenge of the Klan (Indianapolis, 1924), pp. 298–9.

4,000,000,[3] and if this figure is too high for enrolled members, it can hardly be too high if it embraces as well those whose sentiments were represented by the Klan but who lived outside the reach of its organizing efforts. At any rate its influence was used in the service of political reaction; and the popularity of a man like Bryan among the Klansmen in some areas suggests that its followers included large numbers who had once given their support to the cause of rural reformism.

The Prohibition and Klan issues always divided the Democrats more sharply than the Republicans, and it was within the Democratic Party that the ethnic tensions in American life were more dramatically acted out. Moreover, the collapse of the Democratic Party after the war was so severe that it brought about an effectual breakdown of the two-party system and of useful opposition. The Democrats had traditionally been the minority party since the Civil War, but the balance of the parties during the Progressive era had been close enough to force opportunistic politicians within the Republican ranks to stave off public criticism by adopting in some form many of the most appealing Democratic proposals. In 1912 only the Republican split had made it possible for Wilson to put an end to sixteen years of Republican rule, while Wilson's narrow re-election in 1916 rested upon his success in staying out of the war. The political capital based on the cry: "He kept us out of war" was of course altogether dissipated, and in 1920 the national Democratic ticket polled only 34.5 per cent of the total vote, which was the poorest showing of any major-party ticket since the Civil War era.[4] This disaster, followed by the bitter wrangling and the interminable balloting of the 1924 convention, all but finished the Democrats as a serious opposition.[5] It was the wide gap between

---

[3] Ibid., pp. 7–8.
[4] In the popular vote, though not in the electoral college, Cox was beaten by Harding even more decisively than Landon was beaten by Roosevelt in 1936, for Landon had 36.4 per cent of the total vote.
[5] In 1924, John W. Davis, the Democratic candidate, received only 28.8 per cent of the total vote, Coolidge 54.1 per cent, La Follette 16.6 per cent.

the parties that made it easier for the Republican stand-patters to rebuff the farmers, survive the exposure of corruption, and ignore the La Follette revolt of 1924, for it is when the major-party contest is quite close that third-party revolts are most likely to have a serious impact.

It was not so much in the La Follette movement as in the Democratic Party that the most interesting denouement of Progressivism was to be found and in which the problems of future reform politics were most clearly posed. For it was within the Democratic Party that the conflict between the rural Protestant Yankees and the urban machines raged at its highest. It was in the twenties and in the person of Al Smith that urban immigrant Catholic America first produced a national hero. Smith was a paradox, for he was a Tammanyite and yet a Progressive, a product of an urban machine whose name was synonymous with corruption, and yet a political leader whose governorship gave ample evidence of warm interest in popular welfare. A Catholic, a wet, a graduate of the city streets who had never been to college, an adroit politician with a history of genuine achievement, he became a symbol of the possibilities of urban America. With his coarse voice and uncertain pronunciation and syntax he was a perfect victim for American snobbism, but for the same reason he was a sympathetic figure to those who were shut out from the respectabilities of American middle-class life, and above all to the immigrant stocks. Although the gates to further large-scale immigration had been shut, the active power of the immigrants in politics was just beginning to be felt. The first generation had been relatively passive and submissive, but now the second and even the third generation of the descendants of the great wave of the late nineteenth century were coming of age. They were also growing in pride and self-consciousness. Their interest in politics as something more than a medium of the barest adjustment to American life was beginning to be aroused. Many of them had taken an interest in politics for the first time in connection with the European war, which awakened old loyalties, and many had been moved for the first time to violent enthusiasms on one side or the other by the policies of Wilson, which had an intimate bearing on the fate of almost every European country. Their pride, and often their family plans, had been affected by the closing of the gates in 1921. Their leisure and their amusements had been struck at by the preposterous restrictions of Prohibition, and even their sense of security in America was threatened by the antics of the Klan. To the immigrants, thus aroused, Smith became a natural leader, the more esteemed because the snobs of native stock looked down upon him. The ethnic conflict, heightened by the fight over Prohibition, became during an age of prosperity far more acute than any economic issue.

The ethnic battle went through two phases. The first was fought out within the Democratic Party in 1924. The rural representatives, from the old Bryan constituency, and the Smith followers battled over their differences for seventeen days at Madison Square Garden, while Smith and William Gibbs McAdoo deadlocked the convention for 103 ballots. The fierceness of the squabble was heightened by the dead even equipoise between the forces. On the issue of denouncing the Klan by name the final roll-call decided in the negative by a vote of $543\frac{3}{20}$ to $542\frac{7}{20}$. The delegates left after having nominated a man not conspicuously involved with either faction but also without marked appeal to either, and his showing at the polls was pitiful. Four years later the Smith forces carried the day and named their man, and now the ethnic battle was fought out between the major parties rather than within one of them. Although Smith represented more liberal views than Hoover and was supported by the liberal intelligentsia, both parties truckled so openly to big business that no major economic identification was at stake,[6] and

---

[6] Peel and Donnelly: *The 1928 Campaign*, p. 79. It is true, of course, that Smith attempted more to appeal to those groups which were disaffected by their failure to share in the general prosperity, and that Hoover emphasized the Republican claims to the authorship of prosperity.

the election was fought out quite clearly along the division
between the dry-Protestant-rural and the wet-Catholic-
urban-immigrant affiliations.[7]

Smith's overwhelming defeat in 1928 (he was beaten
almost as badly as four years later Hoover was beaten by
Roosevelt) diverted attention from some of the major
undercurrents in American political life. For one thing,
the election inflicted upon American Catholics, in their
civic capacity, a trauma from which they never fully re-
covered and the consequences of which still haunt the nation. Although Hoover, as the candidate of the incumbent
party in a time of prosperity, and the inheritor of the then
normal Republican majority, would almost certainly have
been elected in any case, the dimensions of his victory had
a great deal to do with the personal snobbery and religious
bigotry invoked against Smith. Not only did the election
underline the fact that it was impossible for a Catholic to
be elected president, but the underground campaign im-
pugned the Americanism of Catholics and thus gave a blow
to their efforts at assimilation and at the achievement of a
full American identity.

Of equal importance were the rise of an urban politics,
and the shrinkage of the Republican majority in the great
industrial centers. As Samuel Lubell has pointed out, this
process went on almost unnoticed, under the cover of
Republican victories. But even in those days of Republican
triumph, the Republican plurality in the twelve largest
cities of the nation shrank from 1,638,000 in 1920 to
1,252,000 in 1924 and fell away altogether before a Democratic plurality of 38,000 in 1928. As Lubell remarks, the
Republican hold on the cities was broken not by Roosevelt

---

[7] Cf. the remark of Walter Lippmann: "Quite apart even from the
severe opposition of the prohibitionists, the objection to Tammany, the
sectional objections to New York, there is an opposition to Smith which
is as authentic and, it seems to me, as poignant as his support. It is
inspired by the feeling that the clamorous life of the city should not
be acknowledged as the American ideal." *Men of Destiny* (New York,
1927), p. 8.

but by Smith. "Before the Roosevelt Revolution there was an Al Smith Revolution." [8] The growing Americanization and the increasing political awareness of the urban immigrant had set in motion an undercurrent that was pulling away from the Republican Party, for in most great centers, the working class, heavily immigrant, Catholic, and wet, and "democratic" in its social bias, moved into the Democratic Party far more readily than it did into the party of Coolidge and Hoover.

What was evident, too, after the internal Democratic strife of 1924 and the defeat of Smith in 1928 was that the Democratic Party, when it was finally to have an opportunity really to challenge the Republicans, must make this challenge behind a candidate who could surmount the feuding that had almost torn the party to pieces. No one realized in 1928 how soon and with what favorable auspices that challenge would be made, but it was becoming clear who could best make it. Franklin D. Roosevelt had long been a Smith supporter and had placed Smith in nomination at the 1924 convention, and yet he was not identified with Tammany in the public mind. At the same time he was a Protestant, and an old-family American, an upstate New Yorker who could make some claims to being a gentleman farmer. As an Assistant Secretary of the Navy under Wilson and as Cox's running mate in the ill-fated campaign of 1920, he had roots in the Progressive past and had made friendships throughout the country that he had not permitted the battles of the twenties to destroy. He was, in short, a thoroughly skilled professional politician who had managed to walk the narrow line between the party factions and maintain relations in both camps. It was his gift to be the first major leader in the history of American reform to surmount the old dualism, so troublesome to the Progressives, between the political ethos of the urban machine and that of nativist Protestant America.

---

[8] Lubell, op. cit., pp. 34–5. Lubell's analysis of the ethnic-religious factor in American politics is extremely revealing.

III · *The New Departure*

The Great Depression, which broke the mood of the twenties almost as suddenly as the postwar reaction had killed the Progressive fervor, rendered obsolete most of the antagonisms that had flavored the politics of the postwar era. Once again the demand for reform became irresistible, and out of the chaotic and often mutually contradictory schemes for salvation that arose from all corners of the country the New Deal took form. In the years 1933–8 the New Deal sponsored a series of legislative changes that made the enactments of the Progressive era seem timid by comparison, changes that, in their totality, carried the politics and administration of the United States farther from the conditions of 1914 than those had been from the conditions of 1880.

It is tempting, out of a desire for symmetry and historical continuity, to see in the New Deal a return to the preoccupations of Progressivism, a resumption of the work of reform that had begun under Theodore Roosevelt and Woodrow Wilson, and a consummation of the changes that were proposed in the half-dozen years before the first World War. Much reason can be found for yielding to this temptation. Above all, the New Dealers shared with the Progressives a far greater willingness than had been seen in previous American history to make use of the machinery of government to meet the needs of the people and supplement the workings of the national economy. There are many occasions in its history when the New Deal, especially in its demand for organization, administration, and management from a central focus, seems to stand squarely in the tradition of the New Nationalism for which such Progressives as Herbert Croly had argued. Since it is hardly possible for any society to carve out a completely new vocabulary for every new problem it faces, there is also much in the New Deal rhetoric that is strongly reminiscent of Progressivism. Like the Progressives, the New

Dealers invoked a larger democracy; and where the Progressives had their "plutocrats," the New Dealers had their "economic royalists." F. D. R., asserting in his first inaugural address that "The money changers have fled from their high seats in the temple of our civilization. We may now restore that temple to the ancient truths," sounds very much like almost any inspirational writer for *McClure's* in the old days.[9] On a number of particular issues, moreover, like the holding-company question, monopoly, and public power, one feels as though one is treating again, in the New Deal, with familiar problems—just as, in the crucial early days of 1933, the formation of a strong bloc of inflationist Senators from the West seemed to hark back to the Populist movement.

Still, granting that absolute discontinuities do not occur in history, and viewing the history of the New Deal as a whole, what seems outstanding about it is the drastic new departure that it marks in the history of American reformism.[1] The New Deal was different from anything that had yet happened in the United States: different because its central problem was unlike the problems of Progressivism; different in its ideas and its spirit and its techniques. Many men who had lived through Progressivism and had thought of its characteristic proposals as being in the main line of American traditions, even as being restoratives of those traditions, found in the New Deal an outrageous departure from everything they had known and valued, and so could interpret it only as an effort at subversion or as the result

---

* Naturally there was also some continuity in personnel, for F. D. R. himself was only one of a considerable number of American leaders who had been young Progressives before the war and were supporters of the major reforms of the thirties. However, one could draw up an equally formidable list—chiefly Republican insurgents of the Bull Moose era, but also many Democrats—who had supported Progressive measures and later became heated critics of the New Deal.

[1] Here I find myself in agreement with the view expressed by Samuel Lubell (op. cit., p. 3): "The distinctive feature of the political revolution which Franklin D. Roosevelt began and Truman inherited lies not in its resemblance to the political wars of Andrew Jackson or Thomas Jefferson, but in its abrupt break with the continuity of the past."

of overpowering alien influences. Their opposition was all
too often hysterical, but in their sense that something new
had come into American political and economic life they
were quite right.

Consider, to begin, the fundamental problem that the
New Dealers faced, as compared with the problems of the
Progressives. When Theodore Roosevelt took office in
1901, the country was well over three years past a severe
depression and in the midst of a period of healthy economic
development. Its farmers were more prosperous than they
had been for about forty years, its working class was
employed and gaining in living standards, and even its
middle class was far busier counting the moral costs of
success than it was worrying about any urgent problems of
family finance. When F. D. R. took his oath of office, the
entire working apparatus of American economic life had
gone to smash. The customary masters and leaders of the
social order were themselves in a state of near panic.
Millions were unemployed, and discontent had reached a
dangerous pitch on the farms and in the cities.

Indeed, the New Deal episode marks the first in the
history of reform movements when a leader of the reform
party took the reins of a government confronted above all
by the problems of a sick economy. To be sure, the whole
nineteenth-century tradition of reform in American politics
was influenced by experience with periodic economic
breakdowns; but its political leaders had never had to bear
responsibility for curing them. Jefferson in 1801, Jackson in
1829, and after them T. R. and Wilson—all took over at
moments when the economy was in good shape. While
each of them had experience with economic relapse—
Jefferson in 1807, as the consequence of his embargo policies, the Jacksonians briefly in 1834 and again after 1837,
T. R. briefly during the "bankers' panic" of 1907, and
Wilson with a momentary recession just before the wartime
boom—their thinking, and the thinking of the movements
they represented, was centered upon sharing an existing

prosperity among the various social classes rather than upon restoring a lost prosperity or preventing recurrent slumps.

The earlier American tradition of political protest had been a response to the needs of entrepreneurial classes or of those who were on the verge of entrepreneurship—the farmers, small businessmen, professionals, and occasionally the upper caste of the artisans or the working class. The goal of such classes had generally been to clear the way for new enterprises and new men, break up privileged business, big business, and monopolies, and give the small man better access to credit. The ideas of this Progressive tradition, as one might expect, were founded not merely upon acceptance but even upon glorification of the competitive order. The Jeffersonians, the Jacksonians, and after them most of the Progressives had believed in the market economy, and the only major qualification of this belief they cared to make stemmed from their realization that the market needed to be policed and moralized by a government responsive to the needs of the economic beginner and the small entrepreneur. Occasionally, very occasionally, they had argued for the exercise of a few positive functions on the part of the national government, but chiefly they preferred to keep the positive functions of government minimal, and, where these were necessary, to keep them on the state rather than put them on the national level. Their conceptions of the role of the national government were at first largely negative and then largely preventive. In the Jeffersonian and Jacksonian days it was to avoid excessive expenditure and excessive taxation, to refrain from giving privileged charters. Later, in the corporate era, it was to prevent abuses by the railroads and the monopolists, to check and to regulate unsound and immoral practices. It is of course true that some of the more "advanced" thinkers of the Populist and Progressive movements began to think tentatively of more positive functions for government, but it was just such proposals—the sub-

treasury scheme for agricultural credits and the various
public-ownership proposals—that provoked the greatest
opposition when attempts were made to apply them on a
national scale.

The whole reformist tradition, then, displayed a mentality founded on the existence of an essentially healthy
society; it was chiefly concerned not with managing an
economy to meet the problems of collapse but simply with
democratizing an economy in sound working order. Managing an economy in such a way as to restore prosperity is
above all a problem of organization,[2] while democratizing
a well-organized economy had been, as we have seen, in
some important respects an attempt to find ways of attacking or limiting organization. Hence the Progressive mind
was hardly more prepared than the conservative mind for
what came in 1929. Herbert Hoover, an old Bull Mooser,
while more disposed to lead the country than any president
had been in any previous depression, was unprepared for
it, and was prevented from adjusting to it by a doctrinaire
adherence to inherited principles. F. D. R.—a fairly typical
product of Progressivism who had first won office in 1910
—was also unprepared for it in his economic thinking, as
anyone will see who examines his career in the 1920's;[3]
but he was sufficiently opportunistic and flexible to cope
with it somewhat more successfully.

Hoover, an engineer born in Iowa, represented the moral
traditions of native Protestant politics. An amateur in
politics who had never run for office before he was elected
President in 1928, he had no patience with the politician's
willingness to accommodate, and he hung on, as inflexibly
as the situation would permit, to the private and voluntary
methods that had always worked well in his administrative

---

[2] The closest thing to an earlier model for the first efforts of the New
Deal was not the economic legislation of Progressivism but the efforts
of the Wilson administration to organize the economy for the first
World War. Hugh Johnson in the NRA and George Peek in the AAA
were in many ways recapitulating the experience they had had in the
War Industries Board under Bernard Baruch.

[3] See Frank Freidel's *Franklin D. Roosevelt: the Ordeal* (Boston, 1954),
and his forthcoming volume on F. D. R.'s governorship.

career.[4] F. D. R., a seasoned professional politician who
had learned his trade straddling the terrible antagonisms
of the 1920's, was thoroughly at home in the realities of
machine politics and a master of the machine techniques
of accommodation. Unlike Hoover, he had few hard and
fast notions about economic principles, but he knew that it
would be necessary to experiment and improvise. "It is
common sense," he said in 1932, "to take a method and try
it. If it fails, admit it frankly and try another. But above all,
try something."

To describe the resulting flood of legislation as economic
planning would be to confuse planning with intervention-
ism. Planning was not quite the word for the New Deal:
considered as an economic movement, it was a chaos of
experimentation. Genuine planners like Rexford Guy Tug-
well found themselves floundering amid the cross-currents
of the New Deal, and ended in disillusionment. But if, from
an economic standpoint, the New Deal was altogether lacking in that rationality or consistency which is implied in
the concept of planning, from a political standpoint it represented a masterly shifting equipoise of interests. And
little wonder that some of the old Republican insurgents
shuddered at its methods. If the state was believed neutral
in the days of T. R. because its leaders claimed to sanction
favors for no one, the state under F. D. R. could be called
neutral only in the sense that it offered favors to everyone.

Even before F. D. R. took office a silent revolution had
taken place in public opinion, the essential character of
which can be seen when we recall how little opposition
there was in the country, at the beginning, to the assumption of the New Dealers that henceforth, for the purposes
of recovery, the federal government was to be responsible
for the condition of the labor market as a part of its concern with the industrial problem as a whole. Nothing

---

[4] Characteristically, also, Hoover accepted what might be called the
nativist view of the Great Depression: it came from abroad; it was the
product, not of any deficiencies in the American economy, but of re-
percussions of the unsound institutions of Europe.

revolutionary was intended—but simply as a matter of politics it was necessary for the federal government to assume primary responsibility for the relief of the unemployed. And, simply as a matter of politics, if the industrialists were to be given the power to write enforceable codes of fair practice, labor must at least be given some formal recognition of its right of collective bargaining. Certainly no one foresaw, in the first year or two of the New Deal, that the immense infusions of purchasing power into the economy through federal unemployment relief would be as lasting or as vital a part of the economy of the next several years as they proved in fact to be. Nor did anyone foresee how great and powerful a labor movement would be called into being by the spirit and the promise of the New Deal and by the partial recovery of its first few years. But by the end of 1937 it was clear that something had been added to the social base of reformism. The demands of a large and powerful labor movement, coupled with the interests of the unemployed, gave the later New Deal a social-democratic tinge that had never before been present in American reform movements. Hitherto concerned very largely with reforms of an essentially entrepreneurial sort and only marginally with social legislation, American political reformism was fated henceforth to take responsibility on a large scale for social security, unemployment insurance, wages and hours, and housing.[5]

Still more imposing was the new fiscal role of the federal government. Again, none of this was premeditated. Large-scale spending and unbalanced budgets were, in the beginning, a response to imperative needs. While other schemes

[5] As the counsel for the National Association of Manufacturers put it: "Regulation has passed from the negative stage of merely preventing unlawful and improper conduct, to the positive stage of directing and controlling the character and form of business activity. The concept that the function of government was to prevent exploitation by virtue of superior power has been replaced by the concept that it is the duty of government to provide security against all the major hazards of life —against unemployment, accident, illness, old age, and death." Thomas P. Jenkin: *Reactions of Major Groups to Positive Government in the United States* (Berkeley, 1945), pp. 300–1.

for recovery seemed to fall short of expectations, spending kept the economy going; and it was only when F. D. R. tried in 1937 to cut back expenditures that he learned that he had become the prisoner of his spending policies, and turned about and made a necessity into a virtue. His spending policy never represented, at any time before the outbreak of the war, an unambiguous or wholehearted commitment to Keynesian economics. Here only the war itself could consummate the fiscal revolution that the New Deal began. In 1940 Lord Keynes published in the United States an article in which he somewhat disconsolately reviewed the American experience with deficit spending during the previous decade. "It seems politically impossible," he concluded, "for a capitalistic democracy to organize expenditure on the scale necessary to make the grand experiment which would prove my case—except in war conditions." He then added that preparations for war and the production of armaments might teach Americans so much about the potentialities of their economy that it would be "the stimulus, which neither the victory nor the defeat of the New Deal could give you, to greater individual consumption and a higher standard of life."[6] How remarkably prophetic this was we can now see. There had been under peacetime conditions an immense weeping and wailing over the budgets of F. D. R.—which at their peak ran to seven billion dollars. Now we contemplate budgets of over eighty billion dollars with somewhat less anguish, because we know that most of this expenditure will be used for defense and will not be put to uses that are politically more controversial. But, above all, we have learned things about the possibilities of our economy that were not dreamed of in 1933, much less in 1903. While men still grow angry over federal fiscal and tax policies, hardly anyone doubts that in the calculable future it will be the fiscal role of the government that more than anything else determines the course of the economy.

---

[6] J. M. Keynes: "The United States and the Keynes Plan," *New Republic*, Vol. CIII (July 29, 1940), p. 158.

And what of the old Progressive issues? They were by-passed, sidestepped, outgrown—anything but solved. To realize how true this was, one need only look at the New Deal approach to those two *bêtes noires* of the Progressive mind, the machines and the trusts.

Where the Progressives spent much of their energy, as we have seen, trying to defeat the bosses and the machines and to make such changes in the political machinery of the country as would bring about direct popular democracy and "restore government to the people," the New Deal was almost completely free of such crusading. To the discomfort of the old-fashioned, principled liberals who were otherwise enthusiastic about his reforms, F. D. R. made no effort to put an end to bossism and corruption, but simply ignored the entire problem. In the interest of larger national goals and more urgent needs, he worked with the bosses wherever they would work with him—and did not scruple to include one of the worst machines of all, the authoritarian Hague machine in New Jersey. As for the restoration of democracy, he seemed well satisfied with his feeling that the broadest public needs were at least being served by the state and that there was such an excellent rapport between the people and their executive leadership.[7]

The chief apparent exception to this opportune and managerial spirit in the field of political reform—namely, the attempt to enlarge the Supreme Court—proves on examination to be no exception at all. F. D. R.'s fight over the Supreme Court was begun, after all, not in the interest of some large "democratic" principle or out of a desire to reform the Constitutional machinery as such, but because the Court's decisions had made it seem impossible to achieve the managerial reorganization of society that was so urgently needed. His first concern was not that judicial review was "undemocratic" but that the federal govern-

---

[7] Of course to speak of democracy in purely domestic terms is to underestimate the world-wide significance of the New Deal. At a time when democracy was everywhere in retreat, the New Deal gave to the world an example of a free nation coping with the problems of its economy in a democratic and humane way.

ment had been stripped, as he thought, of its power to deal effectively with economic problems. Nor was this fight waged in the true Progressive spirit. The Progressives, too, had had their difficulties with the judiciary, and had responded with the characteristically principled but practically difficult proposal for the recall of judicial decisions. In short, they raised for reconsideration, as one might expect of principled men, the entire question of judicial review. F. D. R. chose no such method.[8] To reopen the entire question of the propriety of judicial review of the acts of Congress under a representative democracy would have been a high-minded approach to what he felt was a Constitutional impasse, but it would have ended perhaps even more disastrously than the tactic he employed. F. D. R. avoided such an approach, which would have involved a cumbersome effort to amend the Constitution, and devised a "gimmick" to achieve his ends—the pretense that the age of the judges prevented them from remaining abreast of their calendar, and the demand for the right to supplement the judiciary, to the number of six, with an additional judge for each incumbent who reached the age of seventy without retiring.

Students of the Court fight are fond of remarking that Roosevelt won his case, because the direction of the Court's decisions began to change while the fight was in progress and because Justice Van Devanter's retirement enabled the President to appoint a liberal justice and decisively change the composition of the Court.[9] It seems important,

[8] Indeed, in his message calling for reorganization Roosevelt declared that his proposal would make unnecessary any fundamental changes in the powers of the courts or in the Constitution, "changes which involve consequences so far-reaching as to cause uncertainty as to the wisdom of such a course." It remained for the leading senatorial opponent of the bill, Senator Burton K. Wheeler, to advocate an amendment to the Constitution permitting Congress to override judicial vetoes of its acts. Charles A. and Mary R. Beard: *America in Midpassage* (New York, 1939), Vol. I, p. 355.
[9] Presumably it will always be debated whether the new harmony between Congress and the Supreme Court that developed even while the Court fight was going on can be attributed to Roosevelt's Court reform bill. Merlo Pusey in his *Charles Evans Hughes* (Vol. II, pp.

however, to point out that a very heavy price had to be
paid for even this pragmatic attempt to alter a great and
sacrosanct conservative institution. The Court fight alienated many principled liberals and enabled many of
F. D. R.'s conservative opponents to portray him to the
public more convincingly as a man who aspired to personal
dictatorship and aimed at the subversion of the Republic.

If we look at the second of the two great foes of Progressivism, big business and monopoly, we find that by the
time of the New Deal public sentiment had changed materially. To be sure, the coming of the depression and the
revelation of some of the less palatable business practices
of the 1920's brought about a climate of opinion in which
the leadership of business, and particularly of big business,
was profoundly distrusted and bitterly resented. Its position
certainly was, in these respects, considerably weaker than
it had been twenty-five years before. Still, by 1933 the
American public had lived with the great corporation for
so long that it was felt to be domesticated, and there was
far more concern with getting business life on such a foot-
ing as would enable it to provide jobs than there was with
breaking up the larger units. The New Deal never developed a clear or consistent line on business consolidation,
and New Dealers fought over the subject in terms that
were at times reminiscent of the old battles between the
trust-busters and the trust-regulators. What can be said,
however, is that the subject of bigness and monopoly was
subordinated in the New Deal era to that restless groping
for a means to bring recovery that was so characteristic of
Roosevelt's efforts. The New Deal began not with a flourish

766 ff.) argues that the change in the Court's decisions was not a
political response to the legislative struggle. He points out, among
other things, that the New Deal legislation that came before the Court
after the NRA and AAA decisions was better drafted. It is beyond
doubt, however, that the resignation of Van Devanter was precipitated
by the Court fight. Ibid., Vol. II, p. 761. The fact that advocates of
both sides can go on arguing about who won the fight is the best
evidence that the issue was satisfactorily settled. It aroused so much
feeling that an unambiguous victory for either side would have been
unfortunate.

of trust-busting but rather, in the NRA, with an attempt to solve the problems of the business order through a gigantic system of governmentally underwritten codes that would ratify the trustification of society. One of the first political setbacks suffered by the New Deal arose from just this— for it had put the formation of its codes of fair practice so completely in the hands of the big-business interests that both small businessmen and organized labor were seriously resentful. Only five years from the date of its passage, after the NRA had failed to produce a sustained recovery and had been declared unconstitutional by the Supreme Court, did the administration turn off and take the opposite tack with its call for an inquiry into corporate consolidation and business power that led to the Temporary National Economic Committee's memorable investigation.[1] Although at the time many observers thought that the old Progressive trust-busting charade was about to be resumed, the New Deal never became committed to a categorical "dissection" of the business order of the sort Wilson had talked of in 1912, nor to the "demonstration" prosecutions with which T. R. had both excited and reassured the country. The New Deal was not trying to re-establish the competitive order that Wilson had nostalgically invoked and that T. R. had sternly insisted was no longer possible. Its approach, as it turned out, was severely managerial, and distinctly subordinated to those economic considerations that would promote purchasing power and hence recovery. It was, in short, a concerted effort to discipline the pricing policies of businesses, not with the problem of size in mind, nor out of consideration for smaller competitors, but with the purpose of eliminating that private power to tax which is the prerogative of monopoly, and of leaving in the hands of consumers vital purchasing power.

History cannot quite repeat itself, if only because the participants in the second round of any experience are aware of the outcome of the first. The anti-trust philoso-

---

[1] There had been in the meantime, however, the assault upon the holding companies embodied in the so-called "death sentence" of 1935.

phers of the closing years of the New Deal were quite
aware that previous efforts to enforce the Sherman Act had
been ceremonial demonstrations rather than serious assaults
upon big business. Thurman Arnold, who was put in charge
of the anti-trust program, was well known for his belief that
earlier interpretations of the Sherman Act had actually
concealed and encouraged business consolidation. In his
account of the contemporary function of anti-trust prosecution Arnold put his emphasis upon benefits for the consumer and repudiated the earlier use of the Sherman Act:
"Since the consumers' interest was not emphasized, such
enforcement efforts as existed were directed at the punishment of offenses rather than the achievement of economic
objectives. Indeed, in very few antitrust prosecutions was
any practical economic objective defined or argued with
respect to the distribution of any particular product. In
this way the moral aspects of the offense, and that will-
o'-the-wisp, corporate intent, became more important considerations than economic results. Antitrust enforcement,
not being geared to the idea of consumers' interests, became a hunt for offenders instead of an effort to test the
validity of organized power by its performance in aiding
or preventing the flow of goods in commerce. The result
was that although the economic ideal of a free competitive
market as the cornerstone of our economy was kept alive,
no adequate enforcement staff was ever provided to make
that ideal a reality. Such, broadly speaking, was the state
of the Sherman Act from 1890 down to the great depression." [2]

But if such a position as Thurman Arnold's can be legitimately distinguished from the Progressive type of anti-
trust, as I think it can, there are men today whose political
thinking was forged in the service of the New Deal who
go beyond him in repudiating anti-trust action as a mere
attack upon size, and who take, on the whole, an acquies-
cent attitude toward big business. A few years ago John

---

[2] Thurman Arnold: *The Bottlenecks of Business* (New York, 1940),
p. 263.

Kenneth Galbraith made quite a stir with his book *American Capitalism,* whose central thesis was that the process of business consolidation creates within itself a "countervailing power"—that is, that it brings about the organization not merely of strong sellers but of strong buyers as well, who distribute through large sectors of the economy their ability to save through organization.[3] In Galbraith's book, as in most recent literature in defense of bigness, it is not the effort at disorganization but the effects of counterorganization, in labor, agriculture, and government and within business itself, that are counted upon to minimize the evils of consolidation. More recently David Lilienthal, another graduate of the New Deal administrative agencies, has written a strong apologia for big business that followed Galbraith in stressing the technologically progressive character of large-scale industry in language that would have horrified Brandeis and Wilson.[4] It is not clear whether the attitudes of men like Galbraith and Lilienthal represent dominant liberal sentiment today—though it may be pertinent to say that their books brought no outpouring of protest from other liberal writers. The spectacle of liberals defending, with whatever qualifications, bigness and concentration in industry suggests that that anti-monopoly sentiment which was so long at the heart of Progressive thinking is no longer its central theme. The generation for which Wilson and Brandeis spoke looked to economic life as a field for the expression of character; modern liberals seem to think of it quite exclusively as a field in which certain results are to be expected. It is this change in the

---

[3] This is a rather simplified statement of the thesis of Galbraith's *American Capitalism* (Boston, 1952). Students of the history of antitrust ideologies will be particularly interested in Galbraith's strictures on the TNEC Report (pp. 59–60).

[4] Galbraith argues that "the competition of the competitive model . . . almost completely precludes technical development" and that indeed "there must be some element of monopoly in an industry if it is to be progressive." Ibid., pp. 91, 93, and chapter vii, *passim*. Cf. David Lilienthal: *Big Business: a New Era* (New York, 1953), chapter vi. For another such friendly treatment by a former New Dealer, see Adolph A. Berle: *The Twentieth Century Capitalist Revolution* (New York, 1954).

moral stance that seems most worthy of remark. A generation ago, and more, the average American was taught to
expect that a career in business would and should be in
some sense a testing and proving ground for character and
manhood, and it was in these terms that the competitive
order was often made most appealing.[5] Contrariwise, those
who criticized the economic order very commonly formed
their appeals within the same mold of moral suasion: the
economic order failed to bring out or reward the desired
qualities of character, to reward virtue and penalize vice;
it was a source of inequities and injustices. During the last
fifteen or twenty years, however, as Galbraith observes,
"the American radical has ceased to talk about inequality
or exploitation under capitalism or even its 'inherent con-
tradictions.' He has stressed, instead, the unreliability of its
performance." [6]

IV · The New Opportunism

The New Deal, and the thinking it engendered, represented the triumph of economic emergency and human
needs over inherited notions and inhibitions. It was conceived and executed above all in the spirit of what Roosevelt called "bold, persistent experimentation," and what
those more critical of the whole enterprise considered crass
opportunism. In discussing Progressivism I emphasized its
traffic in moral absolutes, its exalted moral tone. While
something akin to this was by no means entirely absent
from the New Deal, the later movement showed a strong
and candid awareness that what was happening was not

[5] See, for instance, the touching letter quoted by Lilienthal (op. cit.,
p. 198), from a university graduate of the twenties: "We were dis-
mayed at the vista of mediocre aspiration and of compartmentalized
lives. The course of a big business career was predictable and fore-
closed. It was also, as the personnel department pointed out, secure.
The appeal of graduated salary raises and retirement on a pension was
held out as the big lure. But in my high school days the appeal had
been to ambition, a good deal was said about achievement and independence."
[6] Galbraith, op. cit., p. 70.

so much moral reformation as economic experimentation. Much of this experimentation seemed to the conservative opponents of the New Deal as not only dangerous but immoral.

The high moral indignation of the critics of the New Deal sheds light on another facet of the period—the relative reversal of the ideological roles of conservatives and reformers. Naturally in all ideologies, conservative or radical, there is a dual appeal to ultimate moral principles and to the practical necessities of institutional life. Classically, however, it has been the strength of conservatives that their appeal to institutional continuities, hard facts, and the limits of possibility is better founded; while it has usually been the strength of reformers that they arouse moral sentiments, denounce injustices, and rally the indignation of the community against intolerable abuses. Such had been the alignment of arguments during the Progressive era. During the New Deal, however, it was the reformers whose appeal to the urgent practical realities was most impressive—to the farmers without markets, to the unemployed without bread or hope, to those concerned over the condition of the banks, the investment market, and the like. It was the conservatives, on the other hand, who represented the greater moral indignation and rallied behind themselves the inspirational literature of American life; and this not merely because the conservatives were now the party of the opposition, but because things were being done of such drastic novelty that they seemed to breach all the inherited rules, not merely of practicality but of morality itself. Hence, if one wishes to look for utopianism in the 1930's, for an exalted faith in the intangibles of morals and character, and for moral indignation of the kind that had once been chiefly the prerogative of the reformers, one will find it far more readily in the editorials of the great conservative newspapers than in the literature of the New Deal. If one seeks for the latter-day equivalent of the first George Kennan, warning the people of San Francisco that it would do them no good to have a prosperous 'own if in gaining

it they lost their souls, one will find it most readily in the
1930's among those who opposed federal relief for the unemployed because it would destroy their characters or who
were shocked by the devaluation of the dollar, not because
they always had a clear conception of its consequences, but
above all because it smacked to them of dirtiness and dis-
honesty. In the past it had been the conservatives who
controlled the settlement of the country, set up its great
industrial and communications plant, and founded the
fabulous system of production and distribution upon which
the country prided itself, while the reformers pointed to
the human costs, the sacrifice of principles, and drew blueprints to show how the job could be better done. Now,
however, it was the reformers who fed the jobless or found
them jobs, saved the banks, humanized industry, built
houses and schools and public buildings, rescued farmers
from bankruptcy, and restored hope—while the conservatives, expropriated at once from their customary control of
affairs and from their practical role, invoked sound principles, worried about the Constitution, boggled over details,
pleaded for better morals, and warned against tyranny.

Lamentably, most of the conservative thinking of the
New Deal era was hollow and cliché-ridden. What seems
most striking about the New Deal itself, however, was that
all its ferment of practical change produced a very slight
literature of political criticism. While the changes of the
Progressive era had produced many significant books of
pamphleteering or thoughtful analyses of society—the
writings of such men as Croly, Lippmann, Weyl, Brooks
Adams, Brandeis, the muckrakers, Socialist critics like
W. J. Ghent and William English Walling—the New Deal
produced no comparable body of political writing that
would survive the day's headlines. In part this was simply
a matter of time: the Progressive era lasted over a dozen
years, and most of the significant writing it engendered
came during its later phases, particularly after 1910;
whereas the dynamic phase of the New Deal was concentrated in the six hectic years from 1933 to 1938. Perhaps

still more important is the fact that the New Deal brought
with it such a rapid bureaucratic expansion and such a
complex multitude of problems that it created an immense
market for the skills of reform-minded Americans from law,
journalism, politics, and the professoriat. The men who
might otherwise have been busy analyzing the meaning of
events were caught up in the huge expanding bureaucracy
and put to work drafting laws that would pass the courts,
lobbying with refractory Congressmen, or relocating sharecroppers.

To this generalization there is one noteworthy exception:
In his two books, *The Symbols of Government* and *The
Folklore of Capitalism*, Thurman Arnold wrote works of
great brilliance and wit and considerable permanent significance—better books, I believe, than any of the political
criticism of the Progressive era.[7] But what do we find in
these works, the most advanced of the New Deal camp?
We find a sharp and sustained attack upon ideologies,
rational principles, and moralism in politics. We find, in
short, the theoretical equivalent of F. D. R.'s opportunistic
virtuosity in practical politics—a theory that attacks theories. For Arnold's books, which were of course directed
largely against the ritualistic thinking of the conservatives
of the 1930's, might stand equally well as an attack upon
that moralism which we found so insistent in the thinking
of Progressivism.

Arnold's chief concern was with the disparities between
the way society actually works and the mythology through
which the sound lawyers, economists, and moralists attempt to understand it. His books are an explanation of the
ritualistic and functionally irrational character of most of
the superficially rational principles by which society lives.
At the time his books were written, the necessity of coping
with a breakdown in the actual workings of the economy

---

[7] Thurman W. Arnold: *The Symbols of Government* (New Haven,
1935), *The Folklore of Capitalism* (New Haven, 1937). By 1941 the
first of these works had gone through five printings; the second, four-
teen.

had suddenly confronted men with the operational uselessness of a great many accepted words and ideas. The language of politics, economics, and law had itself become so
uncertain that there was a new vogue of books on seman-
tics and of works attempting to break "the tyranny of
words," a literature of which Arnold's books were by far
the most important. The greater part of Arnold's task was
to examine, and to satirize, the orthodox conservative
thinking of the moment. This is not our main concern, but
what is of primary interest here is the extent to which
Arnold's thinking departs from, and indeed on occasion
attacks, earlier Progressivism. The deviation of Arnold's
system of values from the classic values of American Progressivism was clear from his very terminology. I noted,
in discussing the Progressive climate of opinion, the existence of a prevailing vocabulary of civic morals that reflected the disinterested thinking and the selfless action
that was expected of the good citizen. The key words of
Progressivism were terms like *patriotism, citizen, democracy, law, character, conscience, soul, morals, service, duty,
shame, disgrace, sin,* and *selfishness*—terms redolent of the
sturdy Protestant Anglo-Saxon moral and intellectual roots
of the Progressive uprising. A search for the key words of
Arnold's books yields: *needs, organization, humanitarian,
results, technique, institution, realistic, discipline, morale,
skill, expert, habits, practical, leadership*—a vocabulary
revealing a very different constellation of values arising
from economic emergency and the imperatives of a bureaucracy.

Although primarily concerned with the conservatives of
the present, Arnold paid his respects to the reformers of the
past often enough to render a New Dealer's portrait of
earlier Progressivism. He saw the reformers of the past as
having occupied themselves with verbal and moral battles
that left the great working organizations of society largely
untouched. "Wherever the reformers are successful—whenever they see their direct primaries, their antitrust laws, or
whatever else they base their hopes on, in actual operation

—the great temporal institutions adapt themselves, leaving the older reformers disillusioned, like Lincoln Steffens, and a newer set carrying on the banner." [8] Respectable people with humanitarian values, Arnold thought, had characteristically made the mistake of ignoring the fact that "it is not logic but organizations which rule an organized society"; therefore they selected logical principles, rather than organizations, as the objects of their loyalties. Most liberal reform movements attempt to make institutions practice what they preach, in situations where, if this injunction were followed, the functions of the institutions could not be performed.[9] Where the Progressives had been troubled about the development of institutions and organizations, Arnold's argument often appeared to be an apotheosis of them.

At one point or another, Arnold had critical observations to make on most of the staple ideas of Progressive thinking. *The Folklore of Capitalism* opened with a satire on "the thinking man," to whom most of the discourse of rational politics was directed; and the thinking man was hardly more than a caricatured version of the good citizen who was taken as the central figure in most Progressive thinking. While Progressive publicists had devoted much of their time to preachments against what they called "lawlessness," one of the central themes of Arnold's books was an analysis of law and legal thinking showing that law and respectability were so defined that a good many of the real and necessary functions of society had to go on outside the legal framework.[1] Similarly anti-Progressive was his attack on the anti-trust laws—a source of some amusement when he was later put in charge of the enforcement of these laws. But Arnold did not deny that the laws,

---

[8] *The Symbols of Government*, p. 124.
[9] *The Folklore of Capitalism*, pp. 375, 384.
[1] Cf. *The Symbols of Government*, p. 34: "It is part of the function of 'Law' to give recognition to ideals representing the exact opposite of established conduct . . . the function of law is not so much to guide society as to comfort it. Belief in fundamental principles of law does not necessarily lead to an orderly society. Such a belief is as often at the back of revolt or disorder."

as they had been interpreted by reformers, had had some use. Their chief use, as he saw it, had been that they permitted the organization of industry to go on while offering comfort to those who were made unhappy by the process. They had, then, a practical significance, but a far different one from that which the reformers had tried to give them. The reformers, however, had had no real strategy with which to oppose the great trusts: "The reason why these attacks [against industrial organizations] always ended with a ceremony of atonement, but few practical results, lay in the fact that there were no new organizations growing up to take over the functions of those under attack. The opposition was never able to build up its own commissary and its service of supply. It was well supplied with orators and economists, but it lacked practical organizers. A great cooperative movement in America might have changed the power of the industrial empire. Preaching against it, however, simply resulted in counterpreaching. And the reason for this was that the reformers themselves were caught in the same creeds which supported the institutions they were trying to reform. Obsessed with a moral attitude toward society, they thought in Utopias. They were interested in systems of government. Philosophy was for them more important than opportunism and so they achieved in the end philosophy rather than opportunity." [2]

Arnold professed more admiration for the tycoons who had organized American industry and against whom the Progressives had grown indignant than he did for the reformers themselves. He spoke with much indulgence of Rockefeller, Carnegie, and Ford, and compared John L. Lewis with such men as examples of skillful organizers who had had to sidestep recognized scruples. "Actual observation of human society . . . indicates that great constructive achievements in human organization have been accomplished by unscrupulous men who violated most of the principles which we cherish." [3] The leaders of

---

[2] The Folklore of Capitalism, p. 220.
[3] The Symbols of Government, p. 5.

industrial organization ignored legal, humanitarian, and economic principles. "They built on their mistakes, their action was opportunistic, they experimented with human material and with little regard for social justice. Yet they raised the level of productive capacity beyond the dreams of their fathers." [4]

Not surprisingly Arnold also had a good word for the politicians, who, for all their lack of social values and for all the imperfections in their aims and vision, are "the only persons who understand the techniques of government." One would prefer a government in the hands of disinterested men, to be sure, but such men are so devoted to and satisfied with the development of good principles that they fail to develop skills, and hence fail to constitute "a competent governing class." Hence society is too often left with a choice between demagogues and psychopaths on one side, or, on the other, "kindly but uneducated Irishmen whose human sympathies give them an instinctive understanding of what people like." [5] Several pages of *The Folklore of Capitalism* were given to a defense of the political machines for the common sense with which they attack the task of government and for the humanitarian spirit in which their work is conducted. [6]

Taken by itself, Arnold's work, with its skepticism about the right-thinking citizen, its rejection of fixed moral principles and disinterested rationality in politics, its pragmatic temper, its worship of accomplishment, its apotheosis of organization and institutional discipline, and its defense of the political machines, may exaggerate the extent of the difference between the New Deal and pre-war Progressivism, but it does point sharply to the character of that difference. [7]

---

[4] Ibid., p. 125.
[5] Ibid., pp. 21–2.
[6] *The Folklore of Capitalism*, pp. 367–72; cf. pp. 43, 114–15; cf. *The Symbols of Government*, pp. 239–40.
[7] There are many points at which Arnold yields to the need to seem hard-boiled and at which (rather like F. D. R. himself) he becomes flippant over serious questions. While such lapses have a good deal of

To emphasize, as I have done, the pragmatic and "hard" side of the New Deal is not to forget that it had its "soft" side. Not all its spokesmen shared Arnold's need to pose as hard-boiled.[8] No movement of such scope and power

symptomatic importance, I do not wish to appear to portray his writing as an attack upon political morality as such: it was not an effort to destroy political morality, but to satirize a particular code of morality that he considered obsolescent and obstructive, and to substitute for it a new one, the precise outlines of which were obviously vague. In my judgment, Arnold did not even successfully pose, much less answer, the very real and important questions that were suggested by his books concerning the relations between morals and politics, or between reason and politics. For a searching criticism see the essay by Sidney Hook in his *Reason, Social Myths, and Democracy* (New York, 1950), pp. 41–51 and the ensuing exchange between Hook and Arnold, pp. 51–61, which to my mind succeeds only in underscoring Arnold's philosophical difficulties. The great value of Arnold's books lies not in the little they have to say about political ethics, but in their descriptive, satirical, and analytical approach to the political thinking of his time, and in their statement of the working mood of a great many New Dealers.

I should perhaps add that my own comments in this area are not intended to be more than descriptive, for there are large questions of political ethics that I too have not attempted to answer. In contrasting the pragmatic and opportunistic tone of the New Deal with the insistent moralism of the Progressives, it has not been my purpose to suggest an invidious comparison that would, at every point, favor the New Deal. Neither is it my purpose to imply that the political morals of the New Dealers were inferior to those of their opponents. My essential interest is in the fact that the emergency that gave rise to the New Deal also gave rise to a transvaluation of values, and that the kind of moralism that I have identified with the dominant patterns of thought among the Progressives was inherited not so much by their successors among the New Dealers, who tended to repudiate them, as by the foes of the New Deal.

[8] I have been referred to David Lilienthal's *TVA: Democracy on the March* (New York, 1944) as an illustration of the idealism and inspirational force of the New Deal, and as a work more representative of its spirit than the writings of Thurman Arnold. Lilienthal's book is indeed more unabashedly humanitarian, more inspirational, more concerned with maintaining democracy in the face of technical and administrative change, more given to idealization of the people. It also shows, however, a dedication to certain values, readily discernible in Arnold, that would have been of marginal importance to all but a few of the Progressives. Like Arnold, Lilienthal is pleading the cause of organization, engineering, management, and the attitudes that go with them, as opposed to what he calls the "fog" of conventional ideologies. He appeals to administrative experience, technology, science, and expertise, finds that efficient devices of management "give a lift to the human spirit," and asserts that "there is almost nothing, however fantastic that (given competent organization) a team of engineers, sci-

could exist without having its ideals and its ideologies, even its sentimentalities. The New Deal had its literature of inspiration and indignation, its idealistic fervor, its heroes and villains. The difference I hope to establish is that its indignation was directed far more against callousness and waste, far less against corruption or monopoly, than the indignation of the Progressives, and that its inspiration was much more informed by engineering, administration, and economics, considerably less by morals and uplift. For the New Deal not only brought with it a heartening rediscovery of the humane instincts of the country; it also revived the old American interest in practical achievement, in doing things with the physical world, in the ideal that had inspired the great tycoons and industry-builders of the Gilded Age but that afterwards had commonly been dismissed by sensitive men as the sphere only of philistines and money-grubbers.

At the core of the New Deal, then, was not a philosophy (F. D. R. could identify himself philosophically only as a Christian and a democrat), but an attitude, suitable for practical politicians, administrators, and technicians, but uncongenial to the moralism that the Progressives had for the most part shared with their opponents. At some distance from the center of the New Deal, but vital to its public support, were other types of feeling. In some quarters there was a revival of populistic sentiment and the old popular demonology, which F. D. R. and men like Harold Ickes occasionally played up to, chiefly in campaign years, and which Harry Truman later reflected in his baiting of Wall Street. Along with this came another New Deal phenomenon, a kind of pervasive tenderness for the underdog, for the Okies, the sharecroppers, the characters in John Steinbeck's novels, the subjects who posed for the

---

entists, and administrators cannot do today." (Pocket Book ed., New York, 1945, pp. ix, x, 3, 4, 8, 9, 79, 115.) In the light of this philosophy it is easier to see that Lilienthal's more recent defense of big business does not represent a conversion to a new philosophy but simply an ability to find in private organization many of the same virtues that as TVA administrator he found in public enterprise.

FSA photographers, for what were called, until a revulsion
set in, "the little people." With this there came, too, a kind
of folkish nationalism, quickened no doubt by federal
patronage of letters and the arts, but inspired at bottom by
a real rediscovery of hope in America and its people and
institutions. For after the concentration camps, the Nurem-
berg Laws, Guernica, and (though not everyone saw this
so readily) the Moscow trials, everything in America
seemed fresh and hopeful, Main Street seemed innocent
beyond all expectation, and in time Babbitt became almost
lovable. Where Progressivism had capitalized on a growing
sense of the ugliness under the successful surface of American life, the New Deal flourished on a sense of the human
warmth and the technological potentialities that could be
found under the surface of its inequities and its post-depres-
sion poverty. On the far fringe there was also a small number of real ideologues, aroused not only by the battle over
domestic reform but by the rise of world fascism. Although
many of them were fellow travelers and Communists, we
stand in serious danger of misunderstanding the character
of the New Deal if we overemphasize the influence of this
fringe either upon the New Deal core or upon the American people at large. It has now become both fashionable
and, for some, convenient to exaggerate the impact of the
extreme left upon the thinking of the country in the 1930's.
No doubt it will always be possible to do so, for Marxism
had a strong if ephemeral impact upon many intellectuals;
but the amateur Marxism of the period had only a marginal
effect upon the thought and action of either the administrative core of the New Deal or the great masses of Americans.[9] For the people at large—that is, for those who

---

[9] Granville Hicks, in his *Where We Came Out* (New York, 1954),
chapter iv, makes a sober effort to show how limited was the Communist influence even in those circles which were its special province.
A complementary error to the now fashionable exaggeration of the
Communist influence is to exaggerate its ties to the New Deal. Of
course Communists played an active part in the spurt of labor organization until the experienced labor leaders expelled them, and in time
Communists also succeeded in infiltrating the bureaucracy, with what
shocking results we now know. But it was the depression that began

needed it most—the strength of the New Deal was based above all upon its ability to get results.

The New Deal developed from the beginning under the shadow of totalitarianism, left and right. F. D. R. and Hitler took office within a few months of each other, and from that time down to the last phases of the New Deal reforms not a year went by without some premonition of the ultimate horror to come. In the earliest days of the Roosevelt administration a great many of its critics, influenced by such models of catastrophe as they could find abroad, saw in it the beginnings of fascism or Communism. Critics from the left thought, for instance, that the NRA was a clear imitation of Mussolini's corporate state. And—though this is now all but forgotten—critics from the right at first thought they saw fascist tendencies in the "violations" of fundamental liberties with which they regularly charged the architects of the New Deal. Only later did they find it more congenial to accuse the New Deal of fostering Communism.

To a sober mind all of this rings false today, for it is easier to see now that Roosevelt and his supporters were attempting to deal with the problems of the American economy within the distinctive framework of American political methods—that in a certain sense they were trying to continue to repudiate the European world of ideology. Between the London Economic Conference and Roosevelt's "quarantine" speech of 1937, the New Deal, for all its tariff-reduction agreements, was essentially isolationist. What it could not escape was the reality of what even some of the Republican leaders later began to characterize as "one world." After 1939 that reality was the dominant force in American life. The beginning of the war meant

---

to put American Communism on its feet and the New Deal that helped to kill it. The Communists, as consistent ideologues, were always contemptuous of the New Deal. At first they saw fascism in it, and when they gave up this line of criticism during the Popular Front period, they remained contemptuous of its frank experimentalism, its lack of direction, its unsystematic character, and of course its compromises.

that Americans, with terrible finality, had been at last torn
from that habitual security in which their domestic life was
merely interrupted by crises in the foreign world, and
thrust into a situation in which their domestic life is largely
determined by the demands of foreign policy and national
defense. With this change came the final involvement of
the nation in all the realities it had sought to avoid, for now
it was not only mechanized and urbanized and bureauc-
ratized but internationalized as well. Much of America
still longs for—indeed, expects again to see—a return
of the older individualism and the older isolation, and
grows frantic when it finds that even our conservative leaders are unable to restore such conditions. In truth we may
well sympathize with the Populists and with those who
have shared their need to believe that somewhere in the
American past there was a golden age whose life was far
better than our own. But actually to live in that world,
actually to enjoy its cherished promise and its imagined
innocence, is no longer within our power.

ACKNOWLEDGMENTS

✿

My first efforts to set down my ideas on these subjects
were elicited by an invitation from the Charles R. Walgreen Foundation. I am obliged to Professor Jerome Ker-
win, Director of the Walgreen lectures, and to a number of
his colleagues at the University of Chicago for making the
occasion of the original lectures a pleasant one. My first six
chapters are revised and expanded versions of those lectures. A somewhat different version was delivered as the
Commonwealth Fund Lectures at University College,
London, in January and February 1955.

For this volume and other work in progress the Behav-
ioral Sciences Division of the Ford Foundation placed at
my disposal a generous grant that has enabled me to examine many more facets of the history of Populism and
Progressivism than I could otherwise have considered and
to complete the work much sooner than I could otherwise
have done.

Thanks are due above all to my wife, Beatrice Kevitt
Hofstadter, who has developed the art of the editor and
the textual critic into a major gift for asking the right
questions. Her advice has been indispensable. Peter Gay
gave hours beyond number to a searching criticism of the
manuscript and to exploring its argument with me; his
generosity with his time was equaled only by his genial
severity with my lapses. Fritz Stern, after reading the
manuscript, went through the galleys meticulously, to my
inestimable benefit.

For advice in revision I am deeply obliged to many
friends. William Leuchtenburg, Seymour M. Lipset, Walter

P. Metzger, C. Wright Mills, David Riesman, and Kenneth M. Stampp went through the manuscript and provided me, section by section and chapter by chapter, with voluminous and detailed criticisms and suggestions that caused me to make many serious modifications, to eliminate some misstatements and overstatements, and to add several observations that brought out more satisfactorily than my own draft some of the implications of its ideas—after which I was still in possession of a fund of unused comments and questions whose pursuit might yield another book. The manuscript was similarly read with care, in whole or in large part, by Daniel Aaron, Stanley Elkins, Frank Freidel, Henry Graff, Alfred A. Knopf, Henry F. May, William Miller, Henry Nash Smith, Harold Strauss, Harold Syrett, David B. Truman, and C. Vann Woodward, all of whom made valuable comments that led to important changes. Lee Benson and Eric Lampard gave me much needed advice on Populism and the history of American agriculture, and gave me cause to hope that some specialists in this field might be more indulgent than I at first had any reason to expect with the rather broad generalizations I have made about the refractory details of economic history. The research assistants who successively served this inquiry, Paul Carter, Gurston Goldin, Eric McKitrick, and James Shenton, gave to it an informed, imaginative, and affectionate attention that went beyond the call of their assignments. I am indebted in particular to conversations with Mr. McKitrick for some of the formulations in chapter v, to Mr. Shenton for some of those in chapter vi.

INDEX